ETHICS
AND THE DISCOVERY
OF THE UNCONSCIOUS

SUNY Series in Transpersonal and Humanistic Psychology
Richard D. Mann, Editor

ETHICS
AND THE DISCOVERY
OF THE UNCONSCIOUS

JOHN HANWELL RIKER

STATE UNIVERSITY OF NEW YORK PRESS

Published by
State University of New York Press, Albany

For information, address State University of New York
Press, State University Plaza, Albany, N.Y., 12246

Production by Diane Ganeles
Marketing by Bernadette LaManna

Library of Congress Cataloging-in-Publication Data

Riker, John H., 1943–
    Ethics and the discovery of the unconscious / John Hanwell Riker.
        p.   cm. — (SUNY series in transpersonal and humanistic
    psychology)
    Includes index.
    ISBN 0-7914-3425-7 (cloth : alk. paper). — ISBN 0-7914-3426-5
    (pbk. : alk. paper)
    1. Ethics—Psychological aspects. 2. Moral development.
    3. Social values—Psychological aspects. I. Title. II. Series.
    BF47.R55 1996
    170'.1'9—dc20   96-41498
                                                              CIP

10 9 8 7 6 5 4 3 2 1

Exploring the unconscious can be a dangerous task, especially if the unconscious contains profound sufferings, forgotten memories of life-threatening events, and anxieties so intense that they threaten the self's integrity. To enter this hazardous territory with its hidden monsters, shifting sands, emotional avalanches, and temptations to infantile grandiosity, one needs a wise and courageous guide. I have been lucky enough in my life to have had three such guides:

Barry Goldmuntz—the psychotherapist whose genius, insight, and compassion first opened the doors to my unconscious, helped tame its many wild beasts, and gave me the possibility of loving and being loved

Karen Wiens Roth—the psychotherapist whose profound patience and unwavering belief in the sacred allowed my self to come out of the dark hiding it had descended into for half a century

Marcia Dunbar-Soule—my cherished wife with whom I daily share a rich dream life, a prolonged, intense discussion concerning the nature of the psyche, and a mutual caring that nourishes our souls and gives meaning, sustenance and joy to life.

CONTENTS

PREFACE

The purpose of this text is not to convince the unconvinced that unconscious motivation pervades human experience. If Freud, Jung, and writers such as Edgar Allen Poe and Födor Dostoevski cannot convince one of the reality of the unconscious, then I surely cannot. Rather, I wish to raise the question of how the discovery of the unconscious affects our traditional ethical concepts of moral agency, responsibility, and what it means to live well as human beings. For close to a century, we in the West have been living with two primary languages for how to interpret human actions: ethics and a psychology of the unconscious. Yet, these two discourses have a fundamental incommensurability, for ethics is founded on a psychology which assumes that humans can come to know and master all their sources of motivation, while the psychology of the unconscious denies this fundamental assumption.

A number of philosophers have seen psychoanalytic theory as destroying the possibility for ethics altogether and have used this as a ground for rejecting the discovery of the unconscious. I think such an approach is misguided. The discovery of the unconscious does not nullify ethics, but does demand a rethinking and reformulating of the primary concepts and categories of ethics. This book is an attempt to provide such a rethinking. It will try to answer the question, "How do we need to reconceive the primary ethical notions of agency, responsibility, intentionality, self-determination, and what it means to live well, given the reality of unconscious functioning?" I hope to show that while forcing us to make substantial revisions in our moral categories, the discovery of the unconscious also lays a firmer ground for answering why one should be moral than is available currently in ethical theory.

Many of the thoughts in this book have been generated by classes at Colorado College, especially Greek History and Philosophy, which I have cotaught for twenty years with my esteemed colleague and treasured wife, Marcia. I thank her for many of the ideas developed in chapter 2 and for her continuous flow of insight into the workings of the unconscious. I also thank my colleague Jonathan Scott Lee, who has provided a cornucopia of thought-provoking and helpful criticism and suggestions. A number of students looked at the manuscript and helped make it readable: Matt Abell, Beth Bacon, Greg Berry, Stacy Gray, Jeff Rydberg, Olando Martinez, and Jenny Frank. Colorado College, a remarkably wise and humane institution, not only provided a summer grant to help work on the book, but also contributed constant encouragement to pursue these ideas. I would also like to thank two editors at SUNY Press for their support: Carola Sautter and Richard D. Mann. Lastly, I am deeply grateful to Barry Goldmuntz and Karen Wiens Roth, the therapists who first helped me discover my own unconscious and taught me how to live with its terrors, joys, and surprises.

CHAPTER 1

_____

INTRODUCTION:
ETHICS AND PSYCHOTHERAPY

Just as volcanic eruptions can suddenly and cata-
strophically change forever their surrounding landscapes, so
conceptual innovations can irrevocably alter the way we
experience ourselves and our worlds. As powerful and shocking as the eruptions at Thera and Pompeii were for Minoan
and Roman cultures, they were minor in comparison with
the great eruptions of thought in classical Athens, the
Italian Renaissance, and the Northern European Enlightenment that transformed our way of living and conceiving the
world. Conceptual innovations are usually quiet events that
happen without battles, changes of political boundaries, or
shifts in power, but they affect our lives far more profoundly. We can no longer be Athenian democrats arguing
politics on the Pnyx, Roman slaves toiling for the Empire, or
Enlightenment scientists probing the secrets of the universe
in our private home laboratories, for the concepts that
fueled these forms of life have been destroyed and replaced
by others.

A recent conceptual revolution portends to be one of
the most powerful ever, for it has shattered a two-thousand-
year-old idea concerning what human beings are and how
the human mind functions. In disclosing how consciousness

1

is only a part of the human psyche, and far from the most powerful part at that, Nietzsche, Freud, Jung, and others can claim the most important discovery in our century of discoveries, for they illumined unconscious processes that had previously never been understood or even recognized. While scientific discoveries have changed our knowledge of the universe and technological discoveries have transformed patterns of ordinary life, these changes would mean nothing if they were not responded to by people's psyches, and no discourse has been able to disclose and alter the processes, powers, and dynamics of the psyche more profoundly than that of psychoanalysis and psychotherapy.

As Freud and Jung acknowledged, the unconscious was well known to poets and philosophers long before its "discovery" at the end of the nineteenth century. Humans have always experienced inexplicable psychic events such as dreams, slips of the tongue, momentary forgetfulness, hysterical incapacities, obsessive rituals, and other behaviors that are irrational, unproductive, and stubbornly resistant to conscious attempts to change them. What was "discovered" in the discovery of the unconscious was that this realm of human experience was far more extensive, systematic, and pervasive in human lives than previously thought. Where formerly the unconscious had been associated with irrational quirks and limited to an unfortunate few human beings or a few sporadic events in a normal person's life, it was now discovered to be part of everyone's psyche and to work so systematically that its processes could be charted, understood, and altered with therapeutic techniques. What previously were anomalous events in human experience that seemed to have no rhyme or reason now became understandable. Even more miraculously, those forms of unconscious activity that were so persistent and debilitating as to be termed diseases were found to be treatable.

However, the discovery of the unconscious has gone far beyond medical applications, for it has transformed our entire way of thinking about human activity. The concepts of psychoanalytical theory have entered many discourses, such as biography, literary criticism, historical analysis, and law, and have taken up residency in ordinary language, where terms such as repression, defense, resistance, projection, neurosis, depression, and Freudian slip are now commonplace. Psychotherapy has become so central in our society that Alasdaire MacIntyre proclaimed the therapist to be one of the three types of life that define our age.[1]

Yet, with the important exceptions of several Anglo-American thinkers, the Frankfort School, and some other Continental philosophers, the discovery of the unconscious has barely been recognized by that field which traditionally has had the function of elucidating human life: philosophy. There are numerous reasons for philosophy's neglect of the unconscious, including its recent turning away from its traditional inquiries concerning the meaning of human existence to more technical epistemological, logical, and linguistic concerns. But we must still ask why the discovery of the unconscious has not affected that branch of philosophy which deals directly with questions of what constitutes human agency, intentionality, and responsibility: ethics.

Most contemporary ethicists either examine the language of morality or argue about the comparative merits of pragmatic ethics, virtue ethics, Kantian ethics, and utilitarianism, attempting to make adjustments to their favorite kind of ethics in light of criticisms raised by those in other camps. But all of these ethical positions presuppose that human beings are free to direct their own lives and take full responsibility for both the values they hold and the actions they perform. They assume that humans can become fully aware of the forces motivating them, determine which of these forces is ethically superior to the others, and act on the basis of this awareness. Yet, this is exactly the psychology that the discovery of the unconscious calls into question.

Paradoxically, rather than challenging traditional ethical notions, many psychoanalytical theorists have adopted a number of the values and concepts of ethics without realizing that the discovery of the unconscious calls these values and concepts into question. The most widely held goal of psychotherapy is to promote the autonomy of patients—to help them overcome impulses, obsessions, fixations, and other unconscious determinations of conscious life and action. In summarizing the key goals of psychotherapy, Erwin Singer said that "health becomes defined by the degree to which a person is free to perceive himself as an independently acting and reacting unit, experiences consciously the choices at his disposal, and makes choices with a conscious sense of responsibility for them."[2] Rem B. Edwards agrees in defining mental health as the attainment of "rational autonomy."[3] Here are the traditional goals of ethics now seen as the aims of psychotherapy. That is, the predominant view within psychotherapy understands this field to be in the service of traditional ethical aims. Yet, the discovery of the unconscious calls into question the psychological theory on which ethics was founded. It not only challenges the possibility of ethical autonomy and personal responsibility but questions the very worth of these values. Yet, the mainstream of psychotherapy has ignored this challenge and merely assumed the same ends as ethics.

The failure of ethicists to respond to the discovery of the unconscious and the reluctance of psychotherapy to question fully the values of ethics has meant that for close to a century we have lived with two conceptual schemes for understanding and evaluating human activity that are in many ways incompatible. Ethics, for instance, assumes that humans are in almost all cases free to control their actions and hence are responsible for them. Thus, illegal, immoral, and antisocial activities are understood as freely chosen, and the proper response to them is some form of censure or punishment. However, the reigning notion in psychotherapy is that such acts are primarily governed by pathological forces working in the unconscious that are the result of flawed developmental histories. Persons with such unfortunate lives need therapy, not punishment.

The conceptual isolation of these two primary discourses concerning human agency enervates the conceptual vitality of the culture and leaves us with a sense of confusion when the two conflict. How should we treat people who commit crimes but are acting compulsively out of unconscious motivations that they do not recognize or understand? They are not insane, but they also are not free. Are they to be treated the same as others who are not so disturbed? Should we amend our social customs and laws to excuse persons from moral and legal responsibilities if the unconscious controls their actions? When alcoholics ruin their families, abuse their children, and harm others, are they to be pitied because they are suffering from an addiction—an unconscious force over which they have no control—or are they to be morally reprimanded? Are self-absorbed narcissists who use other people as means to their own satisfactions to be ethically censured or medically treated with psychotherapy?

Nowhere has this confusion between the two ways of understanding agency, intentionality, and responsibility been more evident than in the first trial of Eric and Lyle Menendez for the brutal shotgun murders of their parents. The prosecution claimed that the brothers consciously intended the acts and were thus responsible for them, while the defense countered with the argument that the sexual and psychological abuse the brothers suffered in childhood created unconscious and uncontrollable urges to kill their parents. The juries' (there was one trial with two juries) inability to come to a decision concerning the guilt of the brothers represents in the most poignant way possible the confusion current American society experiences concerning its understanding of motivation and responsibility.

How do we need to alter the notion of responsibility if we understand all human beings as having unconscious motivations? How are we to conceive of optimal ways of living if we give up the notion that mind is equivalent to consciousness and believe that unconscious factors play large roles in everyone's lives? These are questions of utmost seriousness with which our culture must come to terms if it is going to achieve a coherent set of beliefs about what it means to be and act as a human being.

The most important attempt in recent literature to deal with the relation of a theory of the unconscious to ethics is M. Scott Peck's *People of the Lie*. Peck commences his book with a number of clinical vignettes, one of which concerns Bobby, a fifteen year old boy whose older brother Stuart had committed suicide with a .22 caliber rifle. Although Bobby appeared to handle this tragedy well when it happened, his grades soon went from a B average to failing, he became increasingly noncommunicative, stole a car, crashed it, and was apprehended by the police. Finally, he was referred to Peck's clinic.

Peck found Bobby to be severely depressed. He did not know how he felt about Stuart's death, why he was now failing his courses, or why he stole the car. The only glimmer in Bobby's flat and lifeless speech came when he thought of the possibility of living with his Aunt Helen. Then, without emotion, he related that while he had asked for a tennis racquet for Christmas that year, what he had received was a gun—the same .22 caliber rifle with which Stuart had killed himself!

Bobby's parents were a "quiet, orderly, solid"[4] working couple who kept a spotless house and attended church every Sunday. Yet, in this seemingly normal household, something was so insidious that it drove one of their sons to suicide and another into an acute depression—a kind of living suicide. In their interview with Peck, they said they had no idea why Stuart had killed himself. While they had noticed that Bobby was depressed, they assumed that this was a normal response to Stuart's suicide, would soon pass, and did not call for therapeutic intervention. Bobby's school had recommended counseling, but they did not take this suggestion seriously nor were they terribly concerned about his failing grades. Besides, they said, "It's not that easy for us to take Bobby here or there during weekdays. We're both working people you know. . . . We can't be just taking off from our jobs every day. We've got a living to make, you know."[5]

When the possibility was raised concerning Bobby living with his Aunt Helen, it was rejected, because Helen was only a cleaning woman. Finally, when asked why they gave Bobby Stuart's suicide weapon for a Christmas present, they replied: "It's a good present for a boy his age. Most boys his age would give their eyeteeth for a gun. . . . We couldn't afford to get him a new gun. . . . Money doesn't grow on trees, you know. We're just ordinary working people."[6] To Peck's suggestion that they were giving Bobby the message to follow in Stuart's footsteps, they retorted: "We haven't been to college and learned all kinds of fancy ways of thinking. We're just simple working people. We can't be expected to think of all these things."[7]

Bobby's parents seemed to be so riveted on appearing to have an ideal household, that they had little concern for the growth and development of their sons as individuals. Their sons had to fit their ideal, their time schedules, their understanding of the world. The sons could not have lives of their own. They also appear to lack certain normal emotions. Most parents could not stand to see or touch the gun that killed their son, yet Bobby's parents kept the gun and gave it to their other son as a present. Somehow a concern for money and frugality had overridden their ability to feel grief and rage at their son's death. Ordinarily, I think we would see Bobby's parents as "little" people with a somewhat distorted sense of priorities. But Peck takes two important steps beyond this normal characterization. First, he says that Bobby's parents are evil—morally evil. Second, in being evil, they are suffering from a form of mental illness: narcissism.

The first step is extraordinary, for Peck is claiming that his training and insights as a psychotherapist allow him to make moral judgments concerning whether persons are evil that are not typically available to those not so trained. According to Peck, "evil is that force, residing either inside or outside of human beings, that seeks to kill life or liveliness. And goodness is its opposite. Goodness is that which promotes life and liveliness."[8] Evil people are those who have the desire "to control others—to make them controllable, to foster their dependency, to discourage their capacity to think for themselves, to diminish their unpredictability and originality, to keep them in line."[9] These life-negating people usually do not break any laws or moral codes. Bobby's parents were church-going uprighteous citizens who did not cheat, steal, lie, commit adultery, and so on. Indeed, not breaking laws or moral codes is an essential part of evil according to Peck, for evil people above all want to appear to be good. But, "their 'goodness' is all on a level of pretense. It is, in effect, a lie. This is why they are the 'people of the lie.'"[10]

It is this pharisaic hiddenness that allows evil people like Bobby's parents to persistently and subtly destroy other human beings without being caught or even recognized. Such people are not consciously aware of their evil. If they happen to get a glimpse of it, they deny this awareness with such defenses as projecting their evil onto others, constructing even firmer foundations for appearing good, or, like Bobby's parents, rationalizing any questionable actions, such as giving Stuart's suicide weapon to Bobby.

In his analysis of evil, Peck shows that our ordinary ways of identifying and dealing with evil are inadequate. A Kantian looking at Bobby's parents could find no evil, for no moral law is broken, and utilitarians would find the conscious intentions of their acts to be concerned with producing the most good for all. But Peck sees that the most pervasive and devastating forms of evil do not occur at the level of conventionally defined immoral or illegal acts. Assessment of the moral worth of actions on the basis of agents' conscious intentions rarely is able to detect fundamental and pervasive sources of evil. Bobby's parents thought they were being good parents and, undoubtedly, appeared this way to their friends. But, with the insights and tools of psychoanalytic theory, we can get behind the masks of pretense and see that, in fact, they were systematically (albeit unconsciously) destroying their sons. With our usual focus, nothing looks out of place in Bobby's home—everything is quite normal—but with our psychoanalytic lens we can detect what ethics fails to see: an invisible cancerous evil annihilating everything it touches.

In bringing psychoanalytic theory to the recognition and exposure of evil, Peck creatively interrelates psychotherapy and ethics. Previous to the discovery of the unconscious and its hidden intentions, our ability to deal with the causes of human suffering was severely limited, as it was confined to overt and consciously intended acts of aggression. While common enough, such acts are far less common than the unconscious covert acts of aggression that quietly destroy the wills of others, reduce their positive self-images, make them dependent, undermine their confidence, or control their behaviors. Thus, Peck thinks that ethics will be less impotent in the face of these unconsciously intended acts if it can learn to use the concepts and diagnostic insights of psychotherapy.

However, this step of using the tools of psychotherapy to expose evils that might have remained hidden in conventional moral life leads Peck to another claim which is more problematic: that evil is a form of mental illness, a subcategory of narcissistic personality disorders. People who suffer from this type of narcissism have an overly grandiose sense of self-importance as a compensatory defense against low self-esteem. They get their feelings of importance by appearing to others and themselves to perfectly meet the standards of their society. Hence, they are driven, like Bobby's parents, to maintain a spotless social image, while at the same time taking out unconscious rage for their narcissistic injuries on others in ways that cannot be detected. They are incapable of recognizing the independent worth of others and often intrude into their lives, using them to try to satisfy their insatiable pathological needs for affirmation and revenge.

They recognize no power or standard higher than their own wills. While their narcissism stems from severe injuries or neglect in childhood, Peck also claims that narcissists make a number of choices that bend them on the path of evil.[11]

Peck envisions ethics and psychoanalytic theory conjoining to form a "psychology of evil." This new psychology will retain both the reprobative power of ethical language along with the healing tools of psychotherapy. In dealing with another patient, George, who had made a pact with the devil to free himself from delusions and obsessions, Peck confronts him with a moral judgment ("You are evil") rather than a clinical diagnosis ("You suffer from a narcissistic personality disorder"). Why?

> At such moments we are required to choose a vantage point. When George told me of his pact with the devil, I was faced with the choice of whether to regard it as just another typical neurotic symptom or as a moment of moral crisis. If I chose the first possibility, no immediate action was mandated on my part, if the latter, I owed it to George and the world to throw myself with all the vigor I could muster into the moral fray. Which way to decide? In choosing to see George's pact—even if it was all in his mind—as immoral, and confronting him with his immorality, I certainly picked the more dramatic alternative. Herein lies, I believe, a rule of thumb. If, at a particular moment, we are in a position in which we must choose a particular model, we should probably choose the most dramatic one—that is, the one that imparts to the event being studied the greatest possible significance.[12]

But how are we to define "significance?" Is it that which is most likely to change George? To change George into what? Is our ideal of what George should be psychotherapy's ideal of a healthy human being or the reigning moral ideal of a good human being? This is the crucial question that Peck does not ask, nor does he inquire into whether psychotherapy should be in the business of constructing ideals at all or whether the common moral ideal is an adequate one, given the discovery of the unconscious.

Rather, Peck assumes that the ideals of health and morality will be one and the same and that we can use either language to achieve the same goal, depending on which one has the most dramatic impact on the patient. Yet, when we carefully examine ethics and psychotherapy, we see that these discourses cannot be used interchangeably, for they are profoundly at odds with one another on how we are to conceive of human agency and responsibility.

If we make a 'moral' or 'ethical' claim about what George or Bobby's parents are doing and call it evil, we imply that they freely choose what they do, are responsible for it, and should be censured in some way. But if we make a medical claim and say that these people are suffering from narcissistic personality disorders, then we do not think that they freely choose what they do, but are controlled by unconscious forces. Despite Peck's saying that people partly "choose" to become narcissists (and Freud's saying that persons "choose" to flee into illness rather than face unbearable conflicts), this "choosing" is hardly the same as the free conscious choice that grounds ethical decisions. These "choices" are usually economic determinations made by the unconscious to avoid conflict or interior disintegration. Since narcissists are not acting freely, they are not fully responsible for their actions, and the proper response to their illnesses is treatment, not punishment. There can be no simple equation of evil with illness, for these terms belong to two different "language games" that have different ways of understanding human activity.[13]

Thus, the discourses of psychological health and ethics seem to be deeply at odds in their comprehensions of human activity and ways to deal with it. What are we to do with this conflict? We might, like Nietzsche, want to eliminate ethics as a repressive, dissimulating language that crushes individual spontaneity and coronate health as the reigning value discourse. However, there is nothing in the value of optimizing one's health that would lead one to values of social responsibility or living according to principles rather than individual needs and desires. Such a value system would certainly endanger the fabric of social life.

On the other hand, we could, like Alasdaire MacIntyre and Stuart Hampshire,[14] dismiss the notion of the unconscious as having any relevance for understanding and evaluating intentional activity. But, if we do this, then we lose the most important theory of human behavior developed in the contemporary world and its tools for seeing and dealing with hidden forms of evil. Further, since the theory of the unconscious is now central to the culture, we simply arrive back at our starting place—a culture divided between two incommensurable discourses for understanding and evaluating human actions.

In order to resolve this conflict we need, first, to understand why ethics is so intrinsically bound to a psychology of conscious intentionality and rational control. This we can do by seeing how and why ethics arose in ancient Athens as a value discourse that opposed the reigning normative systems of tradition and desire. Then, we need to analyze the discovery and important mappings of the unconscious to see why the moral psychology of ethics is not only called into question but also exposed as being partially responsible for numerous psychological and social pathologies. Finally, we must find some point of intersection where these crucial discourses can meet and mutually adjust to one another.

I believe this point of intersection is the concept of *maturity*. Maturity is the central concept of psychological health, for health is understood as that which leads to or promotes the achievement of adult functionality. Pathologies are often talked about as fixations at or regressions to earlier stages of development. These regressions prevent us from performing adult functions, enjoying certain facets of adult life, or having mature emotional responses to situations. However, maturity is also the primary value of ancient ethics in general and Aristotle's ethics in particular. Classical ethics is centered on the question of what constitutes the good life, and answers to this question were usually formulated in conceptions of what the life of the fully mature person should be.

Thus, if we return to the question of what a good life might be, of what it means to be a fully mature human being, we can locate a place where the new theory of human nature proposed by the discoverers of the unconscious can intersect with the concepts, methods, and values of ethics. The value system of health needs such a union because its concept of maturity lacks both a moral dimension and a justification for a number of hidden ethical assumptions. That is, although health's concept of maturity is put forth as an empirical discovery, it clearly contains a number of assumptions about what is valuable in life that it can neither justify nor connect up with a coherent system of moral values.

That ethics also needs to return to a theory of the good is not so evident. In fact, most ethical theorists would probably see such a return as a conservative regression to an unworkable and impossibly biased theory, one which attempts to force all people to live according to a narrow ideal that inevitably favors a certain gender and a certain class. Indeed, the primary conceptual ground for the formation of the modern world was the replacement of the classical and Christian theories of the good by the liberal theory that individuals could choose to determine what was good for themselves and pursue this good so long as they did not violate the rights of others to pursue their own visions of the good. Almost all modern ethical systems have either relinquished a theory of good in favor of rights and moral duties or reduced the good to pleasure that people can define or specify as they please.

Yet, modern ethical theories that lack a notion of what constitutes a good life have come under increasingly powerful attacks for their abstractness, unworkable generality, and especially their inability to justify why individuals should act ethically.[15] While encouraging people to define what is good for themselves and pursue it, modern ethical theories also demand that people constrain their pursuits within a system of justice that respects the rights of others. But why should we curtail the pursuit of our own self-interests for the sake of the rights of others? Despite some valiant attempts by contemporary theorists such as John Rawls, Alan Gewirth, and Jürgen Habermas to give reasons for this constraint, none of these reasons can be compelling for people who understand the rational to be that which is most effective in achieving what is in their self-interests.[16] Indeed, without some theory of the good, it is difficult to imagine how such an argument could possibly be made. That is, the only argument that could convince committed egoists, who believe they can get away with unethical actions, is to show them that by becoming ethical persons they will reap more personal good.

This is just the argument I will attempt to make in part 2. I will try to show that the people who are most able to know and realize their own good are those who take an ethical stance toward the world. Crucial to this argument will be replacing the modern view of human beings which sees them as independent entities with a set of unspecified desires by a view that understands all humans to have intersubjective origins and relations throughout life and who have a set of basic needs, some of which can not be realized without becoming a person who respects and empathizes with others. This view of human nature cannot be fully developed without a theory of the unconscious.

While I conceive this enterprise as being a resurrection of Aristotelian ethics, it is an Aristotle after the discovery of the unconscious, Darwin's replacement of teleological biology with an evolutionary one, and the recognition that the grounds for ethics must extend beyond the prejudices of the author's particular gender, race, culture, and class. The current concept of maturity is still firmly based in male/upperclass experience, overemphasizing the values of individuation, autonomy, and self-sufficiency, while de-emphasizing values clustered around interdependency, socialness, and intimacy—values that are seen as more central to the lives of women and ethnic cultures. Our new concept of maturity must take into account the experiences of these peoples.

That is, we must be wary not to reinvent a theory of the good that constricts human well-being to a certain form of life, such as the philosophical life that was advocated by almost all the classical ethicists, or the Christian life of piety. Our ideal of the good must allow for a vast variety of life-styles and choices, but it must also show that no matter what life-style is chosen, it is always to one's benefit to be a moral person. If the discovery of the unconscious can help us establish this conclusion, then it will not be the great enemy of morality as it has so often been taken to be, but, perhaps, its greatest ally. However, we must be careful here, for the moral person we are talking about is not the old conception of a conscious rational agent fully in control of all her intentions, but a new kind of person, one for whom the unconscious is an essential part of who one is as a human being.

PART I

THE DISCOVERY
OF THE UNCONSCIOUS

CHAPTER 2

THE BIRTH OF ETHICS

It matters not how straight the gate
How charged with punishments the scroll,
I am the master of my fate
I am the captain of my soul.

—William Earnest Henley

All individuals and peoples construct their lives according to values; yet, these values can be produced and followed in a number of ways—ethics is only one such way. For most cultures at most times individuals and communities simply reproduce the socially regnant values of their cultures. Ethics occurs when such reproduction is called into question and individuals take on the burden of asking questions such as "Are the values of my culture good ones?" and "What is the best way for humans to live?" Such individuals separate from the given value structures of their cultures, probe into the basis of values, and take on the task of generating values by which to constitute their lives. A society becomes "ethical" when it centers its value discourse around issues of justification and sees individuals as responsible for choices of values and the consequences of those choices.

Ethics is such an essential part of our social landscape that we can hardly imagine what human life would be like without it. Indeed, ethics and Western culture were simultaneously invented in classical Athens, and their coinvention is not accidental—the central values and forms of life that define Western culture come, in large part, from the achievement of an ethical way of living. Yet ethics is absent from many if not most cultures and has characterized Western social existence only for certain classes at certain times and typically has been permitted for only one gender. Until recently, ethics has had to share the production of values with a strong religious orthodoxy and the kind of social conformity demanded by small groups living in more or less isolated agricultural communities. Yet, the strong presence and persistence of an ethical tradition in the West has been a central factor in making it such a dynamic culture, especially since the Renaissance.

1. Fate

To understand both why ethics is such a unique form of human existence and to prepare us for the kind of world uncovered by the discovery of the unconscious, we need to look at the "moral psychology" that existed prior to the Athenian invention of ethics in the fifth century B.C.E., when human life centered on the concept of fate or destiny. By "fate" is meant a conception of life in which every important value, event, and individual activity is determined by forces other than an individual's will or intentions. One's fate is primarily defined at birth by one's gender, place in relation to other children within the family (the lot of the first-born son is quite different from that of the second), the family's position in the social order, the customs of that social order, and events that are caused by disruptive forces exterior to the society, such as attacks by invaders. That is, once we know the gender, ordinal position in relation to other children in the family, social status of the family, and the particular community of a person, we can almost predict what the person must do in any situation.

Fate works primarily through social roles. People do not choose their roles; rather they are born into them or have the roles thrust upon them. There are no universal obligations; rather, roles determine both duties (what is owed others in their roles) and what one is due. There is also no common virtue for everyone, for each social role has a function, and virtue is that which enables one to fulfill one's particular function. Hence, the king must have different virtues from the peasant, and the wife will have different virtues from the slave.

While such a view seems to annihilate the freedom and responsibility of individual human beings, this is not so, for in the world of fate, there are as yet no individual human beings. Rather, human beings feel themselves as part of a group, reflecting its identity in their own identities. Humans are not experienced as isolated atoms having independent existences, but as parts of a vast matrix of social, natural, and supernatural forces that interweave everyone in a common destiny.

Anthropologist Richard Shweder sees such value frameworks as far more common than those of ethics:

> Anthropologists and psychologists who study other people's conceptions of the person and ideas about the self have documented the prevalence among the peoples of the world of a mode of social thought often referred to as concrete, undifferentiated, context specific, or occasion bound. The folk believe that specific situations determine the moral character of a particular action, that the individual person per se is neither an object of importance nor inherently worthy of respect, that the individual as moral agent ought not to be distinguished from the social status she or he occupies, that, indeed, the individual as an abstract *ethical* and *normative* category is not to be acknowledged.[1]

We encounter this world of fate in almost all Pre-Platonic Greek literature. Fate dominates the world of

Homer's *Iliad*, where it is often expressed in terms of a language of the gods. Significant events are accompanied by phrases like "And thus was the will of Zeus accomplished." It doesn't matter how valiantly individual Greek warriors fight or how fine Greek military strategy is; Zeus has promised Thetis that Achilles will be honored, and so the Greeks will be pushed to the brink of annihilation. And regardless of what Hector does, he will be killed by Achilles. Thus, it is fated.

In Herodotus' *Histories*, we find the oracle at Delphi able to "predict" events as small as Croesus's boiling a turtle and a lamb in a bronze cauldron on a particular day[2] and as important as the outcomes of major battles, because events are not the result of free human choices but are, for the most part, determined by inexorable forces acting through humans. When the king of Persia, Xerxes, decides not to attack the Greeks on the advice of his sagacious uncle, Artabanus, a kingly phantom appears to Xerxes in a dream and tells him that he must attack the Greeks. Xerxes ignores the dream and the phantom returns the next night to again tell Xerxes to attack the Greeks. Worried about the dream, Xerxes asks Artabanus what it could mean, and he, as an early precursor to Freud, says that dreams do not come from God but are produced by day remnants: "Nearly always these drifting phantoms are the shadows of what we have been thinking about during the day."[3] However, to appease Xerxes, Artabanus dresses in his clothes and sleeps in his bed. That night the phantom comes to Artabanus and says:

> "Are you the man who in would-be concern for the king is trying to dissuade him from making war on Greece? You will not escape unpunished, either now or hereafter, for seeking to turn aside the course of destiny."[4]

Xerxes and Artabanus then agree that the phantom is the voice of destiny and proceed to their dooms when against all odds Greece defeats the Persian attack.

As a literal account of historical events, this episode is obviously questionable. Yet, it seems to carry an understanding of why leaders do what they do that has far more depth than histories which use only recorded public events, for this dream sequence reveals that Persia forms Xerxes, not vice versa. Given that Persia is the most powerful nation in the world and that its main god is the sun, the king must express Persia's drive for power over all lands that the sun touches, regardless of his conscious choices. Also, Xerxes as king of Persia has no limits to his personal power. His whim is law. How can a person in such a position conceive of proper boundaries as a concept governing action? Even when he tries to hear such a notion from Artabanus, his "unconscious"—the unconscious of any king of Persia—overcomes the conscious, rational decision not to attack Greece. Xerxes' fate is expressed in dreams by a "kingly phantom" because it works at an unconscious level impervious to individual thought and desire. Any king must have this dream, which is why Artabanus dreams it when he is dressed in the king's robes. This is not a world of persons but social *personas*.

Concepts never occur alone; they always cluster. Just as ethics clusters "individual responsibility," "freedom," "intentionality," "choice," and "praise and blame," so fate is webbed with the concepts of "pollution," "purification," and "social identity." In ethics we locate the cause of social disruption in the consciously intended choices of individuals, whom we then seek to censure in appropriate ways for their misdeeds. But in a world of fate where all individuals are knotted together in a common social identity and subject to vast impersonal forces, a disruption of the social order is a pollution or a *miasma*. Just as chemicals spewed into a lake at one place spread to pollute the entire body of water, so a disturbance in the life of one of the key members of a society can affect everyone in the community.

Although pollution might occur primarily through an individual, it is not assumed that the individual intentionally caused the *miasma*. Rather, the individual and group identities are merged; their fates intermingled. The response to pollution is not to blame the offending individual, but to perform the rite or action which will purify the community of the pollution. Sometimes this involves the punishment, exile, or death of the offending party, but often, it does not. The Athenians had an ancient tradition of ridding themselves of the pollution which had gathered during the year by voting on a person—the *pharmakos*—to exile from the community. The exiled person whose leaving purified the city may have been guilty of no crime other than being visible or irritating to the city.

We see this value system of fate/pollution/social identity at work in the beginning of the *Iliad*, when the Greeks suffer a plague of Apollo's arrows which they experience as divine punishment for a pollution in their midst. A seer proclaims the cause of the pollution to be King Agamemnon's taking of Chryseis, the daughter of a priest of Apollo, to be his concubine. He took her because she was the most desirable woman of the conquered city, and as king, he (by fate) not only deserves her, but also must take her in order to fulfill the expectations others have of him as king. The act of purification seems simple—to give her back—but it is not, for if Agamemnon returns her and then has no concubine, he is not living his fate as king; the social order is jeopardized. Hence, he must take another warrior's concubine, chooses Achilles', and thus launches the tragic series of events that will doom so many Greeks and Trojans to their deaths.

It is important to see that Agamemnon is not to blame for intentionally bringing the plague on the Greeks, or for being so dumb as to think that he could take the daughter of a priest and get away with it. He did, albeit without much wisdom,[5] what a king is "fated" to do, and in so doing brought pollution to the Greeks. The pollution is neither accidental nor intentional, but the necessary outcome of a social system in which kings are always tempted to exceed proper human boundaries.

We see in this story another crucial aspect of the world of fate: overdetermination. By "overdetermination" I mean that more than one explanation for why events happen the way they do can be given, and each explanation is complete in and of itself.[6] Oedipus both chooses and does not choose to cause the pollution in Thebes. On the one hand, he was fated, according to the Delphic oracle, to kill his father and marry his mother. He could not have done otherwise. On the other hand, we may ask, why was his first action after learning his fate from the oracle to kill a man old enough to be his father and then marry a woman old enough to be his mother, especially after he had been told that those he thought were his parents in Corinth weren't really his parents? His acts seem to come directly out of his impetuous, raging character whose mind is both brilliant and strangely myopic. Oedipus seems both fated to do what he does and to freely bring his fate on himself. Although these explanations contradict one another, both are correct in the world of fate.

Agamemnon brings the plague on the Greeks because he is personally greedy, lustful, and impious. But the plague also occurs because any ruler, regardless of personal characteristics, must act to make his lot better than anyone else's and thereby always oversteps proper boundaries. Further, the plague seems to occur as part of a wider system in which every event of the Trojan War has been fated even beyond the wills of the gods. These explanations contradict each other, but each is true.

Fate, like a many-headed hydra, strikes through personal character, social role, the *ethos* of a community, and the patterns of the universe. Heroes and heroines of epic, tragedy, and Herodotus' history are almost always both responsible and not responsible for what they do. They both intend (in some way) to do what they do, and do not intend it. What happens to them has to happen; yet they choose to bring it upon themselves.

We who live in a world that esteems individual choice as the highest value must find the notions of overdetermination and fatedness to be irrational and noxious. Indeed, it can be said that one of the major goals of liberal democracy is to fully overcome the world of fate—to give every human being an equal opportunity to social and economic goods regardless of gender, race, class, or even genetic handicap. However, we must also see that the value system of fate has the benefits of recognizing the incredibly complex web of forces at work in human activity and promoting a rigorous social order. The world for many cultures is chaotic enough without the possibility of individual free choice.

The world of fate began to disappear in the sixth and fifth centuries in Greece when two social movements were at work that, for better or worse, began to offer new possibilities for human existence. The first of these movements was a shift in the socioeconomic structure from a rigid aristocracy to a more (Athens) or less (other city-states) democratic polity with a trade-based economy. The new political, social, and economic structures opened up heretofore unimagined possibilities that shattered the traditional allotments of fate.

The second force was the emergence of philosophy which undercut the world of fate by systematically critiquing the existing norms and concepts of the culture. While others, such as the poet Hesiod and the political reformers, had criticized this or that aspect of Greek culture, philosophy invented a thorough and unremitting questioning that was not an event in one's life, but a form of life itself. Values and beliefs were no longer to be merely accepted because they were traditional; rational justifications for them now had to be given. The early pre-Socratic philosophers explored ways of understanding the physical universe without reference to the gods or dark powers of fate. Socrates, the Sophists, and Plato challenged existing moral and social concepts and created a vision of human individuals determining their own personal destinies.

2. Eros

The new democratic Athenians were faced with a question of utmost importance: if the structures of fate were not to govern the patterns of their lives, what was? From what we see in Thucydides' account of the Peloponnesian Wars, Aristophanic comedies (especially *The Birds*), and Platonic dialogues in which Socrates encounters various Sophists and their students, the new, self-determining Athenians found a basis for their actions in desire. Self-determination meant to follow *eros*—to seek that which most deeply aroused one and enlivened his passions.

The clearest statement of this position is given by the sophist Callicles in Plato's *Gorgias*:

> [A]nyone who is to live aright should suffer his appetites to grow to the greatest extent and not check them, and through courage and intelligence should be competent to minister to them at their greatest and to satisfy every appetite with what it craves.[7]

Another sophist, Thrasymachus, mirrors this philosophy in the *Republic* by claiming that everyone really desires to be a tyrant with complete power to satisfy his own desires, unbeholden to any laws or morality.[8] The more we are able to attain this state, the better we are living.

This new self-aggrandizing person bent on the realization of his eros' fantasies is best exemplified by the most important social and political figure in post-Periclean Athens, Alcibiades. The son of a wealthy aristocratic family, Alcibiades was extraordinarily handsome and so gifted with talents of leadership and intelligence that he riveted both the political attention of Athens and the erotic affections of Socrates. Plutarch says of Alcibiades that:

> He intermingled exorbitant luxury and wantonness, in his eating and drinking and dissolute living; wore long purple robes like a woman. . . . His shield, again, which was richly gilded, had not the usual ensigns of the Athenians, but a Cupid [eros], holding a thunderbolt in his hand, was painted on it.[9]

A man's shield, as we know from Homer, is his identity— Alcibiades is eros personified.

Alcibiades's eros led him to extravagantly enter seven chariots in the Olympic games, where he won first, second, and fourth places—an unprecedented feat in Olympic history. He later convinced the Athenians to attack Syracuse on the grounds that it was an ill-defended city of immense wealth and to make him one of the leaders of the armada. However, just before the most important military expedition of the war was to embark, drunken revelers defiled certain sacred herms in Athens and the chief suspect was Alcibiades, who was known to have privately profaned the mysteries. The Athenians let Alcibiades sail with the navy that strongly supported him, and then, in his absence, convicted him of sacrilege and sentenced him to death. Alcibiades learned of his sentence, jumped ship, and went to Sparta where he revealed Athens' plan to attack Syracuse and seduced the king's wife. The Spartans sent just enough aid to Syracuse to defeat the Athenian armada, and from this point gained the upper hand in the Peloponnesian Wars. Later, Alcibiades went to Persia, and there was killed either because the Spartans assassinated him for being too dangerous or because he seduced the daughter of a noble family.

We also meet Alcibiades in Plato's *Symposium*. In a dialogue in which Socrates appears to have the last and wisest words on eros, Alcibiades appears as Dionysus incarnate:

> So the flute girl and some of his followers helped him stagger in, and there he stood in the doorway, with a mass of ribbons and an enormous wreath of ivy and violets sprouting on his head.[10]

This Alcibiades/Dionysus confronts Socrates with the fact that he failed to have sex with him after he had seduced Socrates into bed, and, thus, puts in question whether Socrates really "knows" about eros. His unrestrained life of eros is a foil to Socrates' careful harnessing of eros to philosophical ideals.[11]

Brash, intelligent, handsome, rich, narcissistic Alcibiades holds no limits for himself or for Athens. He accepts no fate, no boundaries. The mysteries can be profaned, Athens betrayed, other men's wives seduced, and luxuries enjoyed beyond one's means. He pursues whatever attracts his eros and if this leads to the destruction of the most creative and dynamic polity in Western history, so be it. While the Athenians despised Alcibiades' personal indulgence, they were also deeply attracted to him and mesmerized by his erotic pursuits. As Aristophanes said, "They love, and hate, and cannot do without him."[12]

However attractive Alcibiades' life of unrestrained eros might have seemed to the Athenians, the limitations and disastrous consequences of such a life are poignantly revealed in Thucydides' *Peloponnesian Wars*, where the erotic pursuit of power, honor, and wealth by both individuals and states is shown to bring disintegration to the Greek world and defeat to its primary practitioner, Athens.

3. Ethics

It was in this culture struggling between fate and individual desire that Socrates emerged, calling for a different form of human life altogether: ethical self-determination. For Socrates, a life based on fate denied possibilities for individuation and negated what made persons distinctively human: their minds. There is no place for the rational direction of life in a world in which human action is dictated by social position and custom, structures which had evolved by chance with no objective justification for them. To allow humans to develop their capacities for self-governance and self-direction, the system of fate had to be overcome.

However, the turning to erotic desire as a way of overcoming fatedness gains nothing by way of individual self-determination, for desires are as arbitrary and tyrannical as the structure of fate. At least the world of fate is predictable; life based on unrestrained erotic impulse is not. According to Plato, to live on the basis of desire uncontrolled by a knowledge of the good is to commit oneself and one's state to anarchy.[13] If the world of fate is bondage to external circumstance, the world of desire is bondage to momentary impulses. Neither offers human beings the possibility of genuine self-determination.

In critiquing the forms of life based on fate and eros, Socrates discovered a new possibility for human existence: ethical self-determination. For Socrates and other Greek philosophers ethical life involved three fundamental components: (1) an ability to critically examine the values of the culture in which one lives; (2) a knowledge of and control over all of the motivating factors in the psyche; and (3) a harnessing of one's desires to values derived through rational thought. The first condition frees us from our fated embeddedness in a web of social values, the second gives us control over our desires and emotions, while the third offers us a justified basis for activity rather than the arbitrary grounds for actions found in fate and desire.

In conceiving an ethical form of life, the philosophers took elements from the conceptual schemes of both fate and eros. From the view that championed life as the unfettered pursuit of individual desire, the philosophers accepted the idea that the source of human action must be internal to individuals, not external forces or arbitrary social customs. From fate they took the notion that there is a permanent moral order in the universe which must be obeyed if individuals and societies are to fare well. This permanent structure is not, however, external to individuals. It cannot be located in social circumstance or the will of the gods, for this would deny the possibility of individual autonomy. Rather, the moral order is located at the very center of who we are as humans, for it is the ultimate object of rational inquiry. We can realize our deepest human powers and become truly happy only when we can use our rational faculties to discover the moral order and guide our lives according to it.

We see how ethics challenges both fate and desire in Plato's *Meno*. When Socrates asks Meno to define virtue, he responds that a man's virtue is governance and a woman's virtue is to care for the household and obey the husband. He indicates that there are different virtues for children, old men, slaves, "and a great many more kinds of virtue."[14] This is an appropriate answer within the framework of fate where one's virtue must correspond to the lot into which one is born, a lot determined by gender, family, and social role. Socrates' demand that he find something common in all these kinds of virtues is a rejection of the old system of fate as a possible way of living in the world.

Meno tries again:

> It seems to me then, Socrates, that virtue is, in the words of the poet, "to rejoice in the fine and have power," and I define it as desiring fine things and being able to acquire them.[15]

In line with the new Athenian ethos, Meno replaces the world of fate with that of desire. Socrates now inquires whether someone could desire what is evil. While Meno thinks this possible, Socrates convinces him that we only seek what we consider to be good and only do what is bad out of ignorance as to what really is good. Hence, desire must be directed toward the good, and the crucial problem for human life becomes how to know the good. Magically, the life of eros transforms into that of ethics.

The same shift from the frameworks of fate and desire to that of ethics occurs in the first book of the *Republic*. Polemarchus claims that justice is giving each person his due—the response anyone should give who resides in the world of fate. Socrates quickly disposes of this definition and its variation—justice is doing good to friends and harm to enemies—by showing that as a virtue, justice can only do good to human beings and never harm. Fate having been destroyed, Thrasymachus leaps into the argument and declares that justice is in the interest of the stronger. Those who have the power to satisfy their desires should do so regardless of what custom or moral principles might say. The best life is satisfying one's eros to the greatest degree possible.

The remainder of the *Republic* attempts to answer Thrasymachus by demonstrating that ethical life is so preferable to the life of desire that even if a person, like Gyges with his magical ring, had the power to satisfy any and all of his desires, he would still choose the life of ethics. In brief, Plato claims that to be happy, one's psyche must function well—must perform its task of directing a person's life. To do this, it cannot be divided and constantly at odds with itself. Since the desires and emotions are tyrannical and anarchic with tendencies to fragment and overwhelm the psyche, they must be controlled by a higher unifying power. This power can no longer be an authority outside the person as it was with fate. The only power within the psyche capable of controlling the desires and giving a wise direction to life is reason. When reason rules the psyche we can act on a knowledge of what is good rather than on the basis of unjustified, irrational, immediate desires and emotions. However, reason by itself cannot curb the appetites. A person also needs to develop virtues—now defined as character traits that enable one to know and realize the good—in order for reason to gain ascendancy in the psyche. Ethical life, the only life in which a person can be self-determining, occurs when the psyche is able to achieve unity within itself by having reason, with the help of the virtues, rule all the psychic functions.

Of course, reason has the right to rule the psyche only if it can attain wisdom about what is truly good for human beings, and, hence, Plato's ethics leads directly to questions of what the good is and how it can be known. Plato answers these questions by positing a realm of eternal unchanging forms that give a moral structure to the world and which can be known by a philosophically trained reason. These metaphysical and epistemological claims are the ultimate assumptions upon which his theory of ethical life rests. Knowledge of the forms not only enables us to direct our lives on the basis of universal principles true for all humans at all times, but knowing them is also the most fulfilling of all human acts, for such knowing grants, in the moment of knowledge, immortality and meaningfulness. The highest good turns out to be knowing the good. This is so because the fundamental principle of ancient psychology holds that the psyche takes on the form of what it intends. If it is always attending to the world of fleeting, changing particulars, it will be chaotic and inconstant without any meaning beyond its brute particularity. However, if it gazes on the world of universal eternal values, then it dons their garb and becomes immortal.[16]

In the *Symposium* and the *Phaedrus* Plato connects this moral psychology directly to eros. In these dialogues, eros is not just one of a number of desires, but the "first-movement"[17] of the soul, a source of motivation beyond the forces of fate and those of desire which, if fully satisfied, gives life the sense of complete happiness. Since eros seeks only what it lacks and what humans lack most is a harmonious unity of their psyches and immortality, eros is drawn toward ultimate forms of unity. However, a harmonious unity is equivalent to the beautiful, and fragmentation (including the fragmentation of life and death) is seen as ugly. Thus, what most deeply attracts eros is beauty. Sexual unions with beautiful others cannot fully complete us, for the merger with others can at best join us with other fragmented mortals and can, if heterosexual, create only more mortals. However, if eros seeks to unify the person with an eternal ideal of beauty or a permanent moral order, then the psyche can become fully unified, fully beautiful, and even achieve a kind of immortality.

> And when he has brought forth and reared this perfect virtue, he shall be called the friend of the god, and if ever it is given to man to put on immortality, it shall be given to him.[18]

The ideal of ethical life, then, is one in which individual human beings see as the only legitimate source of activity their own eros and direct this eros towards a universal ideal of what is good. Aristotle accepts this general scheme of ethical life, but transforms what has mathematical and other-worldly overtones in Plato into a natural biological perspective. Eros is replaced by an *entelechy*—an inner drive that seeks to actualize our human essence. Like all species, human beings have a final mature state which represents the natural *telos* (final goal or mature end) of the species and ethical life represents the fullest realization of the human *telos*.

For Aristotle, mature persons are those capable of living autonomously and rationally. They have wisdom concerning how to act virtuously and effectively in the world, understand the world in which they live, and participate in the life of their communities. This mature state can be attained only by persons developing virtues to curb the power of the passions, acquiring practical wisdom from experience, gaining theoretical knowledge concerning the fundamental principles of nature, and sharing in friendships. Ethics, then, is the art of self-constitution, the art with which we can actualize our essential potentiality to be human. In fate, the world dictates what we become, while impulse and circumstance control our lives when we live by desire. But in ethics we choose our own selves and direct our lives through rational deliberation.

When we constitute ourselves through the development of virtues and reason, we also constitute the communities of which we are a part. These are moral communities, for morality is that part of ethics which says how people ought to relate to one another. It differs from mores or social customs that are grounded in tradition by claiming that its principles have a justification in ethical reasoning. That is, the presence of virtuous, wise human beings is what allows communities to come into being and function harmoniously. Conversely, it is the optimal functioning of a moral community that is able to produce mature human beings. The process of making an ethical individual is also the process by which the moral community constitutes itself. In sum, when we realize the proper human *telos*, we actualize the essence of being human, help create an ideal community, and attain happiness for ourselves and others.

While there were substantial differences among the Greek ethicists concerning what constitutes the permanent moral order and the extent to which an ethical life requires involvement in community, they all agreed that the key for unlocking the possibility of ethical and moral life is the attainment of unity in the psyche, which, in turn, can happen only if reason, with the aid of the virtues, attains hierarchical ascendance and control over the anarchic emotions and desires. The failure to achieve such an organization of the psyche condemns humans to having disunified, fragmented psyches, pulled this way and that by tyrannical desires and emotions that have no master. If external control over desires and emotions—fatedness—is relinquished, then humans must replace this with a mechanism of internal control. If they can't, then they, like Alcibiades, will dissipate themselves and their societies in a myriad of fragmenting erotic attractions.

When virtues curb the power of desires and reason directs activities according to an ideal of human excellence, then we attain self-mastery. Above all else, it is self-mastery that defines what it means to be ethical for the Greeks. With self-mastery, desires do not control us, nor do fated external circumstances; rather, we are masters of our fates, captains of our souls.

Socrates reveals what is meant by self-mastery in his trial and death. He refuses to plead and grovel at his trial, even though such histrionics might have saved his life, for such actions would mean that he cared more about the desire to live and what fate was doing to him than he did about the good. When presented with the chance to escape from prison, he refuses on the grounds that it would be breaking a law, thus injuring both his soul and the city which nurtured him. When confronted with the argument that he will dishonor his friends if he allows himself to be killed by his enemies, he replies that he is not interested in honor from the many, only the good (thereby negating the world of fate). And when he is asked to escape because he has suffered a grievous wrong from the jury, he retorts that others' doing wrong is no ground for his now doing wrong (thereby proclaiming that there are no conditions that abrogate an ethical stance). Impending death and possible torture do not disturb Socrates, nor does he see them as injuring his ability to be good, for good concerns only the psyche's relation to itself.

What Socrates does is to change the concept of personal welfare from one of having honor (fate) or satisfying desires, including the fundamental desire to survive, to keeping one's psyche intact by always intending what is good.

> For I spend all my time going about trying to persuade you, young and old, to make your first and chief concern not for your bodies nor for your possessions, but for the highest welfare of your souls, proclaiming as I go, wealth does not bring goodness, but goodness brings wealth and every other blessing, both to the individual and the state.[19]

Self-mastery is not mastery over the world, but over the self's responses to what the world does to one. If the psyche is well-ordered and always responds by doing what is good, rather than by following one's desires or the demands of others, then one has self-mastery. Since harm is defined in terms of injury to the psyche's relation to itself, Socrates can claim "that nothing can harm a good man either in life or after death."[20] Disease may ravage the body, but it cannot upset the psyche if it has achieved self-mastery. Others may imprison and torture one, but they have no power to harm the psyche that is fully one with itself.

Socrates' proclamation of self-mastery as the highest goal of life is followed by almost all other Greek thinkers. For Epicurus self-mastery produces the highest form of human well-being, *ataraxia* (undisturbedness). For the Stoics self-mastery gave *apatheia* (apathy—the lack of pathos or suffering), the most blessed state a human could attain. With self-mastery the Stoic can overcome the vagaries of fate, and, hence, both the slave (Epictetus) and the emperor (Marcus Aurelius) can achieve the same state of well-being, despite vastly different fates.

Only Aristotle, the fullest, most complex ethical thinker of the ancient world, admits that self-mastery can be altered by the caprices of fate. Good luck in terms of social position, natural beauty, natural talents, wealth, and so on can add to one's happiness, and dire misfortune, such as happened to Priam when all fifty of his sons were killed and Troy destroyed, can ruin one's life. Yet, he still holds that fate cannot give happiness—only self-mastery can—and fate cannot take away happiness except in the most tragic of circumstances.

Since ethical life centers on the self's relation to the self, the primary factor in determining the ethical worth of an action is a person's intentions, for this is the one factor over which a human being has full control. If one's acts produce good by accident, this does not mean the person is good or worthy of praise. Likewise, if one's intentions are good but circumstances frustrate them, one is still good and to be praised. It is the free, unforced, production of intentions grounded in an ultimate source of moral value that defines being ethical for the ancients. When we are in control of our intentions and they are grounded in an objective source of value, we are masters of ourselves, happy and good, regardless what the world does with our actions based on those intentions. It is not one's actions that determine one's worth, as in the Homeric world, but one's intentions. As Aristotle says in a passage that succinctly sums up what it means to be ethical:

> But in the case of virtues an act is not performed justly or with self-control if the act itself is of a certain kind, but only if in addition the agent has certain characteristics as he performs it: first of all, he must know what he is doing; secondly, he must choose to act the way he does, and he must choose it for its own sake; and in the third place, the act must spring from a firm and unchangeable character.[21]

Although ethics undergoes numerous changes in the modern world, it retains the notion of ethical agency that was created in classical philosophy. The most important change is, of course, that the theory of good disappears from the center of ethical life and is replaced by the notion that agents are free to choose their own conceptions of what is good and pursue them, so long as this pursuit obeys certain moral laws or respects the rights of others to pursue their own goods. Hence, the moral psychology of the Greek philosophers is no longer held as the vision of good that every person must achieve to be fully happy. Rather than being a vision of what is good, this moral psychology is used to define what it means to be an agent capable of pursuing goods in an ethical way. Persons seeking their own goods must know the moral limits of these pursuits, be able to control their desires when they conflict with these limitations, and take full responsibility for the intended consequences of their actions. Even if the life of desire seems predominant in our market economy, it is a life that is deemed possible only if it is led by people willing and able to know, control, and limit their motivations according to a rational structure of justice. As the Nuremberg Trials showed, neither social pressures to conform to certain role expectations nor subservience to a distorted set of social norms can be used as excuses for not doing what is right. That is, while we can follow individual eros or conform to social expectations, we cannot do so if they conflict with what is ethical. Ethical agency takes precedence over both fate and desire. In sum, the vision of ethical life created by the classical philosophers has become the reigning form of life for the culture. Regardless of what else we do with life, we are responsible for becoming ethical—for knowing what is right and having the internal control to defeat desires and social forces that might prevent us from doing what is right.

It is the centrality of ethical life that makes the discovery of the unconscious so threatening that we want to deny its occurrence or minimize its importance. But happen it did, and we must now turn to its new understanding of the human psyche to determine how we must begin to reconceive and reevaluate the notion of ethical life.

CHAPTER 3

THE DISCOVERY
OF THE SOCIAL UNCONSCIOUS

Despite the alluring grandeur of its ideal of self-mastery, ethics has a skeleton in its closet, a dark secret in an otherwise perfectly ordered house. Socrates saw the problem at the very inception of ethics, but denied that it really existed. Aristotle attempted to explain it away, but it remains a genuine difficulty in his otherwise coherent system of ethics. The great thinkers of the Enlightenment were sure that reason could overcome it, but the problem did not go away. Rather, it exploded upon the West with such great force during the nineteenth century that we are still reeling from its implications. The Greeks called this problem "*akrasia.*"

1. *Akrasia*

Akrasia is the state in which humans lose power over themselves without obvious exterior agencies forcing them to do so. It occurs when a person knows what is good and is seemingly able to do the good, yet does something other than the good.[1] How can this be? Do cases of *akrasia* reveal that ethics' goal of self-mastery is an illusion or just that self-mastery has not yet been fully achieved by the agent? Do they indicate that the psychology on which ethics is based—that we can know and gain control over all the forces present in the psyche—is fallacious or that proper development of the virtues has not occurred?

Socrates had the most difficulty with *akrasia*, for he claimed in the *Protagoras* that if one has knowledge of what is good, then one will necessarily choose the good. We commit evil acts only because we are mistaken about what really is good. Since "virtue is knowledge," no one does evil voluntarily. Hence, Socrates denies the possibility of *akrasia*: there are no cases in which people know the good and fail to choose it. He seems to adopt this position because he wants to move the realm of value from the world of social fatedness into the workings of the psyche. If the psyche is not capable of self-mastery, then this crucial move has no point. Since knowledge is the most valued state of the psyche, no forces can be allowed to be more powerful than the state of knowledge. Hence, knowledge must be virtue or else the goal of self-mastery is called into doubt.

Rather than elucidating how *akrasia* can occur, Socrates simply denies that it ever happens. Even though Augustine knew it was wrong to steal the pears and wasn't forced to steal them, he stole them, nonetheless. Alcoholics know that if they drink they will produce immense harm for themselves and others; yet they drink. It happens all the time: we know what is good and fail to do it.

Aristotle fares better with *akrasia* because he separates a knowledge of what is good from the development of the virtues needed to moderate emotions and desires. Cases in which individuals know what is generally good, know how to achieve it in particular situations, are not prevented from carrying out the action, and, yet, do not do the good are explained by Aristotle as failures to properly develop the virtues rather than a flaw in the notion of self-mastery. Yet, we can still ask whether it is within an agent's power to fully develop the virtues. Aristotle is quite clear in Book II of the *Nicomachean Ethics* that the character any person achieves is the result of developmental and educational forces operating throughout childhood and youth. We are not virtuous or vicious by nature, but become so depending upon what habits we develop. If the adults in a child's life are virtuous role models and they positively reinforce the child's virtuous acts and punish her vicious ones, then the child will develop into a virtuous adult.[2]

This analysis seems to indicate that a person is dependent upon others for ethical development; this is why ethics is seen as part of politics, for the *polis* creates the conditions necessary for the ethical development of its citizens. However, if the development of one's virtues is dependent on others, then the ground for self-mastery lies outside the self, and we are still in the world of fate and luck. What is most crucial in life is the family and community into which one is born, for it is these agencies that can instill or fail to instill the virtues. It is not the self that determines whether it can be master of itself, but forces in its environment.

Aristotle cannot accept such a conclusion, and, thus, shifts his theory in the third book of the *Nicomachean Ethics* to claim that all humans are in control of and responsible for their own moral development.

> [O]ur actions and our characteristics are not voluntary in the same sense: we are in control of our actions from beginning to end, insofar as we know the particular circumstances surrounding them. But we control only the beginning of our characteristics: the particular steps in their development are imperceptible, just as they are in the spread of a disease; yet since the power to behave or not to behave in a given way was ours in the first place, our characteristics are voluntary.[3]

Why is Aristotle, who is usually so thorough and thoughtful, neglectful of this inconsistency? My guess is that his understanding of the process by which habits develop through mimesis and reinforcement derives from a careful observation of human beings and is, in fact, correct. However, if virtue is dependent on what others do to us as children, then we cannot be in control of our lives and fate, cannot be masters of our destinies. Aristotle will not let us fall back into the tangled world of fate in which a person's happiness and well-being are determined by circumstances beyond the individual's control. He, therefore, proclaims that all adults are responsible for who they become. Self-mastery was too powerful an ideal to be given up, and, hence, Aristotle glossed over this problem.

The lure of the ideal of self-mastery is also, I think, responsible for Aristotle's failure to recognize the dark powerful forces working in or through the psyche. For him, ethics is not, as it seems to be for Plato, the difficult overcoming of chaotic evil forces by the good, but the ability of humans to choose wisely from the plethora of goods available to them in a well-ordered *polis*. Yet, he must have seen virtuous persons who had knowledge of the good get caught in irrational obsessions. He must have known virtuous persons who, like tragic heroes, were overcome by senseless forms of irrationality. Yet, such cases go unrecognized by Aristotle—perhaps by choice. As he says in the *Eudemian Ethics*:

> [T]his is the best standard for the soul—to perceive the irrational part of the soul, as such, as little as possible.[4]

Hence, from its very inception the concept of ethical self-mastery concealed a darkness, an irrationality, a problem it could not face: the possibility that there were forces which were beyond the conscious power and knowledge of the psyche that could affect its activity. The Hellenistic schools that succeeded Aristotle's Lyceum were more aware of powerful forces that could control human destiny, but did not believe that they had a psychic origin and, thus, could be excluded from the life of the mind. Christian philosophy recognized dark forces in the interior of the psyche, but theorized that they had a metaphysical origin and could be adequately fended off with faith. It was not until the Enlightenment's attempt to discover the laws of the passions that the discovery of the unconscious began in earnest.

2. The Enlightenment

The Enlightenment thinkers attempted to solve the problem of *akrasia* in two ways. First, they tried to make the power of reason fully autonomous by separating it completely from the body and the social order. For Descartes (1596–1650) the mind is equated with rational consciousness that has no ground other than itself. The mind can achieve full mastery of itself, for it can eliminate all the influences of the body, including the passions. Since the mind can be fully disclosed to itself, *akrasia* must be explained in terms of failures to structure consciousness correctly. Hence, Descartes sees *akrasia* as a non-alignment of reason and will—we will to do something reason does not fully understand—and thinks it can be corrected with a more rigorous structuring of consciousness.

Spinoza (1632–1677) followed Descartes's lead and held that reason could fully free itself from the passions by attaining a scientific knowledge of and attitude toward the world. Kant (1724–1804) completed the rationalist tradition by proclaiming that human beings, no matter what their background, character, or educational training, can avail themselves of a power of pure practical reason which can know and will the moral law. No longer does the rational determination of experience and mastery over oneself depend on character, which is so problematic to the concept of self-mastery, as its roots lie in conditions beyond the self. Rather, reason is an a priori capacity of the psyche that has full power, by itself, to determine the experience and actions of human beings.[5]

The second approach the Enlightenment thinkers used to solve the problem of *akrasia* was to construct a science of the emotions. With a firm knowledge of how the emotions functioned we could better control them and rid their irrational darkness from our lives. Just as the natural scientists of the Enlightenment dispelled the view that the physical universe had dangerous sources of chaos in it by revealing its hidden laws, so philosophers and psychologists sought to eliminate the felt chaos of the psyche by disclosing the laws of the disorderly element of the psyche—the emotions. This science involved a "mapping" of the emotions in which the causes and effects of each emotion were described and analyzed. For Descartes, the passions were understood to work according to mechanical principles, and for Spinoza they functioned according to laws of strict necessity. While Hume (1711–1776) is not so rigorous concerning the passions (he can't be, given his critique of the principle of necessary connection) and does not believe that reason can control the passions, he, nonetheless, maps them and shows how they have an internal order. While Hume contends that reason and knowledge cannot control the passions, it is difficult to read the second book of his *Treatise on Human Nature* without wondering why these extensive descriptions of the workings of the passions are here if they are not meant to help us regulate the passions and live a moral life.

In short, the aim of a science of the passions is self-mastery. For these thinkers a rational comprehension of the passions could lessen their power over the mind and thereby free the mind from their bondage. Spinoza expresses the power of this kind of scientific understanding when he writes:

> If we remove a disturbance of the spirit, or emotions, from the thought of an external cause, and unite it to other thoughts, then will the love or hatred towards that external cause, and also the vacillations of spirit which arise from these emotions, be destroyed.[6]

However, this science of the emotions presented a paradox, for in its attempt to prove the passions rationally understandable, it was forced to theorize that the systematic dynamics of the passions were unconscious. In ordinary life, emotions appear to consciousness as sporadic, chaotic, and often irrational—exactly as Plato described them. Also, we feel that we have some conscious control over at least the moderate emotions. My friend has betrayed me and I feel hatred for him, but I also feel that if I choose to, I can cease feeling the hatred. Yet, a science of the passions holds that the emotions are really not this way at all; they are not chaotic but lawful. They cannot be changed by any conscious choice, but only in ways that correspond to the lawful workings of the passions. Thus, Spinoza will say that the hatred I feel for my friend who betrayed me is not a matter of choice, for it is a law of the emotions that "[i]f a man has begun to hate an object of his love, so that love is thoroughly destroyed, he will, causes being equal, regard it with more hatred than if he had never loved it, and his hatred will be in proportion to the strength of his former love."[7]

Thus, ironically, it was the Enlightenment's very glorification of reason and quest for a science of the passions that led to the discovery of the unconscious and the overthrow of reason as the unchallenged ruler of the psyche. Since the lawful workings of the emotions are not consciously experienced, these dynamics must then occur in a realm that is not conscious. Descartes, Spinoza, and Hume did not realize this implication of their theories, for they believed that even if emotional dynamics were not available to ordinary consciousness, they could become known by a mind working with a correct methodology, be it rationalist or empiricist.

However, the crucial step had been taken for the discovery of the unconscious. By the "discovery of the unconscious," I mean the discovery that (1) there are forces that motivate us that work beyond our conscious recognition and control; (2) these forces do not work occasionally or sporadically but are systematic and pervasive (that is, they do not cause lapses in self-mastery but deny the possibility of self-mastery altogether); and (3) these forces are at work in all people, not just the mad or insane (hence, they cannot be ignored as mere failures in certain unfortunate humans). The discovery of the unconscious took two paths in the nineteenth and twentieth centuries. Medical theory explored the dynamics of a personal unconscious, while philosophy uncovered the dynamics of a social unconscious. The full power of the unconscious cannot be understood without seeing how both social and personal factors are active within it, for both kinds of forces deeply limit the possibility of self-mastery, and, hence, both have a major impact on the question of the extent to which we can live ethical, responsible lives. Yet, aside from a complex unsystematic intertwining of these two paths in the works of Nietzsche and the continental thinkers he influenced, they have been isolated from one another. The remainder of this chapter will detail the discovery of the social unconscious, while the next chapter will deal with the discovery of the personal unconscious.

3. Marx

Although Hegel (1770–1831) and Feuerbach (1804–1872) made significant contributions to the discovery of the social unconscious before him, it was Marx's vision of this force that, along with Nietzsche's, has had the greatest impact. Hegel's concept of unconscious motivation was too connected to an elaborate metaphysical scheme to sustain itself in an age that turned against rationalistic ontology, while Feuerbach's insights were limited to the exploration of religious experience. While Marx (1818–1883) deeply appreciated Feuerbach's materialistic critique of Hegel, he found that Feuerbach had not come to the insight necessary for the transformation of philosophy:

> The chief defect of all hitherto existing materialism (that of Feuerbach included) is that the thing, reality, sensuousness, is conceived only in the form of the *object or of contemplation*, but not as *sensuous human activity, practice,* not subjectively.[8]

"Sensuous human activity" is, of course, labor. Marx believes that it is a person's position within the realm of labor which determines what values, beliefs, perspectives, and feelings she has. This determination is not consciously recognizable; hence, it occurs at a level of unconscious social causality. That is, people typically believe that they freely and consciously choose their values and beliefs, while, in fact, these are determined by the material conditions of existence present in the culture and the individual's relation to the modes of economic production.

For instance, philosophers from Socrates to Hegel thought they were finding ultimate truths and could care less about economics; yet, their philosophies can be read as part of a vast system of economic repression in which those who could work with their minds (typically, aristocrats) are superior to those who work with their bodies (typically, the lower class), thus justifying the privileges and power of the ruling classes. Theologians thought they were disclosing truths about a transcendent world but were really luring exploited workers into a soporific state in which they accept the misery of this world for glory in the next. Philosophers, theologians, and priests do not consciously intend these exploitative results. Indeed, had exploitation been their intention, they would have been less effective in achieving it, for their texts would appear as manipulations. Rather, material forces were manipulating the constructions of these ideologies.

These material forces not only lie behind our structures of values and beliefs, but also constantly make us mask our real motivations. Capitalists think that they have attained their exalted positions through diligence, intelligence, and industry, but in fact they are unconsciously motivated by greed, a will to domination, and an anxiety about their powerlessness at the very moment they are most dominant. Workers think their belief in a loving god who will take away their sorrows and give them a joyous eternal life for the pains they have endured in this one is motivated by their faith, but it is really a function of the material conditions of their existence.

In short, cultural oppression works through individuals at an unconscious level. Subsequent thinkers have expanded Marx's analysis to show how a number of forces of privilege, including those of racism and sexism, tend to reproduce themselves unconsciously. White upper/middle class men often cannot locate sexist, racist, or exploitative motivations in their fields of conscious intentionality and find themselves blameless of any prejudicial wrongdoing. However, when we examine the unconscious expectations they have for women, the poor, and non-Caucasian races, we often find systematic patterns for asserting their superiority. Likewise, we often find that the victims of such oppression are not consciously aware that they are being oppressed. They cannot point to any clear act of oppression intentionally inflicted against them, but rather feel, for no apparent reason, less vital, whole, or able to assert themselves in the world with confidence. Marx's discovery of social, political, and economic forces working at an unconscious level has transformed our abilities to interpret patterns of oppression, giving rise to an intense age of social critique in which many forms of unconscious exploitations are being unmasked.

Thus, for Marx, *akrasia* is not an occasional aberrant state, for humans are constantly controlled by forces beyond their power and awareness which operate regardless of what virtues and skills of reasoning have been developed. It is not the passions, socially imposed rules, or inadequate objects of knowledge that bind us, but the omnipresent material conditions of existence and the economic structures that we use to deal with these conditions.

The reason that these powerful unconscious social forces have not been previously discovered is that all earlier attempts of reason to critique culture have themselves been controlled by these forces. However, since we are now capable of a fully material and scientific understanding of history and of humanity, it seems (in some of Marx's writings) that these forces can come under human control. That is, Marx retains self-mastery as a possibility for humans and returns to the same theme that has been present since Socrates: that reason can free us from bondage and propel us into a new world. The reason is different now, for it is scientific, material and must complete itself in social action (*praxis*) rather than mere thought, but the goal remains the same.

However, it is unclear in Marx why the reforms of consciousness he proposes are not simply another form of self-deception. If one believes that unconscious forces can determine the contents of consciousness without consciousness being able to know it, there being no marks by which a deceived consciousness can be distinguished from one which is not so deceived, then how can one ever be sure that one's theory of unconscious motivation is not also so deceived?

A second problem Marx faced was understanding how the social unconscious operates. What is the vehicle by which the social unconscious is capable of penetrating individual psyches and manipulating them? For Marx, it is difficult to translate a structure of economic production into psychological processes. How does ownership of the means of production or laboring for a capitalist automatically result in certain psychological orientations? It seems to happen, but how?

4. Nietzsche

Although Marx could not satisfactorily answer these questions, Friedrich Nietzsche (1844–1900) probed them with devastating insight and transforming honesty. He dissolved the first problem of how humans can attain self-mastery over unconscious forces by accepting and affirming that they cannot. He answers the second question concerning how social forces manipulate consciousness by discovering that these unconscious forces are carried in the various discourses we speak. It is language that carries and transmits unconscious social forces, and, since we must use language in all thought and action, we cannot escape these forces. With these insights into the social unconscious

Nietzsche unmasked the pretenses of reason to be objective, self-mastery as the goal of life, and ethics as a language that produces freedom. Further, he did not try to resurrect reason, self-mastery, and ethics in new guises, but called for a way of living that is "beyond good and evil."

Nietzsche understood that all of reason's reasonings were manipulated by a force more potent than it—the will-to-power. Attempts of reason to discover what is distorting or controlling reason—whether they be the logical proofs of Descartes and Spinoza, the dialectical phenomenology of Hegel, the naturalist researches of Feuerbach, or the materialist/historical reason of Marx—are still infected, distorted, and directed by irrational forces. Reason cannot free itself from its self-deceptions, for its captor, the will-to-power, is too strong and pervasive ever to allow reason to escape the labyrinth in which it has been imprisoned.

Thus, when we turn to Nietzsche's unmasking of ethics in *The Genealogy of Morals*, we do not find a rational treatise carefully dissecting the problems with ethics nor a claim to objective knowledge concerning morality. Rather, we encounter a Dionysian torrent pulling us into its currents, swirling us into the cruel, joyous, ever-moving flux of life and dissolving the forms and illusions with which we make bearable the unbearable suffering and chaos of existence. We are made to feel what this alternative way of being might be rather than being given a rational account of it.

In approaching ethics through a "genealogical" study, Nietzsche dismisses altogether the possibility that moral values might be the product of human reason; rather, he sees them as the precipitate and symptom of a natural history of trauma and the play of forces working beneath the level of rational consciousness. Nietzsche gives us three accounts of the origin of morality. The first recounts an historical shift from a value system dominated by the spontaneous and powerful acts of nobles to one structured around the values of those who suffered at their hands, the plebeians. The second tells of a biological shift from a forgetting animal to one who is morally responsible. The final genealogy reveals why humans have submitted to the tortures and limitations of living under moral ideals. Each of these genealogies is an account both of what happened in the development of the human species and what occurs in the development of each person now living in the West. We are all spontaneous nobles as children who then get socialized into plebeian values. We are all born animals and get punished and tortured into becoming responsible human beings. We all run from the void to give life meaning through ethical ideals.

The first genealogy reveals how the Christian ethic of altruism, self-denial, and disinterested justice was generated out of envy, resentment, and trickery. In pre-ethical times noble Greeks and Romans acted spontaneously from the strength of their natures and required no justification for their actions. The recipients of the nobles' instinctive wielding of power were the plebeians—the lower classes, the weak, the disenfranchised—who deeply resented the power the nobles had over them. Since they could not fight back on a physical, spontaneous plane, they took their revenge by creating a new concept of the good person: one who was altruistic, capable of self-denial, and who administered justice in a disinterested way. All acts which inflicted pain on humans now needed justification; they could not be instinctual and spontaneous. Since the nobles did not need to be as sharp-witted as the plebeians ("Among the noble, mental acuteness always tends slightly to suggest luxury and over refinement"[9]), they did not have the mental wherewithal to fight this new conceptual framework and finally succumbed to the plebeian ethic.

We see in this first genealogy that beneath the values of altruism, self-denial, and justice lurk resentment, revenge, the need to destroy those more powerful than oneself, and the negation of a free spontaneous expression of the instincts. The manifest content of Western ethics might be concern and care for human beings, but the latent content seethes with hatred and "ressentiment." That is, morality is seen as demanding that all people hold common ideals and values. Such a demand will have the effects of constricting individual spontaneity when it conflicts with the common values and of funneling everyone into a moral "normalcy"—the herd. Further, the morally good person cannot openly express hatred, anger, and resentment. These emotions become internalized and secretly affect all actions and thoughts. "When a noble man feels resentment, it is absorbed in his instantaneous reaction and therefore does not poison him. Moreover, in countless cases where we might expect it, it never arises, while with weak and impotent people it occurs without fail."[10] For Nietzsche we do not consciously feel resentment and cruelty when we are ethical, but in our use of moral language we achieve the same effects as by acting through those emotions. We level and constrict ourselves and others by placing their spontaneous reactions and emotions in a moral straightjacket.

The second genealogy exposes the darkness and suffering concealed in the concept of "moral responsibility." In a "natural" state human beings are forgetful animals, for only by "forgetting" can they have fully spontaneous responses to the present.

> Oblivion is not merely a *vis inertiae*, as is often claimed, but an active screening device, responsible for the fact that what we experience and digest psychologically does not, in the stage of digestion, emerge into consciousness any more than what we ingest physically does. The role of this active oblivion is that of a concierge: to shut temporarily the doors and windows of consciousness; to protect us from the noise and agitation with which our lower organs work for or against one another; to introduce a little quiet into our consciousness so as to make room for the nobler functions and functionaries of our organism which do the governing and planning. This concierge maintains order and etiquette in the household of the psyche; which immediately suggests that there can be no happiness, no serenity, no hope, no pride, no present, without oblivion.[11]

Here Nietzsche foreshadows Freud's notions of an unconscious created through repression and use of a censor. But for Nietzsche, spontaneous repression of disruptive material is healthy, for it allows consciousness to develop and become strong. However, there is an opposite force to natural forgetting that also allows us to be conscious—memory—but its effect on the psyche is far from purely positive. "Now this naturally forgetful animal, for whom oblivion represents a power, a form of strong health, has created for itself an opposite power, that of remembering."[12] Remembering allows us to make promises and keep them. But to make and keep promises involves "the prepatory task of rendering man up to a certain point regular, uniform, equal among equals, calculable . . . with the help of custom and the social strait-jacket, man was, in fact, made calculable."[13] This making of humans predictable and orderly did not come without pain. Memory develops only when it is forced to. "Whenever man has thought it necessary to create a memory for himself, his effort has been attended with torture, blood, sacrifice."[14]

In this genealogy, Nietzsche reveals what lies hidden in the concept of a responsible ethical agent. While the Greek philosophers understood ethical agency as the path to freedom, Nietzsche saw how responsibility negated spontaneity. Humans do not become responsible by free choice, but by being punished when they fail to keep promises and pay debts. The punishment is not meant as revenge for misdeeds but is used to construct a certain kind of human being—the responsible person. Either we remember what is owed or we suffer. Spontaneity is replaced by memory; humans' instincts are replaced by "their weakest, most fallible organ, their consciousness!"[15]

The instincts, however, do not simply disappear, but turn inward and do to the agent what they were prevented from doing to others.

> All instincts that are not allowed free play turn inward. . . . Hostility, cruelty, the delight in persecution,

raids, excitement, destruction all turned against their begetter. Lacking external enemies and resistances, and confined with an oppressive narrowness and regularity, man began rending, persecuting, terrifying himself, like a wild beast hurling itself against the bars of its cage.[16]

The second genealogy, which is meant both as an anthropological account of the appearance of the moral person and a sociological account of the process each human being must endure to become ethical, discloses that the ethical person is a self-torturing, self-destructive being. Beneath the social ideal of a morally responsible agent lies hidden a dynamic process of self-negation and masochistic self-punishment. The morally responsible person gives a general "promise" to be just, caring, and nonaggressive. On occasions she feels injured by others and spontaneous rage and revenge boil up in her psyche. But her moral ideal demands that she must be kind and good. The rage needs release and so turns inward against the agent. "What an enormous price man had to pay for reason, seriousness, control over his emotions—those grand human prerogatives and cultural showpieces! How much blood and horror lies behind all 'good things'!"[17] The world did not have to wait for Freud's late work to discover the negative dynamics of a superego infused with moral precepts. Nietzsche saw its dynamics almost a half century earlier.

Why would human beings torture themselves? Why would they relinquish spontaneity? Why would an animal turn against itself? The third genealogy answers that we choose to live under a repressive ethical ideal in order to ward off the two forces that most threaten our will to live: meaninglessness and death. "Our will requires an aim; it would sooner have the void for its purpose than be void of purpose."[18] We voluntarily constrict our lives with ethical ideals in order to believe that life has a meaning, a purpose. Nietzsche groups all ethical ideals under the term "ascetic ideal," for they all involve a renunciation of spontaneity and multiplicity. Only one way of life is right; feelings, thoughts, and actions that do not fit the ideal must be forsworn. We accept such an ascetic limitation on life in order to escape the most dreaded of thoughts—that life is void of purpose and meaning. "Life employs asceticism in its desperate struggle against death; the ascetic ideal is a dodge for the preservation of life."[19]

The genealogy of morals is now complete. In exploring the genesis of ethics, Nietzsche discovered what had eluded Hegel, Feuerbach, and Marx: that discourse is the vehicle by which the social unconscious is constituted and reproduced in the psyches of all those who speak it. A discourse conceals within itself the history of its sufferings and overcomings and passes these on to all its users. Language is not merely a harmless tool used for communication but the cauldron in which human beings are forged. What Nietzsche reveals in his analysis of ethical language is a paradox. The very language that was supposed to free us from social fatedness—ethics—is itself the chief carrier of the social unconscious. When we speak the discourse of ethics, we unconsciously assume the resentment, self-negation, punishment, revenge, and loss of spontaneity contained in the language. Thus, not only do we find that the psyche is manipulated by forces of which it is unaware, but also these forces are generated by the very language that was supposed to give self-mastery.

Insofar as ethics demands we construct our thoughts, actions, and character to fit a moral ideal, it limits our spontaneity, rejects our idiosyncratic particularity, and forecloses on the rich multiplicity of thoughts, feelings, and activities that we might experience. Ethics might give life meaning, but it dams the flowing ebbs and leaps of life with the deadly structures of permanent values. Nietzsche affirms the uniqueness of each human being, a uniqueness which is present in our bodily reality. Since ethics presents humans with a universal ideal that all persons should become, it negates our particular reality and replaces it with an abstract ideality. It negates our singularity in favor of a universality. When Plato destroys the worlds of fate and desire, he also does away with unique, spontaneous individuality.

The self-torture we undergo to become moral agents reverberates on others in hidden acts of aggression and resentment. According to Nietzsche, all moral people are "people of the lie," for they all have suffered profound early injuries in being socialized into morality and aggress against others in demanding that they conform to the moral ideal or be rejected. In his genealogies, Nietzsche reveals why Peck's enterprise of uniting traditional morality and psychotherapy is problematic, for it is this morality that is partially responsible for causing the narcissistic injuries that lead to evil.

Should we then cast ethics out of our lives and return to the kind of life championed by Alcibiades and Callicles: the free, unfettered pursuit of individual desire? Nietzsche's answer is that we can neither free ourselves from the bonds of ethics nor would such a state be fully desirable. We cannot free ourselves from ethics, for we are caught in a paradox. To have as our goal "the freeing of ourselves from ethics" is precisely to reinstate ethics, for the core of ethics, as we have seen, is the production of freedom and self-mastery. Also, in order to overcome ethics and the social unconscious it generates, we must use its tools and concepts. Nietzsche knows that the social unconscious pervades all we do, even our unmaskings of the social unconscious. While disclosing the negating forces and values of the ascetic ideal, Nietzsche is aware that it is precisely priestly existence and the ascetic ideal that has made his critique possible. Nietzsche is not a Roman noble freely wielding natural strength, but a person who, like the despised plebeians and priests, uses crafty thought and intelligence in an attempt to move an entire culture to new values. "We have seen that a certain asceticism, that is to say a strict yet high-spirited continence, is among the necessary conditions of strenuous intellectual activity as well as one of its natural consequences."[20]

Nietzsche's aim is neither to eliminate ethics nor reinstate it in a new form, but to make us question ethics. While most commentators wish to see Nietzsche as either an ethicist promoting self-mastery to its highest limits or as a nihilist destroying ethics, he is neither. Rather than accepting or rejecting ethics, Nietzsche calls it into question.[21] For Nietzsche, life resides most deeply in the question, in chaos, in the breaking apart of language with aphoristic arrows that rip open the skin of conventional meanings. That is, Nietzsche's aim is to throw us into a process of questioning out of which no self-constituting structures or answers arise. Nihilism and self-mastery are both answers; what Nietzsche gives us is not a new ideal way to live nor a place of transcendence (two values of the ascetic ideal) but the process of self-overcoming that leaves us forever in ceaseless questioning and motion.

5. Conclusion

Marx and Nietzsche are powerful, seductive thinkers. It is difficult to determine where they hit the mark and where their analyses of the human condition become excessive and one-sided. What seems undeniable is their exposure of how deeply rooted psychic experiences are in political, economic, and social forces that work beneath the level of conscious awareness. Yet, while it is hard to deny Marx's claim that our values are strongly colored by the economic classes we belong to, it is much less certain that they are totally determined by them. It seems true that the discourse of ethics tends to restrict individual spontaneity and to "normalize" humans, and that such constriction can produce self-negation and acts of hidden aggressions towards others in the moral demands we make on them. It is not clear that all ways of formulating morality and ethics are equally productive of this constriction, nor is it clear that putting ethics in question is preferable to some kind of personal/social constriction. In sum, we can conclude from the discovery of the social unconscious that the ideal of self-mastery is, at best, illusory, and, at worst, an ideal that may have deeply destructive elements hidden in its discourse.

We can now understand why, at one level, the problem of *akrasia* is insoluble. We can never attain full mastery over the self because the roots of the self are inherently stuck in the soil of social, economic, political, and linguistic contexts. All attempts at unmasking these discourses and transcending them involve using them. Hence, we cannot be self-constituting beings fully in control of who we are because we are inherently part of a social order whose influences cannot be fully known or overcome.

The problem now facing us is how we need to reformulate our concepts of ethical values, moral agency, and responsibility given the power of the social unconscious, our inability to transcend it completely, and Nietzsche's exposure of its negative dynamics. But this question must be postponed until we explore the second great blow to the ideal of ethical self-mastery: the discovery of the personal unconscious.

CHAPTER 4

FREUD AND THE DISCOVERY
OF THE PERSONAL UNCONSCIOUS

In the course of centuries the *naive* self-love of men
has had to submit to two major blows at the hands
of science. The first was when they learnt that our
earth was not the centre of the universe but only a
tiny fragment of a cosmic system of scarcely imag-
inable vastness. This is associated in our minds
with the name of Copernicus. . . . The second blow
fell when biological research destroyed man's supposedly privileged place in creation and proved his
descent from the animal kingdom and his ineradi-
cable animal nature. This re-evaluation has been
accomplished in our own days by Darwin, Wallace
and their predecessors. . . . But human megalomania will have suffered its third and most
wounding blow from the psychological research of
the present time which seeks to prove to the ego
that it is not even master in its own house.[1]

While nineteenth-century philosophers and social scientists were uncovering hidden social forces that could control an individual's intentions and choice of values, physicians were discovering an even greater challenge to the

concept of self-mastery: the personal unconscious. Healers such as Mesmer, Puységur, Charcot, Bernheim, Janet, Freud, and Jung discovered a realm of unconscious personal dynamics that so profoundly limits, distorts, and controls the contents and intentions of consciousness that consciousness can never again claim full mastery of the psychic household. In fact, consciousness now seems a mere tenant in this house, subject to the whims, fantasies, obsessions, and regressed desires of an eccentric but all-powerful landlord, the unconscious.

Although there were extensive explorations into the personal unconscious for a century before Freud took center stage at the *fin de siècle*, and almost all of his ideas on the nature of the instincts, the meaning of dreams, the ideational foundation of psychological pathology, the healing power of the therapist/patient relation, and the centrality of sex had been anticipated, we still associate the discovery of the personal unconscious primarily with Freud.[2] Freud admitted that "[t]he poets and philosophers before me discovered the unconscious," but that he discovered "the scientific method by which the unconscious can be studied."[3]

I believe Freud's claim to be the scientific discoverer of the unconscious can be justified on four grounds. First, he brilliantly interrelates metapsychological theory with empirical clinical data. His theory, unlike that of the Romantics, developed out of clinical observation, and his clinical observation deepened by being informed by theory. This interaction made Freud a dynamic thinker, one who changed his theory on the basis of new observations and saw new facts on the basis of his developing theory. There are few thinkers who show such a remarkable development of thought as does Freud from his first studies of hysteria with Breuer to his closing works on the structural interrelations of the ego, id, and superego.

Second, Freud took the unconscious out of mental hospitals and revealed its presence in normal human life. Insofar as the unconscious was related only to mental disturbances, it could be marginalized by the culture as a condition affecting only a few unfortunates and lovesick romantics. But Freud revealed how the processes of dreaming, jokes, everyday slips, mistakes, and accidents work according to the same principles as those that produce neurosis and made it unmistakably evident that the unconscious has a place in all psychic functioning.

> But when it came to dreams, it [psychoanalysis] was no longer dealing with a pathological symptom, but with a phenomenon of normal mental life which might occur in any healthy person. If dreams turned out to be constructed like symptoms, if their explanation required the same assumptions—the repression of impulses, substitutive formation, compromise-formation, the dividing of the conscious and the unconscious into various psychical systems—then psychoanalysis was no longer an auxiliary science in the field of psychopathology, it was rather the starting point of a new and deeper science of the mind which would be equally indispensable for the understanding of the normal. Its postulates and findings could be carried over to other regions of mental happening; a path lay open to it that led far afield, into spheres of universal interest.[4]

And so it has been: the language of psychoanalysis not only explores the normal, but also becomes normal by entering many other "regions of mental happening" including literary criticism, social theory, historical explanation, and law.

Third, Freud was the great cartographer of the mind. He produced extraordinary dynamic, economic, topographical, and structural maps of psychic functioning and interwove them into the first systematic theory of a psyche with unconscious processes. Others might have seen the new continent of the unconscious and even touched its ground, but Freud saw it, mapped its territory, and presented his discovery to the world in a way that brought others flocking to this new land. Freud's maps have proven to be so powerful that almost all post-Freudian explorations of the unconscious have started from them. There are no entirely new maps; just redrawings of Freud's old maps to make them fit better with our vastly increased knowledge of how the psyche functions.

Fourth, Freud attempted to systematically define the structure and parameters of psychotherapeutic cure. His techniques of free association, dream and symptom interpretation, and working through of transferences, along with his advice that therapists remain non-judgmental and personally distant, set strict boundaries on the times they see patients, and maintain a scrupulous non-physicality in the relation have proven effective elements in psychotherapeutic practice. Freud's therapeutic practice was interwoven with his theory of the psyche, for the evidence that the theory was correct depended in some measure on whether his patients got better.

Freud's theory of the unconscious is immensely complex, and its complexity is exacerbated by the numerous changes it underwent in the half century Freud wrote on the psyche. What follows is a severely condensed account of his theory of the unconscious with a focus on those parts of the theory that have a major impact on ethics and the understanding of human agency. With a detailed understanding of Freud's theory, we will be able to see both how the unconscious undermines the traditional psychology of moral agency and, later, how it can be used to lay the groundwork for a new theory of moral psychology.

1. Freud's Theory of the Unconscious

Freud discovered that the psyche has unconscious ways of interacting with the world that are totally different from those of consciousness. Like consciousness, the unconscious has desires, intentions, aims, wishes, and thoughts, but rather than functioning in a clear, open, logical domain, they are submerged in the torrential dynamics of primal instincts. The unconscious is many things for Freud—a realm of repressed wishes, the carrier of infantile experiences, and the generator of fantasies, especially sexual fantasies; but, first and foremost, it is the cauldron of the instincts—the driving force of all human activity.

Instincts are stimulated by wishes, build up tensions, and seek objects on which to release these tensions, for the nervous system has "the function of getting rid of the stimuli that reach it, or of reducing them to the lowest possible level."[5] The wishes that mobilize unconscious instinctual activity and govern its behavior work according to a primitive way of thinking that Freud calls the "primary process." Primary process thinking differs from conscious thinking in two essential ways. First, it is under the sway of the pleasure principle rather than the reality principle, and, hence, will choose objects according to what it thinks will give the most pleasure without regard for the availability or appropriateness of these objects in reality. Second, primary process "ideas" (Jonathan Lear calls them "proto-ideas") are expressed in terms of symbols or images rather than discursive concepts. These images function in webs of densely interconnected symbols according to "likenesses" rather than logic. For instance, if a particular woman reminds me of my mother, the unconscious might fuse the two, recall unresolved Oedipal wishes I had for my mother in childhood, and then generate wishes to have the current woman satisfy those desires. The images in the unconscious do not have the clear analytical boundaries of concepts. Indeed, the central rule of all conscious reasoning, the principle of noncontradiction, is absent in primary process thinking. For consciousness a particular person is that particular person and not someone else, but this is not so for the unconscious, where a particular image could stand for two or more persons, and a cigar can be a penis. The association of "ideas" in the unconscious according to likenesses explains why free association rather than logic is needed to follow unconscious thinking.

Condensation and displacement are the two most important "methods" the primary process uses to produce its images. Condensation occurs when several ideas or images are merged into one (as above when the woman and mother are collapsed into a single image), while displacement occurs when significance is taken from one image and given to another or when one image is substituted for another. For instance, one could have a dream expressing a primary wish for an incestuous attachment to one's father, but it would be too anxiety provoking for the father to actually appear in the dream as an object of sexual affection. Hence, the father is displaced by a symbolic substitute or string of substitutes. The person might dream of turning on a faucet instead of kissing the father, for the faucet is connected to a pipe which is a substitute for the pipe the father smokes and is always in his mouth.

The ease with which the unconscious can move from image to image on the basis of the remotest forms of similarity is what allows the instincts, especially libido, to be so labile in the objects they will accept for discharge. Indeed, one can partially satisfy the instincts with psychic events rather than real ones, a process Freud calls "fantasy" or "hallucination."

The paradigm of primary process thinking and hallucinatory satisfaction is dreaming. Complex dreams (the kind most people have once they are past early childhood) are produced when an event during the day—typically an insignificant event—has a likeness to a childhood memory that is connected to a dangerous, previously repressed wish. During the day, the censor can keep this wish from consciousness, but when it relaxes at night, the wish can make its way into experience if it is adequately disguised. It is the function of the "dream-work" to protect the sleeper from waking by transforming the wish through condensation, displacement, dramatization, and symbolization into a fantasy that both expresses and satisfies the wish, but in such disguised ways that it does not offend the ego's censors and wake the sleeper.

While dreams are the primary way the unconscious produces fantasy objects for instinctual fulfillment, we can also see fantasy production at work in waking life. Why does Edward fall madly in love with Elizabeth? He consciously explains it in terms of her attractiveness, intelligence, kindness, and so on, but this does not explain his heart palpitations, visions of bliss, and radiant glow, for many women have such fine qualities that don't cause these "symptoms" in Edward. He is experiencing these unusual sensations because the unconscious has fused Elizabeth with a childhood memory of his mother and is saying "Here is mother, again. Here is another chance to get the nourishment you missed, another chance to merge into uroboric bliss, a chance to more satisfactorily resolve your Oedipal desires than what happened at five years old." None of these connections appear to consciousness. All Edward knows is that he is in love, has to see Elizabeth constantly, has to win her from her nasty boyfriend, and feels lonely, depressed, and empty without her. The Elizabeth he loves is a "fantasy-Elizabeth."

Primary processes are also at work when we find ourselves highly anxious in situations in which we encounter authority. Regardless of whether the person in reality is thoughtful, generous, and concerned for our welfare, we feel fearful and anxious, sure that his niceness is a mere veneer and that aggression could burst out at any moment. In this case, the primary process is establishing some "likeness" to the real and/or fantasized father of one's childhood. The feelings of fear, helplessness, anxiety, and retributive rage that have been repressed from earlier experiences of the father now reappear because the primary process has found a likeness, and we become anxious both about our vulnerability and the possibility of expressing our rage.

We see in these examples that primary process thinking is "timeless." Unconscious processes "are not ordered temporally, are not altered by the passage of time; they have no references to time at all."[6] The unconscious does not care that fifty years have passed since one was a small child not satisfied at the breast; it will still keep seeking for replacement objects—cigarettes, pipes, pens, and so forth as though they could now satisfy this oral need. It does not matter that one is no longer a vulnerable child; the unconscious will make one feel anxious in situations that remind one of times she was aggressed against by her parents.

In contrast to the primary process thinking of the unconscious, conscious or secondary processes are under the surveillance of the reality principle. Their aim is also to produce pleasure, or more commonly, reduce unpleasure, but they do so with real objects. A fantasized breast might partially satisfy the primary process, but real milk is needed to keep the organism alive. Working effectively with the real world involves using articulated concepts rather than symbolic/condensed/labile proto-ideas, and logical connections rather than a free association of likenesses. An employee should get a raise on the basis of superior work carefully evaluated according to objective criteria, not because she has a likeness to a favorite Aunt Mary of childhood. If the latter thinking prevails, it is doubtful the enterprise will.

While it is easy to see why the self-preservative instincts must have real objects for satisfaction, it is not immediately clear why the libidinal instincts need to turn from hallucinated satisfactions to real-object satisfaction. For Freud, adult sexuality must gather the various sexual instincts under the domain of the genitals and seek real objects for reproductive purposes, for without these real objects too much tension remains unreleased in the instincts and too much energy is directed toward the self rather than the world. This unreleased narcissistic energy then turns into anxiety and we fall ill. In order to be healthy one must genuinely love real people, not fantasies.

> Here we may even venture to touch on the question of what makes it necessary at all for our mental life to pass beyond the limits of narcissism and to attach the libido to objects. The answer which would follow from our line of thought would once more be that this necessity arises when the cathexis of the ego with libido exceeds a certain amount. A strong egoism is a protection against falling

ill, but in the last resort we must begin to love in order not to fall ill, and we are bound to fall ill if, in consequence of frustration, we are unable to love.[7]

The need to turn away from fantasy to reality can also be explained by Freud's economic and hydraulic principles for the functioning of the instincts. Freud's psychological economics are never stated clearly in any one section of his work, but they seem to revolve around three principles. The first is the pleasure principle: the psyche always seeks to optimize pleasure and eliminate unpleasure. For every event, the unconscious weighs all of its options according to whether they will produce a gain or loss of pleasure. In general the discharge of an instinct on a real object maximizes pleasure. However, in facing a conflict, the ego can see repression and symptom-formation as gains in pleasure in comparison to the destruction and anxiety that the ego would experience if the conflict became conscious. That is, neurosis is an economic choice, a chosen "flight into illness,"[8] for it is seen as the most pleasureful alternative under the circumstances.

The second economic principle states that pleasure is optimized when the organism is in a state of constancy. "[P]leasure is in some way connected with the diminution, reduction, or extinction of the amounts of stimulus prevailing in the mental apparatus, and . . . similarly unpleasure is connected with this increase."[9] What stimuli stimulate are the instincts, and a stimulated instinct gathers psychic energy that causes discomfort until it can be discharged. Discharge occurs when the instinct can be expressed, preferably in motor activity on real objects. If this is not possible, then a secondary, but not fully satisfactory, discharge can occur on a fantasy object or in a symptom. When unreal objects are used to satisfy the instincts, not all the tension is discharged—a remainder is left that becomes anxiety and expresses itself in symptoms. It is this economic principle that moves us toward real objects and away from living our erotic and aggressive lives in fantasy.

The third economic principle is that of conservation: "it is a matter of general observation that people never willingly abandon a libido position, not even, indeed, when a substitute is already beckoning to them."[10] This principle can also be termed the principle of "saving in expenditure" for "it seems to find expression in the tenacity with which we hold on to sources of pleasure at our disposal, and in the difficulty with which we renounce them."[11] In short, the psyche is a fiscal conservative. If a libidinal attachment and organization has worked in the past, the psyche will wish to remain gaining pleasure from it, even though events and circumstances demand a more mature object choice.

The principle of conservation explains both why we are so ready to regress to earlier libidinal states when tension mounts in our current ones, and why, in the face of the loss of a libidinal object, we form an "identification" with it—make it part of the structure of ourselves so as not to lose it. This principle also explains why we remain neurotic even though this economic position has ceased to optimize pleasure.

> As a rule it soon turns out that the ego has made a bad bargain by letting itself in for the neurosis. It has paid too dearly for an alleviation of the conflict, and the sufferings attached to the symptoms are perhaps an equivalent substitute for the torments of the conflict, but they probably involve an increase in unpleasure. The ego would like to free itself from this unpleasure of the symptoms without giving up the gain from illness, and this is just what it cannot achieve.[12]

Closely connected to Freud's economics are his "hydraulics." Freud sees the instincts as exhibiting standard fluidic behavior. Humans start with a set "reservoir" of instinctual energy. If any amount of it flows in one direction, it cannot at the same time flow in another. Thus, humans are faced with certain basic choices on how to direct their libido and aggression. The more love flows towards others, the less love one has for oneself and one's preservation. This is why the lovesick have so little concern for eating, sleeping, and other ordinary concerns of self-preservation. The opposite is also true for Freud: the more we narcissistically love ourselves, the less we are capable of loving others. Aggression works in the same way: if we do not take our aggressions out on the world, then we must turn them towards ourselves, and if they are turned toward the self, they will not be directed toward the world.

Just as fluids flow best when their paths are unblocked, so the instincts optimally discharge their tensions if the channels between the bodily source and object are unblocked. With free-flowing channels, all the instinctual energy can pour onto the object and we achieve intense, full satisfactions. This kind of free flow of instinctual energy defines humans in the state of nature:

> If one imagines its [civilization's] prohibitions lifted—if, then, one may take any woman one pleases as a sexual object, if one may without hesitation kill one's rival for her love or anyone else who stands in one's way, if too, one can carry off any of the other man's belongings without asking leave—how splendid, what a string of satisfactions one's life would be![13]

While such an unrestricted instinctual state might seem a dream come true for males,[14] it is really a nightmare. If everyone (males) act on instincts, then anyone can be aggressed against at any time. Such a state is so insecure that humans cannot live in it and construct civilization to limit instinctual activity. With the coming of civilization, the instinctual channels can never again be fully free. They get dammed up—sometimes by necessity (reality), but more typically by the moral injunctions of society. Indeed, the primary purpose of morality is to check the free flow of the instincts.

When instinctual flow gets blocked, several alternatives can occur. If the dam is not too strong, the energy can be redirected onto a substitute real object, in which case it would be an act of sublimation for libido or a displacement for aggression. However, if the dam is so powerful that the instinctual flow cannot be discharged on a real object, then it turns back into the self and its fantasy objects. In the case of libido, the return to the self brings about an increase in narcissism and symptom-formation. The return of aggression to the self brings guilt, masochism, and a tendency toward depressive/obsessive neuroses. "When an instinctual trend undergoes repression, its libidinal elements are turned into symptoms, and its aggressive components into a sense of guilt."[15]

Given the lability of objects on which the instincts can discharge themselves due to primary process thinking, what could possibly block an instinct so thoroughly that it could not flow either to an object or substitute object? Reason or rational activity cannot be the chief hindrance, for the "instinctual passions are stronger than reasonable interests."[16] The only thing that can fully block an instinct is another instinct. When this occurs, another field of Freudian energetics comes into play: dynamics.

For Freud the heart and soul of unconscious experience is the conflict of the instincts. In the early and middle writings, this conflict is conceived primarily in terms of a fight between the libidinal and self-preservative instincts. After *Beyond the Pleasure Principle* (1920), the conflict is reconceived in terms of a battle between libido (which has now subsumed the self-preservative instincts in its narcissistic tendencies) and the death instinct. Freud does not analyze the self-preservative instincts in depth, referring to them typically as "hunger," but does give extensive analyses of libido and aggression.

The one instinct that remains from beginning to end in Freud as the primal generating force for human activity is libido. Libido is a difficult and shifting concept. In Freud's early and middle writings, libido has a definite sexual character to it, but in his later works libido is likened to Plato's *eros*, seeking to expand life into ever greater unities. "What psychoanalysis calls sexuality was by no means identical with the impulsion towards a union of the two sexes or towards producing a pleasurable sensation in the genitals; it has far more resemblance to the all-inclusive and all-embracing love of Plato's *Symposium*."[17] Libido seems to be responsible for human initiatives to create, reproduce, grow, and to seek wholeness through achieving wider and fuller unities. What remains "sexual" about libido is that it seems always to be connected, in one way or another, to how the Oedipus complex is resolved.

After Freud's discovery of primary narcissism (1914), which he understood as libido directed toward the self, the self-preservative instincts could be seen as part of narcissistic libido. As such, libido and self-preservation could not have an ultimate conflict, although they could take libido in different directions. Hence, Freud had to posit another instinct to conflict with libido in order to explain psychic dynamics, and this was the death instinct (*Thanatos*). Freud found evidence for this drive in sadistic activity (especially sadistic sexuality), aggression, sleep, repetitive activity bent on mastering some aspect of life, and the self-destructive dynamics of guilt and melancholia (depression).

Freud is never fully clear on what the death instinct is. It first appears as that force "the task of which is to lead organic life back into the inanimate state."[18] In this usage, the death instinct is the moving force behind the economic principle of seeking a reduction of tension and a state of constancy. But Freud also talks as though the death instinct was involved in the attainment of mastery (something akin to Nietzsche's will-to-power) and as a generalized aggression that can have a primary flow both against the world and the self, rather than primarily toward the self with displacements on the world.

The death instinct also fuels the superego and helps impose moral standards on the ego. It is these moral standards that stand as the primary obstacles to the pleasure-seeking of libido and cause the most severe conflicts in the psyche. While libido excites and disturbs the psyche, "bringing about a more and more far-reaching combination of the particles into which living substance is dispersed,"[19] the death wish demands that the psyche return to an absolutely undisturbed realm. Thus, the human psyche is torn between an *Eros* that seeks wholeness through ever-increasing unifications and a *Thanatos* that wishes to achieve wholeness by breaking things apart until the absolutely simple is attained. Much of what happens in an individual's life, according to Freud, depends on which of these primal forces gains the upper hand.

While there has been a great deal of criticism of Freud's death instinct, it has strong precedents in the two major philosophical schools of the Hellenistic era—Epicureanism and Stoicism—and in the most widespread of the Asian religions, Buddhism. For Epicurus, the highest good was *ataraxia*, a state of complete undisturbedness and composure, while for the Stoics the zenith of human life was to be found in *apathia*, a state free of pathos, free of suffering caused by internal or external stimuli. A similar state is the goal of Buddhist meditation, *nirvana*. Humans seem to deeply desire states of quietude. While these similarities between the death drive, *ataraxia, apathia,* and *nirvana* can be made when we think of the death drive as a need for constancy and nondisturbance, they break down when the death drive is seen as generalized aggression.

When the instinctual conflicts between libido and *thanatos* become so intense that they must be repressed, symptoms are formed. Freud describes symptoms in many ways: as frozen reminiscences, the return of the repressed, substitute gratifications, regressions to previous libidinal stages of organization and fixation at this point, symbolic expressions of repressed wishes, and compromise-formations between the repressed desire and repressing force of the ego.

Since the unconscious is reluctant to give up any position that offers it gratification, the symptom constantly repeats itself, becoming a repetition-compulsion. The symptom also represents an earlier phase of libidinal organization because the conflict disallows satisfaction at a current level of sexual advancement. Hence, symptoms are regressions. They are the "return of the repressed" for they express material that is not available for consciousness. Since the symptom expresses a sexual wish, gratification of that wish, defense against the wish, and memory of when the wish was first generated, it is a compromise-formation.

All of these descriptions relate to the fact that symptoms are symbols that make sense to the primary process. Symptoms symbolically express both the forbidden sexual wishes and the need of the ego to repress them, plus offering the unconscious a kind of fantasy gratification for the wishes. "The symptoms constitute the sexual activity of the patient."[20]

An example of a multiply determined symptom is the hysterical cough and hoarseness of Freud's patient, Dora. Freud finds that Dora's symptom expressed her early oral sexuality that was never fully abandoned, disgust for and identification with her father's ill and loose life, erotic attraction to Herr K (in which her throat displaces her vagina as the place of "irritation"), sexual desire for her father and her knowledge that he and Frau K have oral sex, and identification with Frau K both in terms of the recipient of her father's love and also as a gratification of lesbian desires (Frau K nursed Dora's father when he was ill). And these are hardly all the meanings of this symptom: "I can guarantee that this series is by no means complete."[21]

Repression of the conflict of instincts and the conversion of the conflict into symptoms, guilt (in the case of repressed aggression), and a generalized anxiety are all for the sake of keeping the ego intact. The ego's function, along with dealing with reality, is to give "a coherent organization of mental processes."[22] Conflicts that threaten to annihilate the coherent organization of the ego and its ability to deal with reality have to be repressed and defended against in order for the psyche to keep functioning. One might ask why this is not a perfectly satisfactory way of handling psychic conflict. Freud's answer is that the neurotic is incapable of enjoyment and of efficiency—the former because his libido is not directed on to any real object and the latter because he is obliged to employ a great deal of his available energy on keeping his libido under repression and on warding off its assaults.[23]

In sum, the unconscious is writhing with conflicts which must work themselves out according to strict economic, hydraulic, and dynamic principles. Eros and Thanatos are constantly at odds with one another. The instincts seek pleasure and are lured by fantasy, while the ego attempts to come to terms with the moral and biological requirements of reality. These conflicts ceaselessly menace the psyche with disintegration and it must be ever ready to use its tools of sublimation, redirection of aggression, repression, defense, and resistance when the conflicts threaten to get out of hand. All of this unconscious activity is governed by primary process thinking which lacks a principle of noncontradiction, the ability to form clear concepts, or the ability to come to terms with the passage of time. It is a thinking thick with symbolic clusters that condense past and present, sign and event, and myriads of likenesses into images and fantasies of unending intrigue and complexity. Here a hoarse throat can at one and the same time be an irritated vagina, a defense against sexual desire, a wish for oral sex, and a disgust at oral sex.

Consciousness knows nothing of this world. Its perceptions are as Hume describes them: appearances without force, associations without conflict, clearly delineated objects that do not shift or change into one another. For Freud, rational consciousness is a very small island of calm in a sea of unconscious conflicts, dynamics, obscure connections, and conservative economics.

This theory of unconscious functioning is devastating to the aims of ethics and morality. The unconscious is "immoral" in its processes of seeing other human beings merely as objects for drive discharge, of interacting with them not on the basis of who they are or what they've done but according to primary process associations, and of seeking merely pleasure for the self in terms of tension reduction. The unconscious also prevents us from being ethical by disguising what our motivations really are. If Freud is right about how the unconscious functions and that unconscious motivation can be present in all of our activities, then it seems that ethics' concepts of agency, self-mastery, acting according to principles, and responsibility must be severely questioned. However, the matter does not end here, for Freud also has a theory of how morality arose for humanity and how it operates in the psyche. These theories must be examined before we can understand the full impact of Freud's theory of the unconscious for ethics.

2. Freud's Views of Morality

Freud's views of ethics and morality are complex—even seemingly contradictory—for they derive from three different parts of his work. In *Totem and Taboo, Future of an Illusion,* and *Civilization and its Discontents*, Freud attempts to give genealogies for why morality came into existence and the role it plays, for better and worse, in human life. Second, in his post-1920 metapsychological writings, Freud locates morality in the superego and attempts to understand how it functions in the structural dynamics of the psyche. In both of these accounts, morality, while necessary, typically causes people to be guilt-ridden, repressed, and/or constricted. However, in his clinical works where Freud writes about the aims of psychotherapy, he sees increased freedom and the ability to be morally responsible as genuinely worthy human possibilities.

Freud gives two different genealogies of morality. The first occurs in *Totem and Taboo* and is repeated in *The Future of an Illusion*. In the beginning, humans lived in a primal horde, not unlike troops of great apes. In this horde, a primal father ruled all the females and would not let the other males have access to them. Driven by libidinal forces, the disenfranchised brothers banded together, killed the father and ate him, but because they also loved and admired the father, were filled with remorse and guilt at their deed. Out of that guilt arose the first two moral prohibitions: a taboo against killing a totem animal (who is the resurrected father, later to become God) except on ritual occasions that reenact the primal murder and feast, and an incest taboo against sexual relations with the women of the horde. The second taboo was necessary to prevent the new social organization of the band from falling into a war of all against all for access to the women.[24] "Society was now based on complicity in the common crime; religion was based on the sense of guilt and the remorse attaching to it; while morality was based partly on the exigencies of this society and partly on the penance demanded by the sense of guilt."[25] This genealogy reveals morality to be a purely male creation arising out of violence against the father, guilt over the murder, and fear that the social order will collapse into a war of all (males) against all (males) for the right to control female sexuality.

Freud's second genealogy occurs in *Civilization and its Discontents* where he imagines what human life was like before civilization arose. He characterizes it as the freest, most satisfying form of human existence because the aggressive and libidinal instincts are allowed to flow without inhibition.[26] However, since everyone's instincts are uninhibited, no one is safe, and "so in reality only one person could be made unrestrictedly happy by such a removal of the restrictions of civilization, and he would be a tyrant, a dictator, who had seized all the means of power."[27] Yet even this primal father faces grave and ever-constant dangers. Aggression and libido had to be restrained in order for life to be bearable, and, hence, morality began when "[c]ivilized man . . . exchanged a portion of his possibilities of happiness for a portion of security."[28] With this genealogy, we see that morality is a necessary restraint that humans have inflicted upon themselves in order to gain security.

The next crucial moment in the development of morality occurs when the exterior enforcement and sanctions of society become internalized in the form of an interior censor, the superego. The development of morality in the superego mirrors the origins of morality in society. Ontogeny recapitulates phylogeny when a little tyrant, the male child, erotically seeks but cannot have his mother, aggresses against his father, but fills with guilt, fear, and anxiety. He then gives up his claims on his mother, and resurrects his father as an ego ideal in his superego.

To be more precise, the superego acquires its particular ego ideal through two kinds of early identifications. The first, less examined by Freud, is the process of empathic identification by the child with the homogenital parent—the boy with the father, the girl with the mother. The second kind of identification, the one that is foremost in Freud's discussion of both narcissism and how an ego builds character, is a process in which an abandoned libidinal object is introjected into the ego and identified with. These identifications with abandoned libidinal objects give the ego both a reservoir of desexualized libido and an increase in self-esteem. The libido that was once expended on others now flows back into the ego and "[w]hen the ego assumes the features of the object, it is forcing itself, so to speak, upon the id as a love-object and is trying to make good the id's loss by saying: 'Look, you can love me too—I am so like the object.'"[29] (It is instructive to see the relation between the extremely important process of identification and the tenet of ancient moral psychology that held that the psyche takes on the character of what it intends. In Freud, the ancient principle is seen as true, but working only at an unconscious level and typically only in the first years of life.)

Hence, the ego is built by transforming others into a structure of itself. "The 'character' of the ego is a precipitate of abandoned object-cathexes and . . . contains the history of those object-choices."[30] The objects that the child's ego is most likely to take into itself are its parents, and through them their values and the society at large. The parental values and aggression by which they were enforced on the child then break off from the ego and form an "ego ideal" in the superego. In this way, the society reproduces its values in every individual.

> We see, then, that the differentiation of the super-ego from the ego is no matter of chance; it represents the most important characteristics of the development both of the individual and of the species; indeed, by giving permanent expression to the influence of the parents it perpetuates the existence of the factors to which it owes its origin.[31]

These processes of identification, character-formation, and value production culminate in the Oedipus complex. A young boy will, according to Freud, typically feel a possessive and sexual love of his mother, hatred and aggression toward his great rival, the father, and fear both his own aggression and being castrated by an enraged father. The anxiety concerning castration demands that these feelings come to a resolution. In a successful negotiation of the Oedipal conflicts, the boy will form an intensified empathic identification with his father and refuse to identify with his abandoned mother. This father-identification allows for an affectionate vicarious relation to the mother, solidifies the boy's masculinity, and creates a set of values with the forcefulness of the real/imagined father behind them.

Freud had much more trouble understanding how girls go through the Oedipal stage, for they have no fear of castration. According to Freud, a girl's deepest desire is to have a penis, which, in the Oedipal stage is transformed into a desire to have a baby by her father. She seems to give up her Oedipal desires because she fears losing her mother's affections and slowly comes to see that she is not going to be successful in having a child by her father. Thus, a fortuitous outcome for the girl parallels that of the boy. She forms an intensified empathic identification with her mother and refuses to identify with the abandoned father.

The final result of such successful resolutions is still ambivalent, for it contains the joint precepts "'You ought to be like this (like your father)' and 'You *may not be* like this (like your father)—you may not do all that he does; some things are his prerogative.'"[32] Because the father is experienced as more aggressive and castration is more anxiety-provoking, boys supposedly form more rigorous and demanding ego ideals than girls. Freud says this is why women are not as moral as men and are not as interested in the construction of civilization.[33]

While it appears that the ego ideal contains both an ideal to be emulated and a set of prohibitions, Freud rarely speaks of the ego ideal as luring us to achievement. He sees ideals as limiting and restricting humans rather than as visions whose beauty and power can move them to greater development. Humans do things because they are forced to by pressures and conflicts in the instincts or reality; they never seem motivated to act teleologically on the basis of ideals.[34] The ego ideal is merely a restriction on the possibilities and spontaneities of the ego and the id:

> But the ego ideal comprises the sum of all the limitations in which the ego has to acquiesce, and for that reason the abrogation of the ideal would necessarily be a magnificent festival for the ego, which might then once again feel satisfied with itself.[35]

If we inquire as to where the superego gets its energy to aggress against the ego, we do not have far to look. It is the death instinct. "What is holding sway in the super-ego is . . . a pure culture of the death instinct."[36] The death instinct seems to use morality as a way of making the organism curtail its upsetting libidinal impulses to stay on an even, nondisruptive course. While this combination of morality with a death instinct might strike us as distorted, it does have an eminent precedent in Socrates who said that philosophy, especially ethics, was a preparation for death, and whose steadfast adherence to his moral principles at his trial and during his imprisonment led to his own death. To be morally steadfast is to be unchanging in one's structure, but unchangingness taken to its limit is death. Perhaps this is why Socrates in the *Apology* is so unafraid of death—death almost seems a friend—for he has achieved such an unmoving moral character that nothing in life or death can alter him.

Freud seems to have ambivalent attitudes toward the superego. On the one hand, he sees it as the "most precious cultural asset in the psychological field,"[37] for it provides security without the burden of external enforcement. On the other hand, the superego is able to gain interior control of the instincts only by a kind of internal aggression against the ego, one that fills it with guilt. This internal censor is much more powerful than the previous external authorities, for it demands not only the renunciation of instinctual action, but of instinctual wishes.

> Thus we know of two origins of the sense of guilt: one arising from fear of an authority, and the other, later on, arising from fear of the super-ego. The first insists upon a renunciation of instinctual satisfactions; the second, as well as doing this, presses for punishment, since the continuance of the forbidden wishes cannot be concealed from the super-ego. . . . Thus, in spite of the renunciation that has been made, a sense of guilt comes about. This constitutes a great economic disadvantage in the erection of a super-ego, or, as we may put it, in the formation of a conscience. Instinctual renunciation now no longer has a completely liberating effect; virtuous continence is no longer rewarded with the assurance of love. A threatened external unhappiness—loss of love and punishment on the part of an external authority—has been exchanged for a permanent internal unhappiness, for the tension of the sense of guilt.[38]

This is quite a price to pay for attaining security through an intrapsychic control mechanism—"permanent internal unhappiness."

Despite the gloomy dynamics of the superego, they do not lead to illness unless they become excessively harsh. The factors that seem to be involved in whether the superego becomes too harsh are, first, the character and aggressiveness of the father, and second cultural variables such as religion and education.[39] This aggressive aspect of the superego will be further intensified if the moral values of the ego-ideal contain strong prohibitions against aggression towards other humans (as Christian morality does), for then the death instinct cannot find an outlet in the world and must be turned against the self. Also, if the child is anxious about his own aggression and represses it, this aggression will turn inward against himself.

Although many variables seem to be involved in the superego's becoming overly harsh, the core around which they all revolve is the moral system of the social order. An increase in civilization brings expectations for stricter inner control and this in turn leads to a heightened sense of guilt and self-negation. Freud wants to reveal "the sense of guilt as the most important problem in the development of civilization and to show that the price we pay for our advance in civilization is a loss of happiness through a heightening sense of guilt."[40] It is the moral system that makes the father harsh, causes us to interiorize aggression, and limits adult libido to procreation within the bonds of marriage, a restriction Freud blames for modern nervousness and neuroses.[41]

The indictments that Freud brings against morality in his genealogies and metapsychology mirror those of Nietzsche. Both see morality as retaining the scars of a violent social birth and passing these injuries on to all who adopt the discourse. For Nietzsche the birth of morality occurs when the plebeians take revenge on the nobles with their ethic of fairness and love, while for Freud it emerges out of guilt for having killed the primal father and fear of social life being a Hobbesian war of all against all. The structure of these genealogies, however, is almost the same: the strong, spontaneous, unrestricted individual is done in by persons who are weak but socially organized. For both, the interiorization of moral principles turns a human into "a wild beast hurling itself against the bars of its cage."[42] Morality can so bind and constrict human spontaneity and the individual expression of the instincts that it makes us fall ill, become misshapen, and leads to a "permanent internal unhappiness."

However, what Nietzsche deplores in the loss of individual spontaneity and vitality, Freud sees as a regretful necessity. There must be some limitation on the instincts or social life will be impossible. The question is whether the kind of limitation contained in morality is the optimal way to control instinctual activity. Here Freud is ambivalent, sometimes asserting that the traditional aims of ethics are the highest values in human life and at others calling for a new kind of value system that would fully incorporate the findings of psychoanalysis.

3. Psychoanalysis and Ethics

Freud's genealogies see morality as, at best, a necessary evil that causes profound individual unhappiness, while his metapsychology seems to destroy the possibility of rational control over life altogether. The only agency in the psyche that might be capable of rational autonomy is the ego, but Freud sees it as "owing service to three masters and consequently menaced by three dangers: from the external world, from the libido of the id, and from the severity of the super-ego."[43] One would expect Freud to conclude from his genealogies and metapsychology that moral agency is both impossible and undesirable.

Hence, it is surprising to find in his clinical works the aim of producing autonomous rational agents capable of living morally responsible lives. In these aims, Freud reveals himself to be part and parcel of the Western ethical tradition. He still believes self-mastery to be "the highest achievement which is attainable by any human being."[44] The path to achieving self-mastery could have come straight from the works of Plato or Descartes: "Our best hope for the future is that intellect—the scientific spirit, reason—may in process of time establish a dictatorship in the mental life of man."[45]

Although these statements make Freud appear to be aligned with Plato, Aristotle, and other great ethicists, a cursory examination of the kind of self-mastery that is possible given Freud's psychology and the kind of self-mastery demanded by ethics reveals that the two are only nominally alike. Freud's ethical posturings must be separated from what is demanded by his theory of psychic functioning. Freud as an ethicist is rather traditional and unprobing; Freud as the discoverer of the unconscious calls into question the very foundation of ethics and points towards an entirely new way of relating to values.

For both Freud and ethics the fundamental condition for an autonomous, responsible life is the unification of the psyche. The degree to which the psyche has split off parts of itself off into separate realms with independent functionings is the degree to which it is unable to rule its own existence. For both Freud and ethics the key to attaining this unity is a knowledge of and rational control over the fragmented psychic functionings. But Freud claims that knowing the repressed emotions and wishes is not enough, for "[k]nowledge is not always the same as knowledge."[46] An abstract knowledge of repressed emotions does nothing to free us from their power. The kind of knowledge needed to release the psyche from its bondage to repressed conflicts is a re-experiencing them in all their emotional intensities rather than just intellectually understanding what happened at a certain time in one's past. One ceases to be bound when the immoral or unacceptable fantasy/wish is not denied but admitted as part of who the self is. With this self-acceptance, the energy absorbed by the repressed object is released and we cease acting out the fantasy in overdetermined ways. Such a cathartic knowing cannot occur if reason is dictatorial and governs all its affairs with a rational moral principle, for such a principle would not allow the immoral wish to be accepted as definitive of the self.

For Plato, Aristotle, and most of the ethical tradition reason must *rule* the psyche, but in Freud's psychology such a rule is neither possible nor advisable, since a dominance of any factor in the psyche leads to a repression or malfunctioning of other factors. The instincts are necessary for activity, the superego for character and stability, the ego for conscious direction and decisions about how best to achieve satisfaction, given the contingencies and limitations of reality. The rational ego really can't replace the id or superego in these basic functions or achieve overt dominance over them. At best, it can help these parts of the psyche to function better if they are malfunctioning. Integration is always a more or less affair with Freud—never complete, never rigorous, never grounded in just one part of the psyche.

Ethicists also held that self-mastery was possible only if the psyche could ground itself in rationally derived values free of social and biological determinations. Freud finds no mechanism by which the psyche can ground itself in objective values or principles, nor any way by which the psyche can extricate itself fully from its social and biological influences. The great powers in human life are the biological instincts of the id and the cultural values ingrained in the superego. There is no possibility of an independent grounding of values in reason nor a possibility that these values can teleologically guide the psyche. Freud agrees with Hume that reason is not a generating agency, but at best a guiding one. For humans, "arguments are of no avail against their passions."[47] The ego can transform id energy into ego energy through narcissistic identifications and sublimations, but if these stray too far from their original libidinal aims, then psychic disturbance occurs. Even when the ego is able to "borrow" energy for its purposes, it is never able to achieve the kind of full-blown independence and grounding of itself in its own structure of reason required by ethics. The agency which gives values to life, the superego, is not capable of either free choice or radical change. In opposition to Aristotle's claim that we are responsible for our character, Freud sees character as more or less determined by early childhood identifications. While later experiences might alter the superego to some degree, "it nevertheless preserves throughout life the character given to it by its derivation from the father-complex—namely, the capacity to stand apart from the ego and to master it."[48]

Thus, even if the goal of analysis is some state in which the ego achieves more mastery of the other parts of the psyche than occurs in neurosis, it is far different from the kind of mastery required by ethics. Ethical self-mastery and responsibility demand the ability to disengage ourselves fully from our biological and social heritages, be fully aware of what motivates us, have control over these motivating factors, and have a rational ground for establishing values. Given Freud's analysis of the unconscious, none of these conditions can be satisfied. Self-mastery can at most mean the ability to extricate oneself from debilitating unconscious conflicts, partial release of libido from infantile fantasy objects, lessening the power of an overly harsh superego, or acting without excessive obsession.

Thus, even though psychoanalysis can significantly aid the ego in gaining access to and control over the wishes and dynamics of the instincts, the psyche never has the power to know for sure that it is not being manipulated by unconscious forces. The ego no longer has its privileged position in the psyche as the agency capable of knowing and controlling all the elements of the human mind. We can never be sure that any of our actions are simply free productions of conscious intentionality. There is always the possibility of overdetermination and no stance that consciousness can take to assure itself that this is not happening. In short, the ego is "not even master in its own house."[49]

In sum, Freud's psychology calls into question the traditional notions of ethical agency and responsibility by showing that they are founded on an inadequate analysis of psychic functioning. Yet, when we inquire as to what new concept of responsibility emerges from psychoanalysis, Freud is strangely silent. There are some revolutionary statements concerning how our relation to the unconscious must be taken into account in our moral lives—that we are responsible for unconscious intentions and even our dream productions.[50] But there are also traditional separations between normal conditions for responsibility and non-normal, as when Freud draws a delineation between malingering soldiers who are responsible for their cowardice and neurotic soldiers who are not.[51] In general, Freud seems reluctant to generalize from psychology to ethics, holding that "[p]sychoanalysis has no concern whatever with such [moral] judgments of value."[52]

In recent works, David Wallwork, Ilham Dilman, and Jonathan Lear[53] have attempted to see Freud's work as supporting the traditional ethical values of love, justice, autonomy, care for others, and responsibility. They draw on passages from various parts of Freud's work and bring what is marginal to the center. While their work is an important corrective to the prevailing view that Freud's theory destroys morality, it must be remembered that Freud's positive statements about the possibility of humans' attaining autonomy and acting with moral responsibility cannot amount to anything more than a few pages out of twenty-three volumes of work, most of which is dedicated to showing how unconscious forces impinge upon and control human destinies. For every statement asserting the possibility of autonomous self-direction, there are countless more that claim "[o]bscure, unfeeling and unloving powers determine men's fate."[54]

Unlike Wallwork and Lear, I see Freud as siding with Nietzsche in turning away from morality as our preeminent value discourse towards a theory of psychological health. Morality is seen as too strongly connected with the repressive forces of the superego. The central conclusion of the last chapter of his last major work, the *New Introductory Lectures on Psychoanalysis*, is that human life must come to be based on the science of psychology, a science of mental health.

Hence, we have returned to the questions raised in the discussion of Peck's *People of the Lie*. Are we responsible for our wrong acts if evil is a form of illness? Are we responsible for our unconsciously motivated actions or are they simply symptoms of a disease that calls for sympathy and attempts at cure rather than punishment? It is now time to confront these issues directly by turning to the languages of health and ethics and asking whether the discovery of the unconscious entails the death of ethics and the coming of an age in which health dominates the field of values.

CHAPTER 5

THE CASE AGAINST ETHICS

It is difficult to make statements about what is essential to a culture, for the grounds of any culture are multiple, complex, and intricately interwoven; yet, it is hard to imagine Western culture without seeing it as grounded in "Plato's hope." Plato envisioned human beings as being able to break from the bondage of social fatedness and the tyranny of desires to become free persons capable of determining their own lives. Since reason was necessary in order to question social values, control the emotions, and give a coherent direction to life, Plato saw reason's achievement of dominance in the psyche as the key to the creation of this new kind of person. As reason can know and control only that which can be an object for it, Plato hypothesized that reason could both ground itself in an objective structure of rational values and could apply this structure to the whole contents of the psyche. It could do this, however, only if the other elements and forces of the psyche could be brought into consciousness, for consciousness is the only domain reason can rule. If this hope were true, then humans could attain full mastery of themselves and be autonomous beings who were, nonetheless, responsible for the construction of a harmonious social order.

Although the quest for an objective moral structure of values grounded in metaphysical being has been largely abandoned, the goal of becoming masters of ourselves has not. By the time we are adults, we are expected to attain a full control over our motivations and rationally (non-compulsively, non-ignorantly) choose the best course of action available to us. To the extent we cannot freely choose what life to follow, what actions to perform, or what consequences to produce, we are not considered to be fully mature human beings.

The discovery of the unconscious calls this paradigm into question. Not only is the theory that the mind can fully know and control its motivating factors seen as an illusion, but, as we have discovered with Marx, Nietzsche, and Freud, ethics itself is implicated in producing the very things that it claims to be eliminating—human suffering and bondage.The heart of the conflict between ethics' view of autonomous agency and that of the discoverers of the unconscious centers on the concept of whether there can be "overdetermined actions."

1. Overdetermined Actions

An overdetermined action is one that can be fully understood in terms of either conscious or unconscious intentions. It is akin to the overdetermination in the world of fate, for equally good and independent explanations can be offered for actions, depending on whether one accounts for them by looking at unconscious or conscious motivations. Agents will be able to give intelligent reasons for what they are doing, but their acts can also be interpreted as accomplishing unconscious aims that have nothing to do with these reasons. Since unconscious activity can manipulate conscious activity, but not vice versa, it is the unconscious aims that direct overdetermined actions. Thus, in overdetermined actions, persons do not know and cannot control what motivates them. Nor can they know the extent to which they are capable of free choice, for there is no way of determining the extent to which actions are caused by unconscious motivations. So pervasive is the possibility of influence by the unconscious that we can never hold, like Plato, that the mind can be fully disclosed to itself.

Freud has been seen as holding not only that some actions and thoughts can be overdetermined, but also that all human activity is strictly determined. This view of Freud, held by such philosophers as John Hospers, Joel Feinberg, and Paul Taylor, sees him as denying that humans have any freedom to be other than what they are. I reject the determinist interpretation of Freud on a number of grounds. First, Freud was not a metaphysician who carefully considered the problem of freedom and determinism and made a definite statement concerning this problem. Rather, he made a number of statements about psychic phenomena being determined. These can be interpreted in a number of ways, including as denying that psychic events are capricious or occur by chance—a view which is fully compatible with a number of theories of freedom. Second, if Freud is a strict determinist, then neither psychotherapy nor his statements concerning how therapy can free patients from their symptoms and obsessions to live more autonomously make sense. Third, such a global view of determinism is unhelpful, for it does not allow us to see the real contribution Freud makes to discovering what particular psychological factors in particular people take away their autonomy and how these factors might be overcome. As a global determinist, Freud can help us no more than the philosopher or scientist who asserts that we are fully determined by the laws of nature but has no understanding of unconscious processes. Overdetermined actions are of significance precisely because they might be other than they are.[1]

There are four kinds of overdetermined actions that are crucial for seeing how unconscious dynamics compromise our ability to be ethical and which significantly challenge the effectiveness of morality: transference, projection, obsessions, and actions in which we unknowingly reproduce oppressive forms of social/political life.

Freud discovered transference when his patients began to intensely love, hate, or feel ambivalence toward him for no apparent reason. These feelings were being "transferred" onto Freud from his patients' unconscious early childhood feelings for their parents or other important persons. The patient will seem to have "good reasons" for loving or hating the therapist, but the real reasons for the love or hate are the connections being made in the primary process condensing parent and therapist into one.

Transferences are part of ordinary life. Most of the libidinal attachments and dislikes of adult life have some primary process connections to those we most loved and/or despised in childhood. If these connections do not overly distort our perceptions, feelings, and expectations, then they not only are livable, but also give a feeling of connectedness in emotional life. However, when they are grounded in pathological structures of the unconscious, then we find ourselves relating to others in ways they do not warrant. That is, our treatment of them is not based on who they are as persons but on associations they have evoked in the primary process of the unconscious. When we love, hate, aggress against, and cower from persons for no objective reasons, then we cannot be moral agents in relation to these people, for moral agency requires of us to treat others as persons, as ends in themselves. When we relate to them through transferences, we do not see them as persons in their own rights but as objects of our unconscious manipulations.

The second type of overdetermined action with importance for ethics is "projection." Projection occurs when we unconsciously take undesirable feelings, wishes, or character traits that we abhor in ourselves and see them as characterizing someone else or some group. Typically, what is projected is guilt and/or aggression, but it could be greed, sexual perversions, megalomania, envy, and so on. When aggression is projected, the person then feels persecuted, endangered, or embattled in a hostile world in which people are out to get him. Consciously good reasons can be given for believing that others are hostile, but the real source of these perceptions is the unconscious projection of one's own hostility.

Erich Neumann's *Depth Psychology and a New Ethic* reveals a devastating connection between the most destructive forms of projection and traditional Western ethics. Neumann holds that Western morality divides the world into good and evil or light and darkness, and demands that humans associate only with the good or light. However, human beings are not naturally "good"; we all feel murderous rage, greed, envy, illegitimate erotic passions, and so on. To be good we must eliminate these negatives from ourselves either through suppression or repression. Suppression occurs when we consciously rid ourselves of what we consider to be evil. This is the path Nietzsche termed asceticism: the rejection of the multiple possibilities of life in order to live according to an ideal. Because it is a conscious process, suppression has no repercussions beyond the suffering voluntarily chosen. However, when we repress what is dark and unacceptable into ourselves, the evil does not disappear, as the old moral psychology thought it did, but enters into a dangerous unconscious dynamic. On the one hand, we develop a conscious social persona, an image that appears perfectly good, and, on the other, an unconscious "shadow" that contains the aspects of ourselves which we cannot accept. Because we have repressed our shadows, we see ourselves as perfectly identified with our ego ideals. Since the ego ideal is a social construct, our identification with it merges us with the social group and its awesome power. Such merging produces "ego-inflation" and causes us to see ourselves and our group as unqualifiedly good and powerful.

While the ego is inflating itself to unlimited proportions, the shadow must be defended against; otherwise it might contaminate the perfect persona. The major defense against the shadow's infiltrating into consciousness is the projection of it onto others. These others are typically minorities living in our midst, different countries and races, those who don't live up to the moral ideal, and leaders, geniuses, and intellectuals who have the power to stand apart from the collective ideal. To understand how common social projection is in the West, recall how many minorities and foreign peoples have been seen as oversexed, greedy, or power-hungry. Recall how many nonconformists have been persecuted for being perverts and how many wars have been justified on the basis of the aggressive intentions of a neighboring country. How many millions of human beings have been inhumanely slaughtered because of the projection of the shadow?

No stronger indictment against Western ethics can be made. In its radical separation of good from evil and its demands that we lead only good lives and be fully responsible for who we are and what we do, traditional morality prevents us from admitting and integrating our evils in healthy ways. Paradoxically, the discourse created to give self-mastery has, in fact, rendered us less masters of ourselves than we had been before, for it has demanded the repression and, hence, loss of control of human emotions and instincts that previously had been considered to be natural.[2] What appeared to consciousness to be a complete ridding of evil intentions from the self (since it could no longer find them) was in fact a strengthening, intensifying, and loss of control over these intentions. Thus, ethics is implicated not only in the suffering of neurosis but also in the aggressions against peoples, races, nations, and individuals caused by projections. At the doorstep of ethics stand the Holocaust and other Western genocides. Of course, there are complex social, historical, economic, political, and cultural factors involved in these events; morality-induced projection was never the sufficient cause of these evils. However, without projection, it is doubtful they could have occurred.

A third type of overdetermined action that is important for ethics is obsession/compulsion. When humans are obsessional, they must habitually perform certain activities or think certain thoughts, regardless of the effects of these thoughts and activities on themselves and others. That is, obsessions are activities in which humans cannot take account of themselves or others as human beings, but must follow the structure of the compulsion.

On first look, obsessional actions do not appear to have the ethical import of transferences or projections. Yet, even the seemingly harmless case of ritual handwashing wastes countless hours of the obsessional sufferer and is endlessly annoying to those close to her. If one also thinks of addictions as obsessions, then this type of overdetermination takes on a massive importance, for the number of lives ruined by alcoholic, drug, food, gambling, and other addictions is on a scale so large as to make most other forms of evil pale in comparison. For instance, every two years more Americans are killed by drunk drivers than died in all the years of the Viet Nam War. Indeed, as we will see in the next chapter, the abuse of alcohol can be seen as causing more human suffering and damage than almost any other factor in contemporary life. Yet, because such abuse seems from a traditional moral standpoint to be either out of an agent's control or fully within it, morality has either ignored this evil or simply condemned it as an evil. Both responses exacerbate the problem rather than helping it.

The fourth kind of overdetermined act is one that we found in examining the social unconscious in Marx and Nietzsche. It occurs when one is unknowingly a conduit for social oppressions. A number of contemporary thinkers have built on the analyses of Marx and Nietzsche to reveal how oppressive forces reproduce themselves in ordinary, accepted social behavior. For instance, Sandra Bartky shows how a woman who follows the usual practices of making herself "feminine" reproduces a patriarchal power structure by being less assertive than men are allowed to be and by admitting that her body and face are not good enough as they naturally are, but must be slimmed, made over, and so forth to conform to a certain imposed ideal. The feminine woman consciously intends only to make herself look attractive, but unconsciously she is obeying forces that keep the

patriarchy dominant.[3] The manager eliminates fifty positions on the conscious grounds that this will maximize
profit, but the act also has the consequences of keeping
workers in an anxious, and, hence, more submissive state.
Few people are willing to admit they are consciously sexist,
racist, or exploitative; yet, sexism, racism, and exploitation
remain dominant social forces, for they are reproduced
through unconscious overdetermination in ordinary social
life.

When we look at all the harm done by persons acting
out negative or ambivalent transferences, projecting their
shadows onto others and then aggressing against them, losing control of their lives in obsessional/addictive ways, and
unconsciously reproducing oppressive social forces, I think
we might find a great percentage of the suffering human
beings cause themselves and one another. Insofar as ethics
refuses to take account of unconscious overdetermination
in actions, it is impotent to deal with them. Only an ethics
informed by a psychology of the unconscious and armed
with knowledge of how acts can be overdetermined is likely
to have any effect in reducing this kind of unintentional
intentional evil.

Yet, ethicists have in general either ignored overdetermined actions or denied that they make any conceptual
sense, holding that for anything to be an "action" it must be
consciously intended. Perhaps more than anyone else in
Anglo-American philosophy Alasdaire MacIntyre in *The
Unconscious* (1958) and Stuart Hampshire in *Thought and
Action* (1959) drove ethicists away from psychoanalytic theory by arguing, as MacIntyre does, that the concept of
unconscious experience makes no sense (since "experience"
implies "consciousness of something"), or, as Hampshire
does, that "there is a necessary connection between conscious and intended action."[4] Hampshire holds that for any
action to be intentional, a person must be able to answer the
question "What are you doing now?" in terms of specifying
his intentions and beliefs about the current situation. To
"intend" to do something means that one has a desire/want/

aim in doing it, has the ability to it, has the requisite knowledge necessary for doing it, and is consciously aware of all these factors. Since overdetermined actions cannot fulfill these conditions, they cannot be considered part of the class of "intended actions."

Freud responded to MacIntyre and Hampshire long before they wrote:

> This equation is either a *petitio principii* which begs the question whether everything that is psychical is also necessarily conscious; or else it is a matter of convention, of nomenclature. In this latter case it is, of course, like any other convention, not open to refutation. The question remains, however, whether, the convention is so expedient that we are bound to adopt it. To this we may reply that the conventional equation of the psychical with the conscious is totally inexpedient. It disrupts psychical continuities, plunges us into insoluble difficulties of psycho-physical parallelism, is open to the reproach that for no obvious reason it overestimates the part played by consciousness, and that it forces us prematurely to abandon the field of psychological research without being able to offer us any compensation from the other fields.[5]

Yet, if we cannot be aware of our unconscious motivations, how can we ascribe unconscious intentionality to any of our actions? Without some kind of basis for establishing intentionality, anything whatsoever can be read into our actions as "hidden motives" and we return to a psychology of finding demons and devils behind every antisocial or masochistic action.

I suggest that we can make most sense of the concept of unconscious intentionality by paralleling the model of MacIntyre and seeing unconscious intentions as making sense in terms of a person's ongoing unconscious narratives.[6] MacIntyre points out that neither observers nor the agent of an action knows how to describe what the agent is doing or why she is doing it unless there is an understanding of how the actions fit into the ongoing narrative structure of her life—the ongoing story the person tells about herself. A person does something, for instance, plants a seed. But what is the intention? Is it to plant a seed, do gardening, play, copy a parent, or make a living? We cannot say unless we know how this event fits the ongoing narrative of how she understands her life.

Although unrecognized by MacIntyre, we can make sense of the notion of "unconscious intention" within this framework. The unconscious is typically engaged in long term projects, such as finally winning mother's love or destroying father's authority, and numerous individual acts can be interpreted as belonging to these narratives. Unconscious narratives typically have generating experiences in childhood and a history of attempts to satisfy their aims. Unlike conscious narratives, however, they are repetitive; there is no development to them.

Without a history of repetitive attempts to satisfy an unconscious wish, we cannot talk legitimately about someone's having an unconscious intention. We cannot tell from Billy's desiring to take Mary away from Tom that he is acting on the basis of repressed Oedipal desires. However, if Billy repeatedly attempts to take women away from other men, and these affairs cause him excessive guilt, loss of friendships, loss of self-esteem, and ruin all chances for the steady intimacy that he so desires, then we might suspect that he has an unconscious Oedipal intention of winning his mother away from his father. If Billy also has obsessive incestuous masterbatory fantasies, recalls in a therapeutic session a strong erotic bond between himself and his mother, and transfers incestuous desires and aggressions onto the therapist, then we can say with more assurance that Billy has an unconscious Oedipal narrative and that he unconsciously intends in his seductions to "win mother from father."

If Billy unconsciously intends these seductions, is he also responsible for them and the misery they have brought to so many lives? In a way we must say "yes," for it was his actions that destroyed marriages, abandoned women, and aggressed against men. On the other hand, he did not know what he was doing, was not acting freely but compulsively, and had no possibility (given the virulence of the repressed desire) of controlling his actions. As Dilman says, "The man executing an unconscious intention is at once agent and victim."[7] He seems both responsible and not responsible for his overdetermined actions. But which is he? Traditional concepts of ethical agency cannot deal with this question because they only recognize the conscious determination of actions. I will attempt to answer this question in chapter 9 after we have more fully explored what it means to conceive of human beings as having unconscious intentionalities.

2. Summary: The Case Against Ethics

The discoverers of the unconscious brought three major indictments against ethics for its failure to understand how the psyche functions. First, ethics has an inadequate concept of responsibility that makes humans both too responsible for who they are and not responsible enough for what they do. Second, ethics and its progeny, rational morality, produce significant and needless human suffering. Third, ethics is impotent in recognizing and preventing evil.

With the discovery of the unconscious, we found that humans cannot be masters of themselves, for they are thoroughly entangled in economic, conceptual, linguistic, and emotional webs which their cultures and childhood histories weave around and through them. Insofar as ethics proclaimed the possibility that we could be masters of our destinies, it perpetrated an illusion—a crucial illusion, a powerful illusion, an illusion on which the West was built, but an illusion, nonetheless. This illusion made us too responsible, for it held that all humans have control over their own personal destinies and can be anything they want to be, and, therefore, have no reason not to be morally ideal. The inevitable failures to meet the ideal of what we should be produce feelings of guilt and inadequacy, which in turn produce depression and other forms of personal suffering. On the other hand, ethics lets us off too easily by not holding us responsible for acts we do not consciously intend. We are not accountable for any suffering we cause through unconscious intentionalities, and, hence, have little reason either to find out what our unconscious intentionalities are or to work on changing them. If ethics is going to continue as a discourse, then it needs to thoroughly revise its moral psychology and reconceive its notions of responsibility, moral agency, and intentionality.

The second indictment against ethics and morality made by the discoverers of the unconscious is that these discourses have inflicted untold suffering on human beings—the very thing that, supposedly, they were attempting to eliminate from the world. Marx and other political theorists see Western morality as a tool used by dominant powers to justify and protect their power. If everyone has the power to be self-determining, then everyone can be seen as choosing their forms of life, except in cases of direct and evident political restraint. That is, forces of social oppression mask themselves behind a theory that denies social fatedness and asserts the full power of individuals to be self-determining.

Nietzsche and Freud located the suffering produced by ethics in another place: the pain caused by the severe limitation of spontaneous and instinctual activity. In demanding that all persons conform to ethical standards, ethics constrains individuality, spontaneity, creativity, differences, and free play. While ethics does strengthen our wills and gives us vast abilities to control our passions and the world, it does so at the cost of sapping the vital creative energies of life. The imposition of a common moral system has the tendency of ascetisizing everyone into a "herd" (Nietzsche) or producing a tortured internal dynamics of repression and guilt (Freud).

To these social and personal sufferings we must add the vast evils of projection. Insofar as morality makes the acceptance of one's inadequacies and moral failures demeaning and degrading, it has the tendency to force us into a dynamic of repression of the shadow, ego-inflation, and a projection of our darknesses on to others. This projection then gives us reasons to aggress against those in whom our projected evil resides.

The third indictment against ethics made by Nietzsche and post-Freudian psychoanalytical thinkers (including Peck) is that ethics is impotent in recognizing and preventing evil. As we saw with Peck's case of Bobby's parents who systematically but without conscious intention destroyed their sons, evil tends to occur covertly, under the guise of socially acceptable acts.

The boss puts his hand on the secretary's shoulders and says, "Nice work." All is fine except that the glint in the boss's eye and extra pressure on the shoulders give a very different message to the secretary, who feels the imposition of sexual aggression. Did sexual aggression happen? The boss did not consciously intend it, but was merely commending the secretary. Hence, according to ethics no wrong was committed. In its concentration on conscious intentions, ethics misses altogether the confusion, guilt, and victimization felt by the secretary.

Even when ethics can recognize evil in overt criminal and immoral acts, it is impotent to prevent them, for it does not understand how they are produced. From its psychological theory, ethics must assume that these acts are generated by agents freely and consciously choosing to do them. However, evil is not consciously and freely willed, but partly generated by unconscious compulsions arising out of profound childhood injuries and neglect. Until these experiences are exhumed and worked through, the tendency to create evil will remain present. The response of morality to evil is to blame the offender and punish her, but what legal and moral punishment tends to do is further entrench the negative self-images that generate the antisocial behavior.

These indictments by the discoverers of the unconscious—that ethics has an inadequate understanding of psychological functioning, a damaging theory of responsibility, a tendency to limit spontaneous self-expression; causes profound and widespread human suffering; and is impotent in recognizing and preventing evil—are devastating. I will later give some rejoinders for ethics, but the best they will do is mitigate the power of this critique. They cannot overcome it. This is not to say that we can easily conceive of forms of life superior to that of ethics, but that ethics has not produced the ideal world its inventors thought it would, nor can it.

These insights into the underside of morality and ethics turned the discoverers of the unconscious away from ethics toward a different set of values—those of health. Nietzsche proclaimed that persons who were not living well to be "sick and moribund" rather than evil. He saw the ascetic ideal of ethics as "the supreme disaster in the history of European man's health," superseding the other two primary illnesses, "the poisoning of Europe with alcohol" and syphilis.[8] Freud, the physician, also made it clear that the values of psychological health are far superior to the civilized morality that he implicated in all psychological suffering.

Thus, the question now arises: Should the field of psychological health, with its more profound understanding of how the psyche functions, take ethics' place as the dominant value system of the culture?

CHAPTER 6

PSYCHOLOGICAL HEALTH

Do an experiment. Go to a local non-university bookstore and look for the section on philosophical ethics. If you are lucky, there will be part of a shelf devoted to this topic with some classical works by Plato, Aristotle, Kant, and Mill, and maybe a few contemporary volumes. In all likelihood, however, such a section will not even exist. Now go to the section or sections that contain books on personal health. You will probably find shelves upon shelves, if not whole walls, devoted to books on how to have fulfilling sex, an optimally functioning body, a nonstressful life-style, and a self-affirming approach to life. Alongside these will be sections on how to recover from addictions to alcohol, drugs, sex, food, debilitating relationships, and gambling, or how to recover from growing up in a dysfunctional family. The section on a healthy diet alone will outnumber by far all the volumes in philosophy.

The conclusion we can draw from this experiment is that health has replaced ethics as the primary value system of our culture. If more evidence is needed, I suggest turning to other media and repeating the experiment. How many radio and television talk shows are devoted to ethics? How many to personal health? If you want to listen to a good tape on ethics while taking a trip, could you? How many psychological self-help tapes are available? The answers are so obvious they need not be given. One hundred years ago pamphlets on morality were as commonplace as self-help books are now, and presidents of colleges and universities often taught culminating senior courses on ethics. Now presidents have no time for such tasks, and ethics classes are no more special than any other specialized course. In short, when we want to learn how to live well, we turn to the field of health, not ethics.

This shift in the primary value system of the culture is of utmost importance and lies at the heart of what many see as the contemporary crisis of values. Authors such as Allan Bloom, Robert Bellah, and Christopher Lasch bemoan the replacement of the old values of community, responsibility, and commitment to high ideals by the self-centered, non-idealistic values of personal well-being.[1] But we should not prematurely judge this shift. As we have already seen, there are a number of profound reasons why ethics was problematical as the culture's primary value language. Societies rarely, if ever, shift value systems simply out of perversity or decadence. It could be that with the discovery of the unconscious, the field of psychological health has gained more power than any of our previous value systems for understanding how the psyche works and what it really needs.

1. The Value System of Health

Although Freud, Nietzsche, and their successors differ in a number of ways on the values they associate with health; nonetheless, a certain paradigm seems to be emerging that can be called "the value system of health."[2] The primary values of health are the well-being and longevity of the individual. Well-being is attained when the physical and psychological systems of the human organism are optimally functioning, and such functioning increases the possibility of longevity. When a physical or psychological system is optimally functioning, it is said to be "fit." Since fitness gives both the sense of well-being and the promise of longevity, it is the central working value in the system of health.

As we are here concerned primarily with psychological fitness, we will leave the ideal of physical fitness as simply having all the systems of the body optimally functioning. The criteria for what constitutes psychological fitness are, at present, diverse, but the following seem generally accepted. Psychologically healthy people are those who are able, in Freud's words, to "love and work." Erik Erikson adds that "a healthy personality *actively masters his environment*, shows a certain *unity of personality*, and is able to *perceive the world and himself correctly.*"[3] Humanistic psychologists such as Abraham Maslow, Rollo May, and Carl Rogers, along with philosopher David Norton, would emphasize persons' abilities to realize fully their unique talents and natural gifts as essential for being healthy. Most psychologists would expand Erikson's active mastery of one's environment into a general notion of autonomy and add spontaneity of the desires and emotions as crucial criteria for healthy psychic functioning. In sum, persons with healthy psyches are those who are capable of intimacy and productivity, autonomously direct their lives, actively master environmental variables, have spontaneous (non-repressed) emotions and desires, are engaged in activities that genuinely use and satisfy their talents and gifts, and have accurate reality testing.

The key to realizing all of these traits is understood as the development of a strong self. Ever since Freud's late work in which a vital ego is seen as the key to keeping the irrational pressures of the id and harsh judgments of the superego at bay, the idea that the self is at the center of psychological life has been increasingly apparent, culminating in the important work of Heinz Kohut's school of self-psychology. Self-psychologists have attempted to show that almost all psychological pathologies can be traced back to injuries in the development of a core nuclear self. Without a nuclear self and sense of self-worth, none of the other psychological systems can adequately function. A weak self cannot tolerate strong conflicts of emotions and drives and hence must repress them. A self with a negative self-representation will not be able to recognize its needs and abilities nor feel that they have the right to be satisfied. Reality-testing abilities are decreased, for injured selves often distort their perceptions of themselves with narcissistic fantasies of grandiosity and have tendencies to idealize or devalue others.

Hence, the sine qua non of psychological health is seen as having an integral core self. Although this seems to resemble Plato's moral psychology, the differences are telling. For Plato and Aristotle, the core self is made up of the rational faculties and virtues that unify psychic functioning during adulthood. What is unified are the contents and processes of conscious experience. In contrast, the nuclear or core self of contemporary psychology is formed in the first several years of life, functions in largely unconscious ways, and is not susceptible to rational manipulation. In short, for classical and Enlightenment thinkers psychological health could be attained in the psyche if reason could control its conscious motivations, while for modern psychology health is primarily a matter of how unconscious structures are formed and relate to one another. In the ancient world, one might seek out a philosophic school to help cure one of psychological maladies; now we go to psychotherapists trained in dealing with the unconscious.

If the archaic self is intact and development continues to go well, then a healthy emotional system will develop. Like Aristotle, modern psychotherapy holds that healthy people have character traits that neither repress nor indulge feelings and desires, but rather allow the self to feel them fully without having to immediately discharge them. The lack of compulsion demanding immediate discharge means that persons have time to deliberate about how best to respond to situations and can thus tie their responses to their systems of values and evaluate the likely consequences of their possible actions. A person with this kind of character is capable of having, in John Dewey's terms, "delayed actions," and these are what distinguish adult behavior from childlike behavior. Healthy emotions are thoroughly connected to deliberative powers and a mature knowledge of the world, for it is only through these connections that the emotions can be adequate responses to present situations.

If one's self is coherent, and her emotions and desires not significantly overdetermined, then the perception of reality will be more or less adequate for practical living. This is where reason has a function in the value system of health: we need to reason in order to perceive reality and meet our needs. However, the difference with classical ethics needs to be emphasized, for reason had the functions in ethics of ruling the other elements in the psyche, being an end in itself, and knowing universal truths. In health, reason has no such stature. It does not rule the psyche, does not penetrate to the depths of an objective reality, and its exercise is not seen as the highest form of human functioning. Reason is merely pragmatic, serving the ends of physical and psychological fitness.

When a person has a unified, self-affirming core self, character traits that neither repress nor indulge the passions, and adequate reality-testing and practical reasoning, then she can be productive, intimate, autonomous, and express her unique individuality. These identifying characteristics of a healthy psyche are, however, appropriate for only one stage of psychic functioning: adulthood or maturity. Life has a number of developmental stages and a person's actions and character are healthy if they are fitting for the developmental stage she is in and pointing toward the next stage of development. This setting of values in a developmental context is contrary to the main thrust of ethics, which has traditionally held that there are eternal values that are true for all times and places. A developmental philosophy, on the other hand, understands that certain values are appropriate for certain stages of life and inappropriate at others.[4] Being dependent is both good and necessary for a child; it is inappropriate for an adult. Responsibility, sex, labor, and independence—values of adult life—are likely to be evils if they come into a person's life prematurely.

As important as each developmental stage is, all of them are anchored by the stage of "maturity." All early change is "growth," if it leads toward maturity; all change after the attainment of maturity is "growth," if it deepens and expands the mature state. Hence, healthy psychic functioning can be equated with the development toward and attainment of maturity. Acting autonomously, having the capacities for intimacy and productivity, realizing one's unique capacities, and living in reality rather than the fantasies of childhood are all attributes of the mature person. If there is an ethic in the value system of psychological health, it is an ethic that has as its highest ideal the attainment of maturity.

2. Aristotle, Health, and Ethics

We cannot fail at this point to see the remarkable similarities between the contemporary value system of health and the ethics of Aristotle. Both have as their central value the development of mature human beings. Both find that character traits which allow the emotions and desires to surface but not dominate consciousness are essential to the attainment of maturity. Both see accurate assessments of the particular worlds in which we live and abilities to act autonomously in these worlds as defining the mature person. Both see the mature person as capable of intimate friendships and social productivity. Indeed, the values of psychological health are so close to those of Aristotelian ethics, that health may be said to be the successor of Aristotle in today's world. Alasdaire MacIntyre is mistaken in mourning the loss of Aristotelian ethics in the modern world, for it is flourishing—just not in philosophical ethics, but in the primary value system of the culture—psychological health.

Yet, there are important ways in which the value system of health differs from the ethics of Aristotle, and these differences are so crucial that they constitute grounds for saying that psychological health cannot be an ethic in the full sense of that term.

For Aristotle, acts by which we constitute the self are acts which equally constitute the community. The virtuous character traits that allow individuals to mature also ground the social and economic relations of a community. A just person asks only for his fair share, and in so doing helps create a just society; a courageous person defends what is valuable to himself and in so doing defends his community. A generous person gains personal esteem in acts that help distribute social and economic goods. By not taking an excessive amount of social or economic goods, a moderate person will help make these available for others.

While it is probably true that persons who follow the modern value system of health will also be good citizens, the connection between what is good for the person's health and what is good for the community's welfare is not necessary, as it is in Aristotle. Unlike the list of Aristotelian virtues, there is nothing in the notions of self-affirmation and self-development that implies that these traits also serve one's community.[5] The values of health have as their exclusive aim the well-being of the individual; any social benefit is a secondary outcome. The individual acting under the values of health has no responsibility for sustaining the community.

It is the self-absorption of the value system of health that prevents it from being an "ethic" in the full sense of that term. Health asks questions like "How can the individual become optimally fit?" and "How can the individual best meet her needs?" It does not ask questions like "How can the individual develop in such a way as to help her community?" or "What use of talents and skills will best serve the community?" Aristotle, of course, would not have separated these questions, for he thought that self-development could only occur in an optimally functioning community and that an optimally functioning community could be sustained only if its citizens were mature adults.

Aristotle and Plato both lived in Athens, a city-state whose political citizenry was limited to free Athenian males. In comparison to later empires and states, its citizenry was extraordinarily homogeneous. By the seventeenth century, such homogeneous political units were impossible to sustain. The diversity of peoples needed to be incorporated into a coherent social life, the vast number of voices demanding a political say, and the rise of an individualistic economics led to communities being replaced by civil societies. Civil societies encourage individuals to pursue those paths that optimize personal happiness so long as the individuals remain within the boundaries of legal justice and obey the values of mutual toleration, minority rights, and majority decision. While personal development in general benefits the society, there will arise a number of occasions in which the good of the individual and that of others in the society will conflict. It might be to a capitalist's advantage to minimize wages, but this is certainly not to the worker's benefit.

To deal with these conflicts, ethics had to change. It ceased asking how a person should live in order to be an optimal member of a *polis* or Christian community and addressed the questions of what basic rights individuals should have and how conflicts between individuals should be resolved. Character development was more or less forgotten as ethicists attempted to find rules or principles that ought to be followed in conflicts of interests. The two major schools of thought that developed in response to these questions were those of Kant and the utilitarians. For Kant, all interests needed to be subjected to the arbitration of a universal law. That is, neither personal nor social interests should dictate what we do in conflictual situations, even if the conflict is within oneself, as when someone is contemplating suicide. Rather, we should act according to universal principles that we are willing to have everyone follow. The utilitarians took a different approach, attempting to use a naturalistic/scientific outlook and methodology. They declared the major unit of well-being to be pleasure and that the maximization of pleasure is what all ethical acts should aim for. That is, if there are numerous conflicting possibilities, one should select that act which creates "the greatest amount of pleasure for the greatest number of people."

This very general statement of a vastly complex shift in Western culture from community to civil society allows us to better understand the demise of ethics and the rise of health. The values of health have come to be associated with an individual's optimizing his fitness, while ethics is associated with fair and just conflict resolution. The ethics of Aristotle have been bifurcated in modern life into a part concerned with the well-being of the individual (health) and a part concerned with relations to others (ethics).

This split has had disastrous consequences for both health and ethics. Insofar as ethics is no longer connected to an individual's pursuit of happiness, the crucial question becomes why should I be moral, if by being immoral I can advance my interests? Why not be a free rider if I am certain that I will not be caught? Modern ethicists have been unable to answer this question adequately. The best they seem to be able to do is to say that being ethical gives us "dignity" (Kant), or that we must be moral if we are to be rational. They cannot say why a life of dignity or rationality is the best way for humans to live.[6] Indeed, Nietzsche would scorn such values as plebeian impositions and imprisonments. Since ethics no longer has anything essential to say about how one can become happy and cannot justify why it should be the highest value discourse, its ability to inspire human lives has diminished.

Health also suffers from this split, for its lack of a theory of social responsibility makes it a conceptually incoherent value system in two ways. First, it is difficult to imagine how human beings could develop into adults capable of productivity and intimacy without becoming persons capable of responding to the needs of others and handling interpersonal conflicts with justice and integrity. While discourses other than morality can help us appreciate and respond to other humans, none does it with more rigor or concern for all persons as human beings as does ethics.

Development occurs under conditions of optimal frustration. When we encounter obstacles that do not overwhelm us but challenge the ordinary ways we have of dealing with the world, then we can develop new powers to overcome them. How can an individual possibly grow from the self-centeredness of childhood and adolescence to a mature adult without the challenge of an ethical standpoint? What will make us give up the narcissistic orientation of the early stages of life, if it is not the demand that we become morally responsible people who can treat other people as ends in themselves rather than as things to be manipulated for personal satisfaction? Persons who retain an excessive self-centeredness and self-absorption often are successful in socioeconomic spheres, but rarely do we find such people genuinely happy with their adult successes and almost never are they able to enjoy the profound satisfactions of mature intimacy. In short, mature human beings live and interact with other humans who have equal rights and statuses and whom deserve respect and care.[7] Insofar as health concerns itself only with the development of individual fitness and largely ignores moral development, it cannot fully achieve its prime goal of "mature functioning."

The absence of a value of ethical responsibility not only makes development difficult to comprehend, but it also endangers the very conditions that health has found necessary for producing fit human beings. We know from the study of infants and the examination of people suffering from psychic disorders that empathic, consistent nurturance, especially during infancy and childhood, is crucial for the production of healthy persons.[8] This nurturance needs to be provided by adults. Yet, adults seem to be so bent on establishing their individual fitnesses, including economic and social fitnesses, that they seem less able to give children the excruciatingly large amounts of time and care they require. Nurturance is not just for children. We are social animals who throughout our adult lives need and cherish the care and responsiveness of others in intimate relations, social connections, and our places of labor. A harsh uncaring environment produces stress and ill-health; a caring, empathic, just environment produces a sense of well-being. Yet care and nurturance, especially in our economic and professional organizations, seem to be on the wane, as individuals compete against one another for seemingly scarce sources of recognition and material goods in a quest for optimal individual well-being.

In short, health's assumption that the fitness of an individual can be treated as an independent entity endangers the very possibility of there being a world of healthy individuals. This assumption also reveals that the values of health are not based solely upon scientific empirical investigations of functioning human organisms, but contain a number of concepts and values that remain uncriticized and unjustified. Nowhere is this importation of uncriticized values more evident than in the focal value of psychological health: maturity.

How do health theorists know that mature human functioning is characterized by "love and work," "unity of personality," "self-realization," "rational thinking," and "autonomy?" Insofar as health purports to be a science, these traits appear to have been determined by empirical observation, cross-cultural studies, and so on. Yet, this is not so. There are many cultures in which adults do not define themselves by love, work, reason, or autonomy but rather by how well they function in the roles into which fate has thrust them. A number of feminist theorists see women as defining themselves more through caring, interdependent relationships than through autonomous achievement in the productive sphere. It appears that the current notion of maturity in health owes more to Western philosophical theories about ideal human states than it does to empirical observation. As Dilman says, "[i]nevitably maturity is a moral category."[9] In short, health does not have adequate justification procedures for determining or critically evaluating the central concept of its value system, maturity.

One promising response to the problem of health's not having a theory of moral responsibility and a set of justified values to define maturity is Lawrence Kohlberg's attempt to show that normal, healthy development involves a natural development of moral reasoning. For Kohlberg, morality is grounded in a natural developmental sequence in which immature forms of moral thinking are successively relinquished in favor of more adequate and mature forms. Young children exist in a preconventional egoistic stage of moral development in which they are concerned for their own welfare and see as reasons to be moral the escaping of punishments or gaining of rewards. Adolescents typically exist in a conventional stage in which morality is identified with support of group mores or the laws of one's community. The highest stage of moral development occurs when one is able to autonomously formulate universal principles. One now demands that the laws and values of one's culture have a rational justification and will not support them unless such a justification is forthcoming. The zenith of moral development occurs when one is able to follow self-chosen ethical principles on "the belief as a rational person in the validity of universal moral principles, and a sense of personal commitment to them."[10] One can find in Kohlberg's theory the acceptance of autonomy, independence, reason, and universality as the highest values governing moral life.[11] These values are not seen as one perspective of what it means to be moral, but as what any normal human being in a favorable social environment will "naturally" come to hold as a mature adult.

Carol Gilligan's response to Kohlberg is that his core study of eighty-four boys over twenty years has produced results valid only for the male gender. Because women do the primary nurturing or "mothering" in our culture, girls and boys have different developmental patterns which incline women much more toward the values of nurturance and interrelatedness.[12] Women are not concerned with abstract and general principles, but with the concrete relationships in which they find themselves. When conflicts arise, they attempt to solve them by abandoning the conflicting activity, increased nurturance, or personal negotiations, not by appeals to universal moral principles.

Gilligan does not say that women's views of maturity are superior to those of men, for this would be using the male organizational model of hierarchy to solve the conflict. Rather, she thinks that both "voices" need to be interwoven in a concept of maturity that overcomes the limitations of the male and female perspectives. What the male perspective can give to women is a sense of personal integrity that tends to get lost or compromised in identifying so strongly with others. What males can learn from women is the importance of relations, intimacy, and care. Through these values men can overcome the loneliness and emotional shallowness that so often plague their lives. When both genders can hear and speak with both voices, humans will be fuller, happier beings.

While Gilligan finds autonomy, an abstract justice of rights, individuation, universal moral laws, and self-sufficiency to be prejudiced toward the experience of one gender, Anthony Cortese's *Ethnic Ethics* sees them as prejudiced toward the experience of one gender in one class in one culture. His use of Kohlberg's testing procedures for moral development showed "a dearth of postconventional scores"[13] for ethnic groups and Third World peoples. Given these results, Kohlberg must either abandon his thesis that he has found a natural developmental sequence to moral thought or declare that some classes in some cultures are superior in producing moral humans. As Kohlberg's whole enterprise would be ruined by adopting the first possibility, he must conclude that some cultures are deficient in their abilities to produce moral adults.[14] Cortese thinks otherwise: different cultures have different patterns of moral development.

Rather than classifying women, non-Western cultures and ethnic groups as morally deficient, Gilligan and Cortese prefer to draw the inference that Kohlberg has not found a "universal" developmental sequence, but one which generally characterizes only middle-upper-class Western white males.

There is another compelling reason for not accepting Kohlberg's account of a natural sequence of moral reasoning, namely, a conceptual incoherence. There is no way of making a logical connection between the way any set of people happen to be reasoning about moral affairs and the way they *ought* to be thinking about moral affairs. Moral thinking is not like other cognitive abilities, for it has a value attached to it—it is the kind of reasoning people should use in certain situations. If it happened to be empirically true (as it might have been at one time) that the majority of adults reasoned about difficult moral issues by appealing to scriptures or a priesthood, this does not mean that this is how they ought to be thinking about these problems. Sociological studies, whether done by Kohlberg, Gilligan, or Cortese, cannot issue into ethical values. From both this conceptual failure and the empirical one, I conclude that Kohlberg's attempt to put morality into a developmental theory to be a failure.

3. Evil and Disease

The value system of health has not been content with simply redefining what constitutes well-being for humans; it also claims that it can deal with certain forms of evil better than ethics can. In order to understand health's attempt at taking over this part of ethics, we need to examine the second fundamental difference between the value systems of health and ethics. In ethics, the opposite of good is evil, while the opposite of health is disease. According to the value system of health, human beings often commit evil acts, because they are suffering from psychological disorders that stem from early injuries to the developing self. That is, health tends to uphold the Socratic maxim that no one does evil voluntarily. Ilham Dilman in a recent book on Freud says, "evil always comes from a self that is immature [not developed in a healthy psychological way] in one respect or another."[15] Jonathan Lear writes "there can be no individuated [psychologically developed] cruel person."[16] We have already seen Peck associating evil with a type of narcissistic personality disorder and Neumann implying that without the unconscious psychological mechanisms of repression and projection, much of the evil in the world would be eliminated.

Hence, health tends to see evil behavior as a symptom of an underlying disease that calls for cure. If the disease proves incurable, then we must do something to isolate the individual from disrupting the lives of innocent others, but this isolation should not be conceived of as punishment, but more like a quarantine of someone who has a contagious and virile disease.

All of this is, of course, diametrically opposed to an ethical conception of evil. According to ethics, agents freely choose to do wrong; they are not forced by external factors into making the evil choices. If evil acts are dictated by certain character traits, agents are still responsible, for as adults they can recognize what their character traits are, what consequences they cause, and are free to alter them. Given the freedom of the adult agent in choice of both acts and character, the correct response to evil is not sympathy and attempted cure but censure and punishment.

That is, in the world of ethics we are responsible for ourselves and our actions, but in the world of health, responsibility is a possibility only for the healthy. Can evil be dealt with more effectively without the categories of free choice, responsibility, guilt, and punishment? There has been one crucial experiment in which health has taken over a realm of actions that previously were in the realm of ethics, namely, acts committed under the influence of addictive substances.

From Aristotle's assertion that people are ethically responsible for acts they commit while intoxicated to the nineteenth century temperance movement, which saw abuse of alcohol as the primary evil in America, the misuse of intoxicating substances has been understood as a moral flaw deserving of moral condemnation and appropriate censure. However, since the founding of Alcoholics Anonymous in 1935, alcoholism has increasingly been seen as a disease. Although the disease concept of alcoholism had previously been espoused by one of the most eminent physicians in nineteenth-century America, Benjamin Rush, the acceptance of this notion depended on health becoming the primary realm of value in the mid-twentieth century and its adoption by Alcoholics Anonymous. Currently, the disease concept of alcoholism is so widely held that it is the official theory of the National Institute on Alcohol Abuse and Alcoholism (NIAAA), and has led to alcoholism's being serviced by numerous medical facilities and paid for by insurance companies. The disease concept is also spreading to other kinds of addictions such as those for gambling, sex, and drugs.

The misuse of alcohol and drugs is a major cause of suffering in our world. In the United States alone, alcohol abuse is the direct or indirect cause of 100,000 deaths a year, making it the third leading cause of death after coronary problems and cancer. Alcohol is also a significant factor in 30 percent of all suicides, 55 percent of all automobile fatalities, 60 percent of all child abuse, 65 percent of all drownings, and 85 percent of home violence.[17] Psychiatrist Donald Gallant is not being hyperbolic when he says "Alcohol dependence is the most common medical and psychiatric problem in the United States today."[18]

In short, whether we think of alcohol abuse and dependency as a disease or as a self-inflicted free choice worthy of moral disapprobation is extremely important, for we are speaking of a leading cause of death, crime, injury, emotional pain, psychological trauma, and severe disruptions in the lives of millions of people. Here is a cause of human suffering on an unbelievably large scale. If it does not have the dramatic visibility of the Holocaust, Hiroshima, or the racial injustice of South Africa, it is nonetheless deadlier and more damaging than all of these put together when viewed on a worldwide scale year after year after year. What is surprising—indeed, shocking—is the almost total lack of interest of ethicists in this problem.

Much of the damage done by alcohol is done by those who have lost control over their drinking (20 percent of the population drinks 80 percent of the alcohol). This loss of control is the key symptom of alcoholism or alcohol dependency, especially when persons continue to drink after being faced with incontrovertible evidence that drinking negatively affects their health, jobs, family life, and friendships. But what causes this loss of control over alcohol? For ethics, one freely chooses to drink or not, and if one knows that one is likely to lose control when one starts drinking and still drinks, then one is fully responsible for all that happens while intoxicated. But health holds that a number of people suffer from a disease—alcoholism—which controverts their abilities to freely choose whether or not to drink and, therefore, calls into question whether they are morally responsible for their acts while under the influence of alcohol.

What kind of disease is alcoholism? Here there is a great divergence of viewpoints with various genetic, neurobiological, neurobehavioral, psychoanalytic, and social theories seeming to have a part of the truth, for alcoholism is a "biopsychosocial entity."[19]

Those who emphasize biological factors give as evidence studies that show that children of alcoholics are far more likely to become alcoholics than the children of nonalcoholics, even when separated from their alcoholic parents at birth and raised in nonalcoholic families.[20] They also point to the fact that alcoholics metabolize alcohol differently than nonalcoholics. Due to an inherited enzyme deficiency in their livers, alcoholics produce more acetaldehyde, a by-product of alcohol, than nonalcoholics. In the nonalcoholic acetaldehyde is quickly broken down into an acetate which in turn becomes carbon dioxide and water and is easily eliminated from the body. However, alcoholics cannot break down all the acetaldehyde in their bodies, and this dangerous poison enters his blood stream damaging the liver, brain, and other organs. In the brain, it enters nerve cells and bonds with dopamine and norepinephrine to form a neurotransmitter, TIQ (or THIQ—tetrahydroisoquinoline). TIQ is a powerfully addictive substance which, when present in the brain, makes the person feel carefree, elated, and full of life. It is alcohol's production of TIQ in the brains of alcoholics that makes it an addictive substance for them.[21]

Yet, many people who severely abuse alcohol and other drugs do not come from alcoholic parents and do not show the signs of physical dependency (such as acute withdrawal symptoms when alcohol is removed) that are typical of the biological model. These facts and the uniform appearance of other psychological problems in alcoholics have led another group of theorists to claim that alcoholism is a psychological disease, and, indeed, it is listed as such in the DSM-IV.

Gary Forrest in his *Alcoholism, Narcissism and Psychopathology*[22] connects alcoholism with narcissistic personality disorders. He holds that every child has certain narcissistic entitlements: to be loved, affirmed, cared for, protected, fed, and so on. When these entitlements are not consistently met or are actively negated, as is the case with physical and psychological abuse, some kind of psychological illness will develop. If this inconsistent or chronic deprivation of narcissistic needs has not been so severe and early as to cause a psychosis or borderline personality disorder, it will result in a type of narcissistic character disorder.[23] People suffering from narcissistic personality disorders experience intense anxiety, excessive amounts of fear, guilt (they hold themselves responsible for not getting adequate nurturing), anger, and depression. While narcissists desperately want human relations to fill their deep emptinesses, they fear other people and see them as potentially destructive, as their parents were in childhood.

Sometime, usually during adolescence, the narcissist will encounter alcohol or some other drug. For a number of them this will be a magical moment, for unlike human beings who have failed to meet the narcissist's needs and cannot be counted on, alcohol is consistent—it gives a feeling of well-being time after time after time without fail. While high, the narcissist discovers that his levels of anxiety, fear, anger, depression, and guilt decrease significantly. He feels on top of the world and is able to form friendships with his drinking buddies the way he could never form friendships before, while at the same time erecting a barrier to real intimacy, for alcohol both gives the illusion of warm, close friendships while preventing a genuine closeness from developing between people.

Hence, addiction to alcohol and other drugs or activities such as work and sex is explained by the kind of consistent feeling of well-being and power that these substances and activities give—the very elements that the narcissist was deprived of in childhood. As psychiatrist and addiction expert Art Knauert says, alcoholics have a love affair with alcohol. Here is the consistent nurturer they have been looking for their entire lives. Here is something that always makes them feel good, always affirms their grandiosity, and always relieves anxiety, fear, anger, depression, and guilt.[24]

The problem, of course, is that tolerance levels for addictive substances get higher, and increasingly more has to be consumed in order to attain a high. Times of non-high are less tolerable and withdrawal is terrible. The body is damaged, social life becomes limited to drinking affairs, work deteriorates, and the old enemies of low self-esteem, guilt, and anxiety gather strength. In order to deal with them, the alcoholic has only one recourse—the only method he has ever learned to deal with them—drinking! And with this dynamic, the downward spiral begins. Its end is either death, severe debilitation, or painful difficult recovery.

To these biological and psychological accounts we must add a social factor, for it has been shown that the rates of alcoholism differ widely from culture to culture. For Roy Hoskins in *Rational Madness*[25] addiction is a learned way of dealing with problems. All humans face difficult problems throughout their lives, problems that cause them some anxiety and raise fears and doubts about their powers to deal with them. A healthy coping style is one that changes these negative feelings to positive ones by solving the problems. But one can also "solve the feelings." That is, one can get feelings of security, sensation, and power without solving problems by using a "fix" such as alcohol, sex, gambling, or pills.

Not only is using a fix a possibility, it is, according to Hoskins, positively advocated as a way of dealing with life by numerous sources in American culture. None is more powerful than the Madison Avenue advertisers who attempt to convince us that the use of their products will turn our lives into paradise. If you are feeling bad, tired, and angry after a hard day, don't change your life-style, have a drink. When this inappropriate coping mechanism changes from an enhancement activity to a habitual, internalized way of dealing with the world, it becomes an addiction.

All of these theories understand part of the complex truth of alcoholism, and all of them locate sources for addiction outside the conscious control of individuals. Alcoholism is a progressive disease, one which, if there is no intervention, will eventually lead to death, madness, or an almost complete nonfunctionality. There is no known cure for alcoholism, but there is a way to stop the progression of the disease almost fully, namely, to stop drinking.[26] But this is just what alcoholics find almost impossible to do. Of all the attempts to get alcoholics to stop drinking, none has been more effective than Alcoholics Anonymous.

Alcoholics Anonymous was founded when two alcoholics, Bill W. and Dr. Bob, discovered that they could remain sober by talking to one another about their alcohol problems. Since then, AA has grown to immense proportions, involving millions of people in over thirty-five countries of the world. AA meetings and their offshoots—ACA (Adult Children of Alcoholics), AlAnon (for persons living with alcoholics), and others—are so prevalent in contemporary American society that only churches can rival them for voluntary participation in a social group. In short, AA is not

a fringe movement or minor social happening. It is esti-
mated that it has already helped millions of people to stop
drinking and made significant inroads in curbing the devastations of alcohol.

Why has AA been so successful in helping people with
alcohol addictions? I suggest that AA has become such a
powerful social force in dealing with addictions because it is
an effective amalgam of both health and ethics. Like health
and unlike the typical moral community, AA does not
demand a proof of good deeds for membership, but only
requests that a person desires to stop drinking. By treating
alcoholism as a disease, AA eliminates moral guilt from the
alcoholic. It does not blame alcoholics for their loss of control
over alcohol, hence, breaking the cycle in which guilt over
drinking produces further drinking. AA is also a non-hier-
archical community of equals sharing their "experience,
strength, and hope." That is, it does not involve demeaning
hierarchical relationships in which nonalcoholic leaders
show alcoholics the right way to live. The AA community is
the heart of the recovery process, for it replaces the consistent affirmation found in alcohol with the consistent acceptance and affirmation of a community of like-persons. (The
above is obviously an idealized statement of an AA meeting—some meetings better realize the ideal than others).

The AA community is capable of establishing or dupli-
cating itself at any meeting anywhere in the world because
all meetings are founded on "the twelve steps," as are
almost all the self-help groups that have sprung up like
mushrooms from the soil of AA. In relation to our examination of the relation of health and ethics, the steps are of
vital importance. The first three steps are:

1. We admitted we were powerless over alcohol—that our
   lives had become unmanageable.
2. Came to believe that a Power greater than ourselves
   could restore us to sanity.
3. Made a decision to turn our will and our lives over to
   the care of God as we understood him.

In these first steps the traditional goal of ethics—self-mastery is relinquished. Alcoholics admit that self-mastery is for them a sham, for they are suffering from a disease over which they have no control. Since they cannot master themselves, alcoholics think it is better to place their lives in the hands of a "higher power" than the power of alcohol. This higher power is not unlike the "higher principle" that ethics seeks, but it is not part of self-mastery. Rather it belongs to the religious tradition of giving up one's ego to do the will of God. It must be emphasized, however, that AA allows almost any concept of a higher power to be used by alcoholics, from a traditional Christian God to the meeting itself. After having declared alcoholism to be a disease and giving up the traditional goal of ethics, it is shocking then to read the next seven steps:

4. Made a searching and fearless moral inventory of ourselves.
5. Admitted to God, to ourselves, and to another human being the exact nature of our wrongs.
6. Were entirely ready to have God remove our shortcomings.
7. Humbly asked Him to remove our shortcomings.
8. Made a list of all persons we had harmed, and became willing to make amends to them all.
9. Made direct amends to such people wherever possible, except when to do so would injure them or others.
10. Continued to take personal inventory and when we were wrong promptly admitted it.

Step eleven then asks for deepened and renewed contact with the higher power and twelve bids the alcoholic "to carry this message to alcoholics and to practice these principles in all our affairs."

These steps seem to have one general goal: the construction of a moral individual! Alcoholics are asked to take a "fearless moral inventory," eliminate their moral shortcomings, and rid themselves of past and current guilts by making amends to all those they have harmed. They are no longer to act on their narcissistic willfulness and desire but to ground their lives on a higher power and set of principles which they are to practice in all their affairs and take to other needy alcoholics. In short, I see the twelve steps of AA as the attempt to produce moral individuals in a moral community.

This is certainly a surprising conclusion to the "takeover" of a realm of ethics by the field of health, for it reinstates the life of ethics in the strongest possible way. Yet there are major differences between the moral community of AA and ethics. One difference we have already seen—the end of AA is not self-mastery but continued reliance on a higher power and a continued humility about the powers of self to control its own destiny. A second difference is that one gains admittance to a typical moral community on the basis of good deeds or the promise of such deeds. Entrance into AA is gained by admitting one has a disease and desires to recover. Even if an alcoholic continually backslides, she is always welcomed back into AA without censure or reproach. Wrongs done to others are confessed without punishment or imposition of guilt. The reason one is not censured for backsliding or wrongs committed and why amends can be made without moral embarrassment is that the alcoholic *is not responsible* for her backsliding or wrongs, since she suffers from a disease. That is, AA is a moral community that does not work according to the ethical/moral principle of guilt. A major purpose of steps five through ten is bringing unconscious and conscious guilt into awareness and developing a practice of ridding oneself of guilt as soon as it occurs.

What a strange amalgam of ethics and health this understanding and treatment of alcoholism is. What other "disease" involves as part of its "cure" the taking of a moral inventory and making amends for wrongs one has done? What kind of disease is it that is cured by becoming a moral person in a moral community? Either we are dealing with something that should not be called a "disease" or perhaps we are looking at the beginning of a new paradigm for disease. Of course, the understanding of disease as a moral, social, psychological, and physical phenomenon is hardly new, as it is the paradigm for disease in most non-Western cultures and characterized premodern Western medicine. Modernity's radical split of the mind from the body and invention of a purely physiological medicine for the body is an anomaly in a world in which disease is typically related to moral and psychological problems and the cure often involves the reestablishing of the individual in the community.

However, in the West, it makes little conceptual sense to try to cure a disease through establishing a moral identity in a moral community. Diseases need medical cures; becoming moral is a response to moral failure, not a medical failure. Thus, AA makes little conceptual sense. However, it works. Although AA and the disease model of addiction have strong detractors,[27] they seem to have had far more success in dealing with alcohol abuse and dependency than either the ethical strictures of earlier centuries or a straight medical model of detoxification, education, or some form of drug therapy such as antibuse. It seems that the combination of a disease model for interpreting failure and a moral model for gaining recovery has some promise at least at a pragmatic level. Conceptually we can understand why this combination might be so effective by seeing that it eliminates guilt as a primary factor in the evaluation of wrongdoing—guilt that, as Freud and Neumann have shown, leads to self-destructive behavior and projection.

Alcoholism and other addictions are not only significant forms of personal and social disorders, they represent a paradigm for the complex of causes that go into most evil behavior—behavior that destroys humans' abilities to live fully. That is, evil actions are probably caused by interwoven complexes of early psychological injuries, genetic predispositions, social variables, and individual choices. There are undoubtedly strong obsessive forces working at an unconscious level in evil acts along with conscious intentions. Because there is this complex of factors generating evil, neither the abstract disapprobations of morality which understands acts as only consciously intended, nor a straight disease approach which has no way of constituting moral agency seem able to handle evil actions. Rather than hauling out moral maxims and blaming offenders or finding narcissistic personality injuries behind all antisocial acts, we need to reconceive our normative systems.

What might help both in the confrontation of evil and the construction of a social order in which the causes of evil are less likely to occur is an ideal of maturity that grasps how unconscious forces work and clearly reveals why being ethical is part of living a deeply satisfying life. Like the process of recovery used by AA, this ideal of maturity will be a hybrid of health and ethics, for it must both include a notion of what constitutes optimal human fitness and have a theory of social responsibility. Only such an ideal can have the complexity and power to deal with the multiple aspects and levels of functioning that go into human activity. We have discovered that our moral values and the value system of health are too abstract and narrow to fully motivate human quests for an ideal or deal with significant failures of social behavior. A new vision of human maturity that interweaves the strengths of both health and ethics has the possibility of accomplishing these goals.

4. A New Moral Psychology

We have come to two fundamental conclusions. First, the discovery of the unconscious has revealed the inadequacy of traditional moral psychology and the tremendous costs of traditional western morality. Second, when we try to replace the value system of ethics with that of health, we find that it is unable to support any theory of social responsibility, unable to justify its concept of maturity as a purely empirical discovery, and that its notion of disease cannot adequately replace the notion of evil or moral wrong. In short, we can no longer legitimately support traditional ethics as a viable discourse nor can we supplant ethics with the discourse of health.

Yet, both health and ethics have genuine goods that we should be reluctant to give up. Health has the most thorough understanding of how the human psyche functions that has ever been developed and a powerful theory of what constitutes a well-lived life based on this understanding. On the other hand, ethics still is the only language that promotes self-determination within a framework of social responsibility. Without it we seem to be faced with patterns of social conformity, as with the system of fate, or patterns of unconstrained pursuit of individual desire. The task for a new moral psychology is then clear: to combine health's understanding of the complex dynamics of a psyche grounded in an unconscious with a theory of agency, responsibility, and what constitutes "the good" from a restructured ethics.

This synthesis of health and ethics cannot take place insofar as we conceive of ethics as a set of universal principles governing actions and health as concerned solely with individual fitness. However, if we retrieve the ancient notion of ethics as a discourse whose aim is to produce human beings who most deeply realize the fundamental human capacities, then such a synthesis can be accomplished, for both health and ethics will have as their goals the production of mature human beings.

Ideals of maturity inherently involve elements of both health and ethics. On the one hand, maturity has the sense of being the apex of a developmental sequence in which the human powers that were latent in childhood and adolescence come to full fruition. In drawing on such fields as psychotherapy, emotion theory, developmental psychology, and early childhood studies, health is able to give a kind of empirical grounding to the concept of maturity that philosophical ethics by itself cannot. Most importantly, these studies can give us knowledge and methods for recognizing, understanding, and dealing with unconscious intentionalities and thereby eliminate the greatest failing of ethics.

However, ideals of human excellence can never be just empirical concepts, for they represent how humans ought to live. As such, they need the support of normative justifications. Just because a certain state "x" might represent optimal psychic functioning doesn't necessarily mean that it is ethically good. One cannot simply go from a fact to a value, from an "is" to an "ought." For instance, suppose, as Freud and Nietzsche seem to have, that the psyche functions best if it can actively rid itself of aggressions by perpetrating violence on others. This might be optimal functioning, but I doubt we would call such activity "good." Ethics examines values not just in relation to the internal functioning of individuals, but to other values as well, including values of how to live in a world of individuals whose interests conflict.

In the second part of this book, I will attempt to elaborate a conception of maturity that is based on a recognition that human beings have unconscious psychic forces that are omnipresent in thinking and acting. With this new theory of human nature, I hope to show that one cannot achieve a full degree of mature functionality without adopting a discourse that requires one to legitimate the reality and needs of other people and accept responsibility for who one is, regardless of the vicissitudes of one's developmental history. It will be a theory that appears to be a combination of health and ethics, but both will be quite different from their present conceptual formulations. The theory of maturity will be strange from health's perspective because it requires an ethical relation to others in order to be fully healthy. The theory of maturity will be strange from the viewpoint of traditional ethics insofar as it will understand humans to be incapable of fully knowing and controlling their intentional behavior and insofar as it divorces responsibility from its ground in freedom and from judgments of guilt when wrong is done.

In formulating this new ideal of human maturity, I will be proposing a theory of the good, a theory that states how human beings ought to live if they are to live well. The great pitfall of such ideals is that they select certain forms of human life as better than other forms and hence judge certain ways of living to be inadequate, thereby limiting the multidimensionality of human existence. We must avoid this pitfall, but not at the cost of allowing all individuals to generate their own concepts of what is good, for this path cannot offer individuals significant reasons not to pursue their personal advantage when it conflicts with the goods of others.

I will attempt an intermediate path between ideals of excellence that select one form of life as best and liberalism, namely, one which specifies a number of basic psychological structures that must function well in order for a human being to feel whole and fulfilled. These structures can be developed in many forms of life, from hunter-gatherer tribes to corporate offices in New York, although some environments and cultures will be much more amenable to their functioning than will others. I will also try to show that some of these psychological structures cannot develop fully unless one becomes the kind of person who is capable of acting ethically. Hence, this theory of good is an attempt to reinstate the ancient notion that people cannot adequately constitute their personal good without also constituting a viable social world.

I term this new concept of maturity an "ecological" vision of maturity because it understands the psyche as an ecosystem set into wider social, cultural, and natural ecosystems.[28] What I mean by an ecosystem is an environment in which the main inhabitants are involved in a complex set of interdependencies and feedback-relations, such that each inhabitant has its own importance in the system and this importance is internally connected to the functionings of all the other inhabitants. The traditional ethical concept of maturity emphasized independence and a hierarchical structuring of values and psychic functions. Hence, autonomy is seen as the highest goal and reason is seen as superior to the other functions of the psyche and given the function of ruling all the other elements. In an ecological psyche, basic needs, emotions, cognitive capacities, and various structures of the self are seen as interwoven in a dense fabric in which each has an essential role to play in the optimal functioning of the psyche. These psychic functions are not seen as something inside an isolated person but as formed out of profound social interactions and always responsive to the environments in which they operate. It is only with such a notion of ecological connectedness that a theory of maturity can adequately begin to interrelate unconscious forces with conscious reason, and individuals with their social and natural worlds.

PART II

AN ECOLOGICAL CONCEPTION
OF MATURITY

CHAPTER 7

MATURE NEEDS AND EMOTIONS: A RECONSTRUCTION OF THE ID

Concepts of maturity are statements about what constitutes optimal human functioning. As we have seen, such statements of excellence are often arbitrarily prejudicial, especially when maturity is defined in terms of certain kinds of behaviors such as love and work, or character traits such as rationality and productivity. For instance, if mature people are defined in terms of intimacy and productivity, then the Zen monk living by himself is, by definition, grossly immature. If maturity is defined by autonomy, then there are no mature people in a tribe whose members share a common social identity.

One might retort that humans have to work in order to survive and love in order to reproduce. If these aren't part of what it means to be mature, then how can the species survive? It is true that work must be done and reproduction occur, but not every mature person must do them. Much of the labor of the ancient world was done by slaves and women, so that "mature" males would have time for politics, war, and education. Are we to call celibate monks and nuns of the Middle Ages, who were seen in their culture as paradigms of human excellence, immature and undeveloped because they did not engage in reproduction? It appears that no matter what behaviors or character traits we use to define maturity, there will be some adults in some societies who do not have them and yet who are considered mature—even optimally mature—in those societies.

The problem with these theories of excellence is that they have been constructed using a hierarchical model of organization and value. That is, certain activities, social functions, or singular character traits are selected to define maturity and then placed in ascendance above all other possible values. The psyche will be well arranged if and only if it allows the selected function or activity to optimally occur. Rather than using a hierarchical model by which to understand the optimal functioning of the psyche (reason must rule the appetites, etc.), I will attempt to understand how the psyche can best function as a coherent ecosystem. Since ecosystems take into account the idiosyncratic characteristics of particular landscapes, an ecological account of human excellence can find optimally functioning humans living many different kinds of lives.

The key to our new account of what constitutes optimal psychic functioning is the incorporation of unconscious processes and structures. The seminal concept of the unconscious is, of course, Freud's. Yet, when we turn to Freud's theory for an account of how maturity can develop in a psyche grounded in unconscious structures and dynamics, we get little assistance. Freud, too, overvalues reason as the savior of the psyche and, surprisingly, has no theory of development that can ground a full notion of maturity. In his earlier works, Freud has a developmental sequence for sexuality, but this reaches its zenith in puberty when libido falls under the rule of the genitals, is directed toward a non-familial person of the opposite sex, and has as its primary activity coitus for the purpose of reproduction. Such a development can be completed by a sexually precocious teenager.[1]

All other development for Freud is the result of the sublimation of frustrated libido or the demands of the environment for work in order to survive. If we could satisfy our libido as we wished and the conditions of life were easier, there would be no internal impulse toward development of any of our capacities. We would remain more or less permanently teenagers in our development.

> It may be difficult, too, for many of us, to abandon the belief that there is an instinct towards perfection at work in human beings, which has brought them to their present high level of intellectual achievement and ethical sublimation, and which may be expected to watch over their development into supermen. I have no faith, however, in the existence of any such internal instinct and I cannot see how this benevolent illusion is to be preserved.[2]

Since Freud, psychoanalytic theory and other human sciences have made substantial strides in understanding the developmental processes of psychic structures. Carl Jung explored the process by which humans achieve individuation, Erik Erikson elaborated an important pattern of psycho/social development that occurs throughout the span of a lifetime, and others, including Klein, Winnicott, Horney, and Kernberg, turned away from Freud's emphasis on the internal dynamics of the psyche to concentrate on how children's relations to others and their internal representations of those relations influence the development of the psyche. Heinz Kohut made the development of the self, as distinct from the ego, the focal point of theory and therapy.

Hence, before we can elucidate a concept of maturity based on the development of psychic functionality, we must make substantial changes in Freud's theory of the psyche as elucidated in chapter 4.[3] In general we will accept Freud's account of the unconscious as functioning according to primary process thinking and the dynamics of repression, defense, symptom-formation, resistance, and so forth, and consciousness as working according to secondary processes. However, we must make significant alterations in his structural and economic maps of the psyche. In this chapter, we will remap the id. In the next chapter, we will incorporate ego and superego functions into a developmental

psychology of the self and change the economics of the psyche from a pleasure/pain calculus to an account of happiness
that is derived from the fulfillment of ideals of human excellence.

1. Basic Needs

Freud's theory that the primal forces of the id consist of
libido and the death drive has been severely criticized. If
libido retains its strong sexual meaning, then all positive
cultural and social achievements must be seen as sublimations of frustrated sex. Culture is merely a consolation for
disappointed sexual lives. If, on the other hand, libido drops
its strong sexual connotations, it becomes so general a term
as to lose most of its meaning and the grounding Freud
wanted it to have in Darwinian biology. Neither of these
consequences are acceptable.

The death drive—*thanatos*—fares no better. While
humans do seek tension reduction in times of overt stress, in
general they seek stimulation, especially when life is stable
and unthreatened. Also, it seems highly improbable that
the major relation of the ego to an ideal is to be constrained
and depressed by it, or that human aggression against other
humans is to be explained in terms of the psyche turning its
self-aggression onto others. It is far more likely, as the
object-relation theorists have shown, that internalized
self-aggression is the result of repressed anger at others.

Part of Freud's problem with aggression is that he con-
fuses drives with emotions (indeed, there is no clear theory
of the emotions in Freud). Drives are constantly operative;
emotions arise only in relation to specific circumstances. It
makes a major difference in our understanding of aggression if we consider it the result of anger which is aroused in
situations of injury and deprivation rather than a basic
drive that must be constantly discharged.

In addition, the viability of a model in which drives
build up tension to the point of such irritation that an object

must be found on which to discharge the energy is questionable. Perhaps sexual desire and hunger work like this at times, but other prime motivating forces such as the needs for love, beauty, and order seem much more constant, both in their demands and in the objects that satisfy them. Mature human beings do not seem to be driven by cycles of strong sexual and aggressive build-ups and releases, but are characterized by a more steady state of well-being.

Finally, Freud seems to have had a certain romantic model of the drives as great unruly forces of nature which without civilization would so dominate human existence as to make it impossible.[4] Freud's id places humans in an impossible bind: to feel happy they must allow the drives to fully discharge themselves, but to feel secure they must painfully harness the drives. Rather than seeing the id as dark, unsocialized forces of nature, I prefer to see it as incorporating motivations to be social. As the sociobiologists have so poignantly shown, we are biologically encoded to be social. For instance, I believe we have as basic a need for social recognition and friendship as we do for sex. We also have such basic emotions as shame, jealousy, and happiness—all of which require us to operate in a social environment. While such a vision of the id makes it less romantically exciting and dramatic, it makes human life far more livable.

I prefer to see basic needs and emotions, rather than drives, as the prime motivating factors of the psyche. Basic needs are unlike Freudian drives in that they are constantly operative and can have a steady fulfillment rather than build-up/discharge cycles that are strongly responsive to internal and external stimuli. For instance, once one achieves a satisfying place in the social order, the need for social recognition can be more or less constantly fulfilled, giving a sense of well-being over time. Conversely, when a need is not being met, the dissatisfaction is typically chronic rather than acute. A lack of feeling comfortable with one's sexuality sometimes is experienced acutely, but typically is present as a chronic low-level lack that reduces one's sense of vitality and lessens one's ability to function as a human being.

Needs are also less labile than drives. They seek certain specific ends and are frustrated when these ends are not attained. While libido can be partially satisfied by almost any object or activity, each basic need seeks a definite end and is not satisfied by the substitution of other goods. Just because we satisfy needs for intimacy and autonomy does not mean we will feel satisfied about our place in the social order nor feel that we have enough zestful adventure in our lives. We might feel our worlds as full of beauty yet feel the absence of sacredness. This concept of multiple basic needs each with its specific end explains why we can feel very fulfilled in some aspects of our lives and dissatisfied in others. The theory of libido is too general to explain this mixed state of well-being.

Needs also differ from basic emotions. Emotions are responses to definite interior and exterior conditions while needs vary less with changes of context. Normal persons will not feel fear unless threatened, nor angry unless injured or deprived; however, they will feel somewhat constant needs for sexual identity, order, social recognition, and intimacy. We can also experience a need as being in a more or less constant state of satisfaction. In short, the basic needs are always present, while the basic emotions constitute a monitoring system that arises only in response to the environment or our interior states that call for adjustment or action.

I believe that a theory of basic needs is necessary for establishing a strong connection between personal well-being and ethics. This connection cannot be made if basic human motivation is seen as drives which seek sexual gratification or aggressive outlets, for, as Freud said, it is precisely these satisfactions that are opposed by ethics. Nor can the connection be made if we adopt liberalism's theory of basic human motivation as whatever desires an individual happens to have, for there is no reason why these desires should include satisfactions from friendship, love, or living in a social order that one relates to as part of herself. Only a theory that postulates that everyone has certain basic needs, such as those for intimacy and social recognition, can show that personal well-being necessitates adopting an ethical way of being in the world. That is, I will try to demonstrate that one cannot satisfy various of the basic needs fully unless one is willing to be an ethical person.

How does one "prove" a theory of basic needs? Concepts like needs or drives are theoretical constructs we use to explain why humans do what they do. They are not the kinds of things that can be empirically verified or which are conceptually necessary. Typically, philosophers and scientists try to reduce all basic human motivation to one or two basic needs or drives, such as Freud's *eros* and *thanatos*, sociobiology's reproductive fitness and survival, or Nietzsche's will-to-power. Such reductiveness makes for elegant theories that have little relation to the vast complexities of lived experience. It is hard to believe that all culture arises out of frustrated sex or that the will-to-power governs all human affairs including friendship and the love of beauty. Here I have postmodern sympathies: the needs and human experiences they give rise to are multiple and conflicting, pulling us in many directions. It is the multiplicity of needs that has made us such interesting and unusual beasts and pushed the species to develop consciousness, reason, and complex selves in order to deal with the myriad of conflicts they cause.

I believe that human beings have ten basic needs: (1) survival, (2) reproductive fitness, (3) order, (4) adventure, (5) social recognition, (6) autonomy, (7) intimacy, (8) knowledge, (9) sacredness, and (10) beauty. My grounds for claiming each of these to be a basic need are that one or another of the special sciences have found it to be so; it has been recognized by profound thinkers—poets, scientists, and/or philosophers—to be a primal source of motivation; and/or it explains lived experience better than any other theory of motivation. I have tried to give the needs in general and each one specifically a justification in *Human Excellence and an Ecological Conception of the Psyche.* I do not wish to repeat that justification here, but to explore how the basic needs and emotions can function in a theory of maturity.

Although I will give brief descriptions of each of the basic needs, it must be remembered, first, that as "atomic," individual needs are abstractions. Needs occur in the ecosystem of the psyche and have internal relations with one another. That is, humans don't have a need for survival, but need as sexual, social, intimate, knowledge-seeking beings, and so forth to survive. Without such a complex understanding of the need to survive, suicide and sacrificial forms of death are incomprehensible. Second, not all the needs are felt with equal strength at all times in all human beings. Different needs or clusters of needs become ascendant in different ways at different times for individuals. What becomes ascendant depends on a number of variables such as where one is in a developmental history (is one a child, youth, or an elder?), environmental conditions (when survival is threatened, the other needs typically go begging), and what needs are favored by the culture in which one lives.

(1) Survival

The need for survival is generally recognized as basic to all living creatures, including humans. Yet, in humans this need is transformed from what it is in other living creatures, for we become conscious of our inevitable mortality. While biologists emphasize the need to perform various activities to satisfy the material conditions for survival, psychotherapists (especially existential psychotherapists such as Lacan, Binswanger, Frankl, and Yalom) find that adult humans have a fundamental need to encounter and accept their mortality. Unless we come to terms with our mortalities, a number of defenses, such as intellectualization, appear that remove us from the rich particularity of life. The need for survival, then, calls on us both to secure the material conditions of life and to resolve ourselves as mortal beings.

(2) Reproductive Fitness

Evolutionary theorists claim that the primary need in all living creatures is to optimize gene production. Freud's concept of libido, while far more labile than the sexual drive of biologists, is meant as an expression of this need. However, this need is not equivalent to having sexual relations, for we are not just animals instinctively moved to sex, but animals who are aware of their sexuality. What for biologists is a reproductive need, for psychotherapists is a need for sexual identity. Just because one engages in sexual activity—even a great deal of sexual activity—does not mean that one enjoys it, feels secure in it, and is deeply satisfied by it. Indeed, hypersexual activity is typically a symptom of a neurosis or an addiction. What it means to have a sexual identity is still greatly disputed among psychological and social theorists. At this point we can only say that it involves accepting and loving the particular body that one has and not being engaged in significant repressions of one's sexual desires, whatever they might be.

(3) Order

All organisms require a certain amount of internal and environmental order. Freud's death drive reflects this need: when too much chaos or tension enters our lives, we become anxious and attempt to restore order to our worlds or psyches by reducing the stimuli causing the chaos. Nietzsche's goal of becoming a constantly self-overcoming being is humanly impossible: we need homeostatic order in our bodies, our psyches, and our environments in order to live. Too much chaos in the environment can drive us mad (the Indo-European root of "mad" is "mai," which means "change"). Too much chaos and conflict in the psyche causes us to repress disturbing emotions or dissonant beliefs.[5] How much disorder a person can tolerate varies from person to person and is dependent upon such factors as how secure the self is and/or how good one's defenses are against experiencing chaos.

(4) Adventure

Too much order is as harmful as too little. Human beings need change, adventure, newness, creativity. Extolled by Nietzsche and romanticism, adventure pours zest and excitement into our lives and makes us feel renewed. Humans need to break stifling orders, be creative, and engage in diversity and multiplicity. There is good evidence that this need, like the previous three, extends into other species of animals. Rats, for instance, if they are well-fed, like to explore mazes rather than just run the route they have been trained to.

Order and adventure are conflicting and balancing needs. The emotion of boredom tells us when order is too dominant; anxiety informs us when there is too much chaos and change. Unchanged order is as deadly as chaotic change.

(5) Social Recognition

We are social animals and need a recognized place in the social order. Aristotle, Chinese philosophers, the great Enlightenment social philosophers, social psychologist Erik Erikson, sociologists Rom Harré and Irving Goffman, French psychoanalytical theorist Jacques Lacan, and sociobiologists all recognize this need as basic. Even outcasts from society tend to form alternative rebel communities in which each person has a recognized place. They often also accept as their social role that they are rebels. Most of us gain social recognition by adopting certain of society's accepted role structures: marriage, a position in the economic world, membership in various organizations, and so forth. Although our intense individualism makes us see role-playing as fake and dishonest, it is as much a part of human life as autonomous self-assertion.

(6) Autonomy

The most heralded need in the West and the central value of ethics has been autonomy. Adult humans need to be able to direct their own lives and activities rather than having them controlled by others. However, what it means to be autonomous has been the subject of major philosophical debates. The ancients held that the achievement of autonomy was primarily a function of the proper arrangement of the psyche—autonomous agents were those who could control their desires and make decisions on the basis of practical wisdom. On the other hand, modern thinkers have viewed freedom as a function of environmental conditions. Expanded possibilities for individual pursuit in the social, political, and economic environments is what constitutes freedom. We will speak more about autonomy in the following chapters, but for now we need to emphasize that it has been too often stressed as our only need or our highest need. It is one among ten and often conflicts with other needs such as those for social recognition, intimacy, and sacredness.

(7) Intimacy

Human sociality is not confined to sex or social role-playing; we also need intimate friends. By intimacy I mean having a relationship with another human being in which both persons can reveal themselves fully and be accepted, have a sense of cherishing one another as special individuals that cannot be replaced by any others, and have a profound mutual empathy with one another. While a side of us wishes to be fully independent, another part of us longs to be so deeply entwined with another human being that life loses its isolation. Experience that is deeply shared with another takes on an added fullness and meaningfulness that gives joy the way little else can. While intimacy conflicts with autonomy in its intertwining of identities, it also aids the development of autonomy. In intimacy we can be present to another person in our unique multidimensionality and have this affirmed, while in all other human encounters we must play roles or be present only in part of our personalities. Hence, intimacy both connects us with humanity in the profoundest of ways and helps make us strong individuated persons. As Aristotle says, "Without friends, no one would choose to live, though he had all other goods."[6]

(8) Knowledge

We are not animals who act in the world according to set instinctual patterns. Rather, we must engage in learning in order to adapt to and survive in the various environments in which we find ourselves. Nature did not leave such learning to chance, but placed within us a need to inquire and know. Indeed, we do not know in order to dwell in a place; rather knowing is part of dwelling. Knowing a place, as language tells us, makes that place a home for us. The root of "know" is the Greek *gnosis* which, in turn, has as its root *nos*—a longing for home as in *nostos* (what Odysseus constantly feels for Ithaca and his family) or the English nostalgia. The need for knowledge is not a need for abstract data or technological methodologies, but a need to find that which turns the alien into the familiar, the foreign into home.

(9) Sacredness

Our secular age denies the need for the sacred despite the fact that anthropology has found it to be a central experience in all cultures of the world. This denial of the legitimacy of a need for the sacred seems grounded in a confusion of sacredness with one particular expression of sacredness—that which interprets the sacred in terms of a singular, all-knowing, all-powerful personality. God might very well be dead for a significant portion of the West's population, but the need for humans to experience and believe in something greater than their own individual wills is not. The secular is defined by the marketplace in which everything has an exchange value or in which the self determines the value of things. But the sacred is ultimate: its value is seen as beyond exchange, as not grounded in anything other than itself, and as not controllable by personal desire. For some love is sacred, for others it is the moral law, beauty, or nature. Even that murderer of God, Nietzsche, did not want to renounce the sacred. His *Thus Spoke Zarathustra* is clearly meant to be the bible for a new age in which the great forces of creativity and destruction set in a pattern of eternal recurrence replace God as what is sacred.[7] While Freud's scientific bent made him reject religion as a product of neurotic forces, Carl Jung found that a number of neuroses originated in the loss of the sacred and that health, in part, depended on finding an adequate relation to the sacred.

(10) Beauty

One of the great wonders of human existence is the depth of our response to beauty. Beauty lifts our spirits and ugliness dampens them. A walk through an autumn wood, a Mozart aria, an article of clothing that is "just me," the brilliant flash of an oriole's body, the grandeur of Greek architecture, the humanity in a Rembrandt portrait—how these move our psyches and refresh zest for life. While some might try to explain our need to experience and create beauty by showing its efficacy for reproduction, at least Whitehead thought it the other way around: we are moved to reproduce because the world is beautiful.

Our need to experience and create beauty is so primal that philosophers and poets from Plato through Whitehead have extolled it as the central need in human existence. We can see why the Greeks and classical Chinese thinkers equated beauty and good, for the psyche functions optimally when its various components work together to produce intense, nonfragmented experiences—when its parts act in concert rather than in opposition to one another. This ecological functioning is mirrored in the values of beauty, for the experience of beauty is the experience of nonconflicting, non-trivial harmonies of diverse elements.

2. Basic Emotions

The emotions are a biologically engendered system whose function is to monitor the internal state of the organism and the relation of the organism to the environment.[8] In particular, emotions tell us how our environments relate to our basic needs and whether our needs are being fulfilled or not. To perform these monitoring tasks, the emotions have three components: cognitive assessments of internal states and external situations in respect to the needs and coherence of the self-system, particular emotional feelings based on these assessments, and action tendencies based on those particular feelings. For instance, the cognition of danger produces the feeling of *fear* which in turn triggers the action tendency to fight or flee. *Anger* tells us we have been injured or deprived and urges us to aggress against the offending agent. A chronic sense of *boredom* indicates that our lives are in general too orderly and need adventure. *Anxiety* arises from internal conflict and calls for either resolution or repression. *Guilt* lets us know that we have broken an internalized value and need to become more consistent with our ideals or change them. *Shame* is the emotion we feel when society catches us offending its values and has the tendency to make us lose self-assertion in order to repair our break with the social order. *Sadness* is our response to loss and causes withdrawal. *Interest* is a response to finding that our environment is safe and stimulates exploration.

All the emotions mentioned above are basic emotions. To them can be added *joy* (felt after a sharp drop in tension and an increased harmony between oneself and the world), *surprise* (a clearing of the nervous system in preparation for responding to fresh and unexpected stimuli), *disgust* (a response to something that has deteriorated or spoiled), *contempt* (the emotion which occurs when one appraises something as inferior), and *happiness* (what we feel when our lives cohere with our ideals).

Unlike the list of basic needs, the list of basic emotions is not firm, for research into this field is fairly new and there is still some disparity as to what the basic emotions are. What is crucial at this point is the recognition that emotions are not social constructions (although how we express them often is socially determined), but biological systems whose optimal functioning depends on completing the full cycle of cognition, feeling, and expression.

The emotions are webs. They weave together cognition, feeling and action into complex patterns and interrelate facets of the inner world with each other and with the outer world. In contrast to thought which distances us from ourselves and the world in order to achieve clear concepts and long-range pragmatic strategies, emotions make us feel alive, connected, involved with the world, and living in the present. Their repression and consequent malfunctioning means not only that we lose our primary monitoring system, but also lose that *joie de vivre* that makes life so worth living. Persons who feel isolated and distant from themselves and the world typically have malfunctioning emotional systems.

All of us struggle with emotional complexes, for emotions tend to obey Freud's principle of conservation: they want to repeat assessments based on a few succinct clues that correspond to past situations and to repeat successful responses of the past. That is, emotions tend to be rooted in primary process thinking in which "likeness" plays a crucial role. If the present situation is "like" one of the past in which I was bitten by a dog, then I will tend to feel fear, even though the dog is not the same and I am now old enough to defend myself. If the present situation is "like" a childhood situation in which one had a parent who was inconsistent in loving—overly erotic sometimes, totally distant and unavailable at others—and one could more or less successfully control the parent's response through seductive behavior, then intimate situations will tend to create anxiety and produce seductive behavior.

Emotions carry their histories of learned responses with them. What we feel is rarely just a response to the present, for it is always webbed with the past. Emotions are like plants, only part of which are above ground. Their life sustaining roots spread out through the soil of unconscious primary process connections, bringing the past and present together in ways that rational thinking abhors.

As difficult as it is, the emotions can mature. Old assessments are replaced by more accurate ones that better understand the complexities of situations, and responses become increasingly governed by deliberation. This is not to say that the unconscious associations disappear altogether, but that we can achieve a relation to the emotions in which the unconscious connections do not overly skew the response to the present. With mature emotions, the unconscious connections can make us feel whole, for we have both a connection to the past and an adequate response to the present.

3. The Id

The needs and emotions are the primal forces that drive all human activity. They are rooted in the unconscious and operate according to its dynamic principles, usually beneath the awareness and control of consciousness. Freud called these forces "Das Es"—the it or id, because they exist prior to the development of personality and are experienced as impersonal forces. As impersonal, the needs and emotions are felt as dangerous forces by the self, for they can fall outside of personal control and overwhelm the self with their power and demands. A person may not want to think about her ambivalent sexuality, but it haunts her with anxiety until it is faced. I want to be strong, but fear overwhelms me.

The needs and emotions are also felt as dangerous because they are so multiple and conflicting. Freud tended to see all psychic dynamics arising out of the conflict between libido and the death wish. How much more threatening and confusing it is to have ten basic needs and a myriad of basic emotions, all of which can conflict with one another and with the structure of the self.

The needs and emotions are dangerous in yet a third way, for they are immersed in primary process thinking, which is an anathema to the logic of consciousness. The images and symbols of the unconscious can overwhelm us with their force, as when a man's childhood imago of his mother falls on a woman and he is driven mad with passion. All the emotions carry images of their previous histories with them. These primary process connections invade our experience with fantasies, such that knowing and dealing with concrete present reality is difficult.

The needs and emotions, then, are both the vital motivating forces of human life and its greatest internal dangers. When the needs, emotions, and/or conflicts these cause threaten to overwhelm the self, they get repressed and enter into the psychodynamics of symptom-formation, defense, and resistance. While Freud has shown how our sexual need can be repressed, others have indicated how the inabilities to cope with mortality (Lacan, Binswanger),[9] sacredness (Jung), intimacy (object relations theory and self-psychology), and autonomy (Erikson) can result in neurotic symptoms. It takes little imagination to see how a parent's inordinate fears of a child's attempt to explore the world outside the parent's control can result in the repression of adventure, or how the need for order might be repressed in an alcoholic household where inconsistency reigns. Rejections by others in early attempts to enter the social order outside the family can cause the need for social recognition to go underground (consciously we just don't care what others think of us, while unconsciously we are desperate for recognition). The impossibility of home life can make our relation to knowledge abstract, boring, and something to be avoided. Having to grow up in harsh, ugly conditions can make one develop a defense against the experience of beauty. To really feel how beautiful the world can be and then to realize how impossibly dreary and misshapen one's environment is can be too much for a psyche. It is better not to respond to beauty.

Emotions are also repressed when they become internally overwhelming or conflictual. Children can especially become terrified of their anger because they think it can magically kill their parents. When emotions become repressed, they fragment off from the rest of psychic functioning and cannot participate in the development of the cognitive faculties or character traits. Hence, repressed emotions remain infantile or regressed. When we have significant repressions of a particular emotion or an intensity level of that emotion, then we either tend not to feel it at all, chronically feel it in terms of symptoms, and/or have it burst out with inappropriate intensity at inappropriate times. Rarely are we able to assess situations that involve that particular emotion accurately, feel the "right amount" of the emotion, and respond appropriately. If, for instance, the desires and emotions connected with early Oedipal sexuality overwhelm the nascent self with conflicts and become repressed, they are likely to torment adult love relations with fears of being subsumed by the partner, guilt about incest, impulsive attachment, expectations of total nurturance and oceanic oneness, and constant attempts to flee the relation.

Not only can specific needs and emotions become repressed, but the needs and emotions in general can be repressed, especially when the assertion of them in early childhood was met with rejection, punishment, or scorn. Many people have an inability to know what they really need, want, or feel. They cannot easily tell the difference between the different needs or feel that they need much of anything. They can confuse emotions such as anger and love, interpreting aggression towards them as interest in them. They often prefer to be told what to do or to meet the needs of others rather than assert their own needs and feelings.

So far, this concept of the id sounds very much like Freud's cauldron of drives seething with energy and power, controlled by infantile primary process thinking, always in a state of conflict, and involved in the unconscious dynamics of repression and defense. But unlike Freud's *eros* and *thanatos*, the needs and the emotions can be educated and develop into mature forms. It is these forms which are crucial for our new concept of maturity.

4. The Id and Maturity

The simplest way of defining maturity in relation to the id is to say that mature persons are capable of satisfying their basic needs and that their emotions are fully operational—fully able to monitor internal dynamics and external contingencies. In short, mature persons do not have significant repressions of the needs and emotions. Hence, a mature person is one who has come to terms with death and attained a firm sexual identity, found a way to balance order and adventure, has intimate friends and achieved a satisfying place in the social order, is capable of directing her life, has knowledge of her significant environments, appreciates beauty, and allows questions of ultimate concern to penetrate her practical life. Since all of these needs can be more or less satisfied, we can continue to deepen our satisfactions of them as we mature through adulthood. Maturity of the needs is not accomplished at a moment, but is a continuing process in which development can occur throughout a lifetime.

It is important to note that at least three of the basic needs require us to acknowledge the importance and worth of either other human beings or something more important than the self: intimacy, knowledge, and sacredness. We cannot have an intimate relation with someone that we cannot treat as a person worthy of full respect. We cannot have knowledge that will make us feel that our environment is a home if it is merely a realm of exploitation. We cannot acknowledge anything as sacred so long as we make ourselves the center of all of life. Hence, these basic needs—unlike the selfish desires of a liberal understanding of human nature—cannot be satisfied if we continue to have only a narcissistic orientation to the world. As I will attempt to show in the next chapter, neither these needs nor the self can attain a mature functioning without the adoption of an ethical stance.

Satisfaction of each of the needs is not enough to constitute an ecological maturity, for the needs might be abstracted from one another and satisfied as independent entities. Indeed, the presence of "atomism" in Western culture keeps such isolated satisfaction a strong tendency. The pornography industry, along with advertising firms bent on the production of desire, encourage us to isolate our sexuality. Sacredness is reserved for an hour on Sunday in a church, knowledge is confined to the classroom, and adventure occurs on holidays. But the sexual need does not have sex, a person does—a person who also has needs for intimacy, beauty, sacredness, and so forth, and who has idiosyncratic talents, desires, hopes, and concerns. Depending on who one is with, the situation, the time, and so forth, a sexual encounter might be either profoundly satisfying or leave one feeling cold, empty, and conflicted. Our human complexity cannot be solved as we solve complexity in the socioeconomic world—by analytically dividing up tasks and specializing in them. When experience becomes an attempt to satisfy needs in isolation from one another, then it can feel thin and meaningless. Immature persons tend to isolate need satisfactions; mature persons interweave needs in an attempt to make experience full.

Like the needs, the emotions can develop from immature to mature levels of functioning. What develops about them is not so much the particular emotional feelings, but the cognitive appraisals of situations and the kinds of responses we have to them. As we saw in Freud, the cognitive appraisals of a child can interweave fantasy and reality factors, for primary and secondary thought processes are not clearly distinguished yet. Children often have a fear of things that cannot harm them and feel sadness when things are absent, but not lost (as when a parent is in a different room). As our reality-testing abilities improve, our appraisals of situations become more accurate. With ordinary development, appraisals move from more or less unconscious immediate responses to situations to judgments based on consciously attained data and logical thought processes.

Our developing cognitive processes also take into account our growing abilities. The sexual teasing that can so enrage teenagers who are acutely sensitive to their nascent sexualities becomes the benign camaraderie of a sexually secure young adulthood and is accompanied by laughter. We visit the great wood that frightened us in childhood to find it a small forest in which we could not get lost if we tried.

Our action tendencies can also develop. Childhood responses to emotions tend to be immediate: loss produces tears; anger aggression, joy a smile, and shame a running away and hiding. As we mature, we gain control over the action tendencies of emotions through the development of character traits—general patterns of response we have to situations and the complexes of needs and emotions that they arouse.

The Greek tragedians and philosophers discovered the key to successful character traits over two thousand years ago: *sophrosyne*.[10] There are no adequate English translations of this term; moderation, sobriety, and temperance all come close to its meanings of "nothing in excess" and "being safe-minded." We are *sophron* when we refuse to get caught up in the immediacy of a situation and respond in forgetfulness of future considerations. If we become enraged and immediately become physically aggressive, we might later find ourselves in jail or with the guilt of having cost a friend an eye or a tooth. If we become overly excited by the allurements of a seducer or seductress, we might later find ourselves enmeshed in a sordid affair or with an intractable disease. *Sophrosyne* allows us to feel the emotions but to delay our responses to them until we have used our practical wisdom to judge what is the best response.

Hence, when Aristotle says that virtue is the mean between deficiency and excess, he means that we need to develop character traits that allow us to feel our desires and emotions without being overwhelmed by their demands and impulses for immediate discharge. In psychoanalytic terms, a person should neither repress nor give infantile indulgence to the emotions and desires. It is good to feel hunger; it is not good to have to eat whenever food appears. It is good to feel danger rather than rashly proceeding regardless of the situation or shying away from all situations in which one is challenged.

With such temperate character traits, our responses to emotions, desires, and complexes of the two can be suited to the situation. Sometimes humor is the best response to a conflictual situation, sometimes rational understanding and strategy, sometimes withdrawal, and sometimes aggression. There is no one right response, for each situation has different persons in different moods with differing abilities to respond. Humor does little good with humorless people; reason does little good with irrational people.

In sum, mature emotions are those based on accurate assessments of situations, whose intensity of feeling is proportional to the situation, and whose response is flexible and occurs after some deliberation.

5. Emotions, Needs, and Self

As we have seen, the fundamental obstacle to the development of the basic needs and emotions into mature forms is repression. Why do emotions and needs become repressed? Freud's answer is that they produce a conflict that causes the ego anxiety and threatens to fragment it. Why does conflict cause the ego anxiety? What is the nature of the ego such that it can fragment and be injured by the fragmentation? The id is comfortable with conflict, for primary process thinking does not recognize contradictions. The superego can hold conflicting values without feeling anxious. What is there about the nature of the ego, whose primary function is to engage in reality-testing, that makes conflict threatening and anxiety-producing?

Freud has no coherent answer to this question, for his use of the German *Ich* is ambiguous. Sometimes it refers only to the ego and its specific functions of promoting survival by finding real objects to satisfy libido and by negotiating between the superego, reality demands, and the pressures of the id. However, at other times *Ich* seems to refer not to a part of the psyche, but the whole person. It is this person that is the subject of experience and this person that needs to keep its various parts in some kind of coherent arrangement in order to function.

If we use this latter meaning of ego and equate it with the self and see the self as having as its primary function the harmonious interweaving of the various components of the psyche—the id functions (needs, emotional complexes), ego functions, and superego idealizing functions, then we can understand why conflict threatens the self and produces anxiety. We can also see why the process of repression/symptom-formation/resistance is so crucial to the psyche as a protection against the dissolution of the self. The psyche cannot "know" in early childhood that ego functions need protection, for it does not have them. However, the process of forming a central core by which the multiplicity of psychic functions can be organized is absolutely crucial if the ego or any other part of the psyche is going to be able to function later in life. Hence, the psyche is "wired" to defend against psychic events that have the possibility of fragmenting the nascent self.

In short, we have found that for the needs and emotions to mature, we must develop a self strong enough to deal with conflicts without massive repressions. Hence, our search for maturity leads us to explore what constitutes a mature self.

CHAPTER 8

THE MATURE SELF:
A RECONSTRUCTION
OF THE EGO AND SUPEREGO

Theories of the self usually attempt to explain how the multiple aspects of a person are able to achieve a unity of functioning over time. Despite the fact that experiences can change dramatically from one moment to the next, most of us feel as though the same person is having the experiences. Even though almost everything about us can change over time, we still experience ourselves as the same persons. How can this personal identity be explained?

From Plato until the twentieth century, the reigning paradigm for explaining the unity of the self has been to say that self is a special mental substance or soul. This paradigm has been severely criticized in the twentieth century for being unable to explain how such a nonmaterial, non-changing substance can be in such a thorough interaction with the ever-changing corruptible body and for producing "ghosts in machines" or strange homunculi (persons inside persons). A further problem with such theories is that they are unable to account for phenomena opposite from unity: selves falling apart or selves that achieve only partial unity. Some people are said to have strong selves, others weak selves, while others seem to have multiple selves dwelling in a single biological body. The substance theory of the self cannot account for these ordinary experiences of the disintegrating, weakening, or splitting into multiples of the self and is, therefore, inadequate.

For contemporary psychoanalytic theory the self is a set of psychic functions that are the product of a developmental process. If this process goes well, the self attains unity; to the degree that it doesn't go well, various pathologies and defects will develop that make the self less able to function in a coherent way. I believe that there are three distinct stages to the development of self, all of which must be completed for a fully mature self to come into being. The first of these is the development of a primary "nuclear" self, then a psychosocial narrative self, and finally an ego that has consistent sets of beliefs about reality and norms for directing actions.

The early development of the self gives it an archaic self-representation and nascent organization of energies and ideals. This "nuclear self" is largely unconscious and is the foundation for the other two structures of self. The narrative self brings the nuclear self into an alliance with society and creates a psychosocial unity. The ego allows a person to critique her nuclear values and social narrative and gives a certain power of transcendence over earlier formulations of the self. Ego functions allow a person to be self-monitoring and self-directed. In sum, a person attains unity by having a self-affirming, dynamic nuclear core that develops into a strong psychosocial narrative, which in turn is complexified and monitored by a coherent set of beliefs and values that allow for a self-critical functioning. The development of each of these aspects of the self is crucial in the production of mature human beings.

The uniqueness and originality of the concept of self here proposed is the integration and interweaving of all three kinds of unity into what I call "the ecological self." Philosophers tend to look for the self in conscious ego functions; social psychologists concentrate on how narratives form identity, while psychotherapeutic thinkers focus on the formation of self in the first years of life. Most want to see their version of the self as the Self, but none by itself is adequate to explain how a mature self attains full unity or how a self loses or fails to gain unity.

This concept of the self differs from other theories in another way, namely, that it refuses to arrange the components of the self in a hierarchical pattern of worth. In the ecological self, the ego does not supplant the nuclear and narrative unities as the highest form of self, nor do nuclear or narrative functions always have priority in cases of conflict. Rather the ecological self is a Hermes traveling between the ego, narrative self, and nuclear core trying to negotiate settlements, listen to the needs, respond to emotional inputs, and arrive at compromises which allow for the optimal functioning of the whole human organism.

1. Kohut, the Bipolar Nuclear Self, and a New Economics

The most fully developed psychoanalytic theory of the self is that of Heinz Kohut and his school of self-psychology.[1] Kohut began his psychiatric practice as an avowed Freudian; however, he found that he could not develop traditional transference relations with a number of his patients, for they did not treat him as a separate individual but as a part of themselves. From these patients, Kohut hypothesized that he was replacing functions of the self that had been injured in early childhood and fragmented off from the conscious workings of the psyche. Patients typically asked him to perform two functions: the first was to have infantile grandiosity affirmed. The response of the primary caretaker (usually the mother) is internalized by the child as its own self-representation. Hence, Kohut calls primary caretakers "selfobjects," for they are experienced by infants as being part of themselves. In fact, they become part of the self through the process of "transmuting internalization." If the selfobject's response is one of empathic, joyful acceptance, then the child will develop a positive archaic self-representation which, with the help of gentle frustrations, will give rise to ambitions and self-assertiveness between the ages of two and four. Persons with unambivalent positive self-images feel that the world welcomes their self-assertions, act to satisfy their needs without guilt, and have a vast reservoir of dynamic energy available for activity in the world.

The second primary need in the child's development of self is for an "idealized selfobject"—a caretaker who is experienced as calm, protective, and in full control of both the world and her own emotional responses. The child's incorporation of this selfobject gives it strength, stability, and an ideal self-representation. Between the ages of four and six this internalized ideal selfobject becomes, with the aid of gentle, appropriate frustrations, an ideal of the kind of adult the child wishes to become.

Kohut's theory of the nuclear self reveals that there are two primary sources of human activity: desires and ideals. The grandiose pole organizes and transforms the needs into a set of personalized wants and desires. Its voice says "This is what I want." The idealized pole, on the other hand, asserts "This is what you ought to become." In other words, humans have as part of their natural constituencies both "desire-based motivation" and "authoritative motivation."[2] The "ought" of the idealized pole is what can later mature into the "ought" of morality. Being moved by ethical and moral considerations is not an imposition of society on the self, but as natural a part of the self as are personal desires.

This analysis of the nuclear self also reveals that the self is inherently social. In early life others perform the functions of the self, and their performances become incorporated into the very being of the self. Here is a radically different self from the isolated atomistic entity of liberal theory; it is a self intrinsically intertwined with others and a self motivated by "oughts" rather than just "wants." It is the kind of basic self that can mature into an ethical person.

There is a tension between the two poles of the nuclear self. The positive self-representation of grandiosity gives the sense that as a particular being I am absolutely adequate and entitled to have my needs met. The idealized pole stands in opposition to the self-satisfaction of grandiosity by holding up an ideal of what I might become, but am not. This tension is mediated, according to Kohut, by the particular idiosyncratic talents and abilities that the person has which can ground ambitions (the transformed needs) and be used to realize the ideal. The particular talents and abilities give definiteness to the ideal and transform a vague general notion of what a good human being is into a particular ideal for what I as an individual self can achieve. This concretizing of the ideal allows the self-assertive ambitions to focus on definite ends. When the energy and liveliness of the grandiose pole align with a particular bent of character and set of skills in pursuit of an ideal for which they are particularly suited, then a fully integral archaic self is born. This self is what David Norton calls a person's "daimon" or inner self, the full actualization of which provides the deepest, happiest form of life.

One can see some similarities between Kohut's two poles of the nuclear self and Freud's libido and superego, for the grandiose pole provides the energy and élan by which to live (libido) and the idealized pole contains values that constrain and direct the energies of the grandiose pole, as Freud's ego ideal does. But the differences are telling. The grandiose pole is not primarily sexual but a general reservoir of energy available for any number of ends (in my terms, the various needs), including sexual ones under appropriate conditions and stimuli. Freud's libido seems to be a blind biological force unconnected to a self or person, while Kohut's grandiose energy is intrinsically tied to a vulnerable self-representation.

Similarly, the idealized pole is like and unlike the superego. Like the superego, it is built from identifications with the parents and incorporates the values of the parents. It is used to limit and direct the ambitions of the grandiose pole. But Kohut's idealized pole is genuinely teleological—it lures the individual to development rather than imposing a harsh and punishing constraint on libido. Freud has some sympathy with a positive ego ideal in "On Narcissism" (1915), "Mourning and Melancholia" (1916), and *Group Psychology and the Analysis of the Ego* (1921). In these works, the ego ideal is seen as replacing the early state of narcissism and represents the perfection of that stage. We feel "triumph when something in the ego coincides with the ego ideal,"[3] for we momentarily reestablish the perfection of the narcissistic stage. However, with the development of his structural psychology in *The Ego and the Id* (1923), the ego ideal is almost completely replaced by the repressive, guilt-producing superego.[4]

For Freud, the libidinal id and moral superego seem always to be in conflict, driving the person to seek a state of respite through regression, repression, or renunciation. But for Kohut there can be a productive and joyous dialectical development between the grandiose and idealized poles of the self, with the ideal luring ambitious energy into more complex and mature forms of attainment.

The grandiose pole represents the personal desire for self-gratification emphasized by the Sophists (Callicles, Thrasymachus) and interpreted by Nietzsche as the dynamic, driving will-to-power that seeks to free itself of all obstacles. The idealized pole represents the ethical universal championed by Socrates, Plato, and Aristotle. Both positions saw a part of the basic truth and both mistook their part for the whole truth of human nature. The Sophists' overemphasis of grandiose desire without an ideal leads to immature patterns of gratification that are nondevelopmental. On the other hand, Socrates' overemphasis on the ethical ideal can negate the particular vitality of the individual, lead to guilt, depression, and the imposition of an ideal self in place of a real one.[5] It is only when both poles are fully operative that optimal growth and maturity can occur. Of all the philosophers it was Hegel who saw most clearly that ethical development consisted of a sustained dialectical struggle between the particularity of who one is and the ideal of what one might be. The ideal lures us into more complex states of existence and the grandiose positive self-representation prevents us from falling into depression and guilt for not yet being the ideal.

This bipolar understanding of the self demands a new economics of the psyche. If the self is seen as motivated only by desire, then an economics of pleasure is adequate; but a self with a dual motivation of needs and ideals requires another kind of accounting: an economics of happiness. The difference can be put succinctly: pleasure comes with the satisfaction of desire while happiness occurs when the felt particularity and personal ambitions of the grandiose pole cohere with the values in the idealized pole.[6] Kohut often uses the term "joy" to designate this experience, but it is more in line with traditional usage to term this coherence of the self "happiness." "Joy [happiness] relates to experiences of the total self whereas pleasure . . . relates to the experiences of parts and constituents of the self."[7]

The gods are pure ideals without desires and live in joy; animals have desires but no ideals and live for pleasure. Humans, as the Greeks used to say, occupy a strange realm between the gods and the beasts, for they have both ideals and desires, a god-like mind and an animal body. Their proper end is the coherence of these two, which is happiness. To identify life with desire and pleasure is to fall into animality. To live only through ideals is to mistake oneself for a god. To be human is to live the paradox of being an animal/god. Pushed by needs, pulled by a teleological ideal, we try to make the two meet in lives that often fail and are tragic. Gods and beasts cannot be tragic.

The difference between pleasure and happiness is an everyday phenomenon. We all know people who indulge in somewhat thoughtless pleasures—typically sex and drugs—and mire themselves ever more deeply in unhappiness. We also know people who are in constant pain—Gandhi and Martin Luther King in prison or Socrates facing death—who are nonetheless happy because they are living their ideals.

In his attempt to make psychoanalysis scientific, Freud invented an economics of the psyche that worked for all animals and used the "scientific" quantities of pleasure and pain to make the workings of the psyche available for mechanical analysis. Hence, he could not include a teleological functioning in the psyche, could not have an ego ideal that inspired us to achieve goals rather than punishing us with its force. The superego could only constrain and negate libido, never lead it. Without a notion of a teleological kind of causation in the psyche, Freud could not see nor understand how happiness functioned in human life.

Kohut has other profound differences from Freud, especially concerning how to view narcissism. For Freud, humans must redirect libido away from the self to other objects in order to mature, for there is a set quantity of libido available, and if this is directed towards the self, then it can't be available for others. Indeed, narcissistic self-love is seen by Freud as the ultimate place of regression, for it characterizes the worst of the psychological disorders, the psychoses. In contrast, Kohut finds that object-love is possible only if there is a healthy self-love. Only when we love ourselves can we fully love others. Maturity is not a matter of renouncing narcissism, but of its transformation from infantile self-centeredness to adult forms of self-assertiveness.

While Freud sees the origins of neurosis in the unresolved drive conflicts of the Oedipal period, Kohut understands drive conflict, Oedipal difficulties, and organ fixations as disintegration products that arise from failures to construct a coherent nuclear self. For Kohut, drive phenomena are not primitive but symptoms of a fragmented nuclear self. An injured self uses drives "in the attempt to bring about the lost merger (and thus the repair of the self) by pathological means."[8] For instance, when the grandiose pole is injured, the child can become driven by Oedipal fantasies and desires for a merger with a parent to make up for the merger that did not take place adequately in earlier childhood. When the idealized pole is injured, it will act very much like a harsh superego and aggress against the self and world, both expressing its rage at being injured and attempting to control the inner and outer worlds to make them safe. Freud's Oedipal libido and harsh superego aggressions do occur, but they are not ultimate structures of the psyche. Rather, they are secondary products caused by early injuries to the self. Likewise, concern with erotogenic zones such as the mouth, anus, or genitals is also a symptom in which the fragmentation of the self is symbolized by treating the body as a set of separate parts.

Kohut holds that the Oedipal stage cannot be entered without some coherence of the self—at least enough self-esteem to feel that one deserves the heterogenital parent and to aggress against the homogenital one. For a normal child with responsive parents who recognize, greet, and sensitively frustrate the Oedipal urges rather than overstimulating them or crushing them, the Oedipal phase is a time for remarkable growth and consolidation of self-worth. However, if the nascent nuclear self is shaky and the parents are either threatened or stimulated by the child's Oedipal wishes, then Freud's classic scenario of drive conflict, repression of libido for the heterogenital parent, and transformation of the homogenital parent into a harsh superego can occur and issue into a neurosis. Thus, neurosis, while centered in Oedipal conflicts, has its grounds in problems of the self. What the child fears in the Oedipal conflicts is not castration but the possibility of self-disintegration.

Kohut did not think Freud was wrong in his diagnosis of patients, but that his particular clientele skewed his vision. Freud dealt mainly with patients from middle-upper-class Viennese homes in which emotional overcloseness between parents and children and intense, often conflicted, emotional relations between parents produced irresolvable inner conflicts for selves who had a somewhat solid nuclear foundation. However, today's American family is characterized by parental absence from the home, distant emotional contacts, and a tendency of parents to use their children to meet their own unmet narcissistic needs. This sociological configuration of the family accentuates problems with the construction of a self and produces general symptoms of loneliness, emptiness, repression of rage, and an intense need for erotic stimulation to feel alive.

The nuclear self is the foundation for all later accretions to the self. If it is solid, then barring massive problems, the rest of the self can be built and mature in a normal fashion. But if the nuclear self has been injured, later developments will either be arrested and/or have to serve defensive purposes along with constructive ones. In worst case scenarios chronic abuse, distance, and neglect in the first two years of life produce death or the inability to form a self, which characterizes the psychoses. Where the deprivations are less severe and/or later, borderline disorders appear in which the ability to form a self is lacking as in psychosis, but an effective set of defenses has been constructed that allow the person to function. If the abuse/deprivation is later or less pronounced than with psychotics and borderlines, narcissistic personality and behavioral disorders can appear. In these disturbances enough of a self is formed to give a substantial coherence to the person, but either the grandiose pole and/or idealized pole has suffered a major defect. Narcissistic disturbances are often associated with highly effective defenses and compensations that allow the person to be successful in the socioeconomic realm, but the successes are rarely gratifying as they cannot overcome the deep lack of worth in the nuclear self.

Narcissistic injuries often lead to an exhibitionist style of living in which one must constantly be the center of attention to compensate for a lack of inner worth. Conversely, these kinds of injuries can lead to a protracted withdrawal from social life and intimacy for fear that if the narcissistic needs are stimulated they will overwhelm the person. Narcissistic injuries also generate strong tendencies towards addictive behavior in which substances or compulsive activities are used in attempts to fill the inner void. Whatever the symptoms, persons suffering from narcissistic disorders feel a primal lack of self-worth and/or meaninglessness in the face of dead ideals. They have profound problems recognizing the existence and rights of other human beings and are constantly using others in desperate attempts to satisfy their needs to be recognized and affirmed. Otto Kernberg describes narcissists as follows:

> These patients present an unusual degree of self-reference in their interactions with other people, a great need to be loved and admired by others, and a curious apparent contradiction between a very inflated concept of themselves and an inordinate need for tribute from others. Their emotional life is shallow. They experience little empathy for the feelings of others, they obtain very little enjoyment from life other than from the tributes they receive from others or from their own grandiose fantasies, and they feel restless and bored when external glitter wears off and no new sources feed their self-regard. They envy others, tend to idealize some people from whom they expect narcissistic supplies and to depreciate and treat with contempt those from whom they do not expect anything (often their former idols). In general, their relationships with others are clearly exploitative and sometimes parasitic. It is as if they feel they have the right to control and possess others and to exploit them without guilt feelings—and, behind a surface which very often is charming and engaging, one senses coldness and ruthlessness.[9]

The inability to treat others as persons derives from early narcissistic deprivations being so severe that one is constantly attempting to replay the initial situation and get one's narcissistic entitlements met in a vain attempt to fill emptiness. Others must be exploited to meet these needs. One is forced by these injuries to be exhibitionist, even if this is demeaning; to merge with idols even though this threatens what little self there is. The narcissist can treat neither himself nor others as ends in themselves.

Whatever else ethics is, it involves the ability to treat ourselves and others as ends, not as means for manipulation and exploitation. This is what severe injuries to the nuclear self prevent us from being able to do. Hence, the ability to mature into an ethical person is dependent on the formation of a vital nuclear self. Not everyone can be ethical, only those who have been fortunate enough to have been given this self. While narcissists might be able to follow abstract rules—or at least think they are following those rules in their conscious intentions—early deprivations will overdetermine the actions with unconscious manipulations. A person might consciously follow the moral rule to help others in need but unconsciously do so to reap their adoration and make them dependent on him.

Thus, the capacity to be ethical is not an a priori possibility for all individuals as Kant and a number of Christian ethicists have held, nor is it an ever-present possibility that needs only education or reinforcement as the utilitarians taught. It is a developmental achievement dependent in particular on the formation of a coherent nuclear self. However, the possibility of being ethical is not the same as actually being ethical, nor is the possibility of having a mature self the same as actually being mature. A nuclear self might give the possibility for people to be ethical, but other things must happen in order for this possibility to be realized. Persons who are actually ethical are both able to see other human beings as ends in themselves and to acknowledge that they must set limits on their self-aggrandizing actions. Persons whose initial narcissism fully matures retain their vitality and ideals while accepting the concrete finitude and limitations of existence. How does this transformation take place? How do grandiose childhood ambitions and received ideals from others transform into mature motivation, social responsibility, and critically held ideals?

Kohut and other psychoanalytical thinkers provide little help with these questions, as they are mainly concerned with the conditions that produce psychic disorders that cannot be repaired by simple readjustments to patterns of living. To move from the nuclear self to a fully mature self that can satisfy the adult forms of the basic needs, sustain an identity through time, and adapt to the real conditions of social and natural life, two further accretions to the self need to be made: the narrative self and the ego.

2. The Narrative Self

Mature persons are typically seen as those who can function within the social and economic systems of their cultures. While this notion is invariant across cultures, the skills and education needed for such functioning vary greatly from one culture to another. The fourteen year old male hunter-gatherer is prepared to be an adult on the basis of an intensive training period for several months followed by an initiation ritual. By comparison, a youth wishing adult status in the middle or upper classes of an advanced technological society must undergo almost two decades of classroom education in order to have a minimal competence to deal with the massive complexities of society and technology that she will encounter. Tribal members who participate in a common social identity probably only need strong nuclear selves in order to function, but such a combination of nuclear self and common social identity is not enough to sustain the unity of a person in more complex social existences. Hence, as soon as we find tribal cultures complexifying beyond a subsistence economy, we find the development of a mythology where the narratives are not just about gods and the creation of the world, but about individual heroes. Under conditions where merger with a common tribal identity is no longer possible because differentiated role structures have come into being, narrative is born.

Narratives are stories people tell others and themselves about who they are and what their lives mean. In order to give meaning, narratives must have both a social template—a general pattern of life that is recognized by the society as worthy—and an openness in the details as to how the pattern is to be realized by the individual. Agamemnon, Achilles, Aias, and Odysseus all follow the template for being Homeric heroes, yet each has an individualized story for how they accomplish this pattern. Thus, narratives both allow persons to have individual identities and keep them within the value structure of the society. For Erik Erikson, an individual's finding a way to express her personal identity in terms of acceptable social functions is crucial if maturity is to be attained. Unless individuals find a way to express their idiosyncratic talents, propensities, defenses, libido-cathexes, and so forth in the social order, their lives generally become reduced to meaningless isolation.

Not only do narratives give us our primary relation to the social order and establish our social identities, they are also the most powerful vehicles we have for providing a continuity of the individual self through time and space.[10] The nuclear self also gives a continuity through time, but of a different sort. Because it is unconscious, the nuclear self tends to be timeless and repetitive, even in its positive, non-neurotic aspects. In general, we keep the same archaic self-representation that was developed in the first few years of life. It provides a kind of blueprint for the development of the self, a development that occurs when stimulated by the challenges of forming a narrative self. It is the stories we tell about ourselves that incorporate the important shifts in our lives and provide a dynamic element to our identities. Even though we are vastly different as adults than we were as children, we can feel a sense of continuity if these alterations are part of a coherent story we tell of ourselves.

People can sometimes lose their narratives, as when one suffers such traumas as divorce, loss of a job, or loss of an ability on which one's narrative depended (such as an athletic skill). When our narratives are seriously disrupted, we often feel lost and adrift, even if the nuclear self is intact. Neuroses probably will not develop unless there is a preexisting weakness in the nuclear self, but a sense of meaninglessness and acute depression can overtake us until we find a way to restore our narratives. Narratives are the ways we make sense of ourselves to ourselves and others; when they are lost, so are we.

The power of narrative in our lives is so impressive that it has convinced many theorists, including Goffman, Harré, and MacIntyre, that narrative constitutes the essence of personal identity.[11] This it does not. Many people with successful narratives are desperately unhappy and unfulfilled as selves because their nuclear selves are injured and cannot be repaired by successful narratives. Also, narrative structures do not have the means to handle the vast varieties of decisions a person in technological societies must make. A coherent set of epistemological and normative beliefs is also needed, and this kind of unity is given by the ego.

Finally, narratives can be dangerous both because they can be used as an illusion of self and because they are the primary carriers of the social unconscious. When there are injuries to the nuclear self, one can adopt the narrative self—one's social position—as a replacement for the nuclear self. Rather than acting from internal motivations, I become "the professor" and act according to the script of what a good professor does. That is, I identify with my primary role or roles. Given the status of the position identified with, this can be a very powerful move to make, for positions carry more authority than mere individuals. However, such a full identification with the narrative self is severely dehumanizing both for the self and others affected by the person. For one, the injuries of the nuclear self do not disappear but convert into symptoms, including the conversion of narcissistic rage into a harsh use of authority. Second, the tendency to narcissistic inflation as a defense against injury can be greatly heightened by an identification with a powerful position and this inflation makes one imperious towards others. However, such inflation can never make a person really happy for all one has done is converted himself into an impersonal role. Far beneath the surface of the imperious self-certain veneer is an injured, deeply unhappy self that can neither be recognized nor affirmed. It is this kind of person who, in Peck's terms, is likely to perpetrate evil in the world as a "person of the lie."

The second danger associated with the narrative self is that it carries with it the social unconscious. When we take on a social narrative, we unconsciously tend to assume the values, perspectives, and prejudices of the class and social order in which the narrative occurs. If the ego develops only enough to ask how the narrative can best be realized (a not uncommon phenomenon), then the narrative self acts as a conduit for the social unconscious and the person can become enmeshed in both the negative internal dynamics that Nietzsche so brilliantly uncovered and the social injustices that Marx and other political theorists found.

These dangers of identification with a narrative have become increasingly apparent for the middle and upper classes in America, where a destabilized family life that injures the nuclear self is combined with the powerful mythology that a narrative in one of the esteemed professions will make one fully happy and content. Not only does this cause intense competition and the anxiety that goes along with it for the top positions, but people often feel as though they are personal failures if they fail to attain one of the esteemed narratives.

Although professions can meet some of the needs, such as providing for the material demands of survival, social recognition, some limited adventures, some order, and the ability to be self-supporting, they have little to do with our abilities to come to terms with death, accept our sexuality, engage in intimacy, attain the kind of knowledge that makes the world a home, achieve a profound sense that we, and not exterior forces, are directing our lives, relate to the sacred, or create beauty. Professions also have little to do with the maturing of the emotions into deep vital ways of living and give little credence to the needs of the nuclear self. Most important, a professional narrative can never replace the nuclear self nor can it heal injuries that are there. The increasing identification of self and profession is one of the major reasons why so much dehumanized and oppressive activity is present in the workplace, and why there is increasing personal despair as persons discover the failures of professions and work to make them happy.

We might do better if we adopt as an essential part of our primary narrative a developmental story concerning how we are achieving maturity. Rather than asking as the central narrative question, "What profession should I choose?," one could ask questions like "What kind of person am I becoming?" "How do I stand now with my mortality?" "Has my sexuality and sex life become fully satisfying?" "Am I more autonomous, more profoundly individuated than I was as a youth?" "How do I relate to my environment, others, and the earth—do I have satisfying intimate relations, feel connected to a community, and relate profoundly to nature?" "Do I appreciate and create beauty?" "Is my emotional life vital with a full range of intensity and subtle nuances of feeling?"

When questions like these become the focal point of one's narrative constructions rather than questions about profession, then a great deal of anxiety concerning whether the socioeconomic world will provide one with a self or crush it disappear. Since professional narratives usually do not have any recognition of unconscious motivation, such a reconception of a primary narrative more adequately allows for conscious and unconscious narratives to be woven into a single tapestry. Dreams, real events, fantasies, genuine triumphs and failures can all be part of a development into maturity. The needs and emotions of the id, character traits, and conscious faculties can all grow with the result that experience can deepen, intensify, and become more profound.

However, it remains true that without some important intersection with the socioeconomic world isolation will occur that can be devastating. Hence, the developmental narrative I am advocating cannot be the sole psychosocial narrative, for it does not connect strongly enough to socioeconomic role structures. We need both: without a developmental narrative, the importance of social positions gets overemphasized; without narratives in the socio-economic world, we have the tendency to be reduced to isolated individuality.

3. The Ego

Neither the nuclear nor narrative self has the capacity for handling all the complexities of living in a technological society. Narratives give a general direction to life, but they cannot handle the numerous everyday decisions one must make. I have a narrative of being a college professor but this does not tell me if I should marry or whom to marry, to have a religion or not, what car to buy, if any, what insurance to carry and how much, and so forth. To keep the self together in the face of these innumerable everyday problems, one needs to have a unified belief system and a coherent set of values. These epistemological and normative systems constitute the primary structure of the ego. The more complexity a person encounters in life, the more central an ego identity becomes.

It is not the purpose of this book to undertake the difficult evaluation of the strengths and weaknesses of the various epistemological methodologies that have attempted to lead us beyond personal and social fantasies and prejudices, but it is worth noting how crucial epistemologies are in the construction of health. Although most of us normally believe that it is others who live in fantasy while we have a good understanding of what is real, the power of the primary process to distort cognition should not be underestimated, especially in situations that invoke the problems of early childhood, such as those of intimacy and authority. The pursuit of reality is a never-ending vocation, but there is nothing else that makes one feel more grounded and firm than when a fantasy passes and one realizes what the reality of the case is—even if it is terribly painful. It is the ego whose vocation it is to find reality. Without a healthy ego we would probably be constantly falling into fantasized worlds.

The ego's normative work involves critically adjusting the ideals and needs of the nuclear self and their transformations in the narrative self to fit complex environmental contingencies. It does this by developing a workable normative methodology to solve conflicts between the various competing sources of value in the psyche and society so that it can guide the numerous decisions that confront us in daily existence. Since life is constantly changing, this process of adjustment is a continuous affair that demands an ongoing monitoring of intentions, actions, and values of the self.

These processes, if performed well, result in a mature ego-ideal and the possibility of an ethical life. The ideals of the nuclear and narrative selves need not be critically held nor do they involve recognizing the legitimate existence of other humans. Nuclear ideals are focused on the possibilities of the self; narrative ideals tend to recognize as worthy only those who constitute one's social group. It is with the processes of the ego that the authoritative and normative source of motivation matures into a self-critical set of values that has the possibility of transcending early influences and narcissistic prejudices to become genuinely moral.

For Freud, a person's value system tends to be dominated by the value structure of the superego. Unlike the mature ego, Freud's superego does not have a self-adjusting power. It is merely the repository of early identifications, a nexus of social value imposed on the biological organism. Yet, it is as evident as any fact of human life that early value formations and nascent narratives can be opposed and altered by a process of critical thought. Because Freud could not find a place for critical reflection that transcended early conditioning, he could not understand how value construction could mature. But for ethicists, it is precisely the ego's ability to take a critical stance towards values that creates the possibility for ethical life.

This is not to say that complete transcendence, such as the pure practical reason of Kant, is possible. It is not. However, the lack of complete transcendence does not mean that important critical adjustments of values cannot be objectively made by human beings. Piaget and Kohlberg were on the right track in seeing that moral thinking undergoes a developmental growth pattern similar to those of other cognitive powers. In general there is the growth noted by Kohlberg away from a narcissistic early stage (nuclear self values), through a social stage (narrative self values), to a rational critical adult stage (ego values). Where Kohlberg goes astray is in forgetting that the nuclear and narrative selves must retain their vital places in a person's life, for they have ways of relating to values that are as important as ego judgments. The ego does not replace these earlier values with better ones, but modifies them, enhances them, resolves conflicts between them, and relates them to a world of other human beings in a critical way. Ethical values without narcissistic input lack the vitality, zest, and individual creativity that Nietzsche so championed as the essence of life. Ethics without narrative connections lacks a crucial social dimension: it characterizes the isolated individual autonomously willing abstractions rather than a human being immersed in the rich flow of social intercourse. However, as important as nuclear and narrative values are, without the critical adjustments of the ego, they cannot fully mature. The ego's power can partially free persons from their initial embeddedness in family and social life and give them the possibility for greater individuation.

The ego's first function in regard to values is to act as an arbiter in cases of conflict. Freud understood this function when he saw that it was the ego that had to resolve conflicts or repress them. The multidimensional psyche portrayed here has far more potentiality for conflict than Freud's battles between libido and reality or libido and the superego, for the needs, emotions, and various stages of the self can all enter into profound differences.

The second normative function of the ego is to internalize development. Childhood development is based on optimal frustrations being presented by the environment, but adult development is contingent upon a person's being able to produce healthy oppositions within herself. The ego is the principle of internal opposition, which can generate a lifetime of continual growth.

Given its two functions of adjudicating intrapsychic conflict and promoting development, it is easy to see why the ego has its characteristic marks of being distant and abstract. If the ego were closely webbed to the emotions, particular needs, the nuclear self, or narrative self, then it could not perform its critical and oppositional functions. To solve conflicts and to provide opposition to these earlier aspects of the self, the ego must remove itself from them.

The distancing of the ego from desires, emotions, and social embeddedness of the person presents it with a grave problem: on what ground can it resolve conflicts of values and critique the values it currently holds, if it cannot rely upon personal preferences or strong desires? This is the problem Plato discovered when he wrote the first moral psychology. He saw that if the psyche were a mere power complex and was ruled by whatever need or aspect of the psyche was dominant at the moment, then there would always be major distortions, repressions, and lack of development in the psyche. The only way out of these distorting power matrixes was for the ego to act on a principle of justice—of letting each part of the psyche perform its proper function.[12] I believe Plato was correct in this insight; unfortunately, he tied justice to an hierarchical model for organization and the rule of justice turned into a dictatorship of reason. However, when justice is connected with an ecological model of organization, then the kinds of distortions and repressions that occur when rational consciousness becomes overly dominant are avoided.

We can now understand why Plato, Aristotle, Kant, Mill, and others thought that the ego must ground itself in a universal principle of justice rather than a part of the self. Particular needs, emotions, desires, or parts of the self cannot be used as grounds for the ego's performing its functions, because it is precisely the battles between these elements that must be adjudicated and their current states that must be opposed for development to occur. In order for the ego to adjudicate intrapsychic disputes requires a principle of justice, a principle that recognizes the "rights" of all the psychic elements and voices. It is important to see that this crucial argument for a principle of justice at the heart of the psyche rests on the theory that both the self and its constituent parts are multiple. If the self is seen as a singular identity, then there is no personal reason why it should not have as the ground for all its decisions, "Do what is best for me."

Thus, the goal of personal health—the optimal functioning of the psyche—brings us to the necessity of incorporating an ethical principle of justice. So also do the basic needs, and they move us to extend the principle of justice to others. In order to satisfy the needs for intimacy, autonomy (which requires a recognition of the difference between oneself and others), and the sacred, we need to overcome early forms of narcissism. A failure to give up early narcissistic grandiosity also makes us unable to come to terms with death, and frustrates us in a major form of reproductive fitness—the actual having and raising of children. Adventure becomes difficult, for the only persons we meet are ourselves. I could examine the rest of the needs, but the result will be the same: insofar as we remain unable to give up self-centeredness and are incapable of treating other human beings as equally worthy as ourselves, we will continue to seek immature satisfactions of the needs. If Peck is right in claiming that the key characteristic of malignant narcissism is "an unsubmitted will,"[13] then the key to overcoming a narcissistic orientation is the ego's placing itself under a principle of justice.

Philosophers have tried to answer the question of "Why be ethical?" ever since Plato proposed ethics as the highest form of human existence. Most recent answers cluster around the argument that it is irrational not to have a rational principle by which to direct one's life. But, as Bernard Williams has shown, the life of rationality is a particular form of life that has certain benefits and deficits.[14] One can rationally choose not to live rationally. Hence, these arguments fail. The reason given here for being ethical is far more substantial: adopting an ethical view of life—a life in which one takes into account the existence of other human beings as ends in themselves—is the only way in which the needs can be fully satisfied and the self can internalize development. Why do we want our needs satisfied and our selves to develop? Because this is the only way we can be happy and feel the full vitality of life. This is the answer Plato and Aristotle gave to the question "Why be moral?", but it is only with recent psychology that we can make full sense of the claim empirically.

This is not to say that what moral values require of us in particular circumstances will always coincide with what is in our best interests, for this is not so. Nor am I saying that it is always right to be moral in cases in which self-interests and moral principles collide, for there is no way to establish that morality always has overriding precedence.[15] However, I am claiming that the kind of person who can most deeply satisfy her needs and achieve the fullest development of her powers is the kind of person who becomes moral.

What I mean by "moral" is very general, for it consists merely in taking into account the existence of others, of treating others as ends rather than only as a means to one's personal satisfactions. This recognition of the legitimacy of the other takes two forms: empathy and acting under a principle of justice.[16] Empathy is a process whereby we recognize the feelings of others in the most profound way possible, by mirroring them in ourselves. This kind of empathic response is so powerful and affirming that Kohut has claimed it can, through a process of transmuting internalization, repair the injured sectors of a nuclear self. It is the empathic responsiveness of the therapist which is primarily responsible for the healing of narcissistic injuries.[17] Empathically responding to the feelings, needs, and sufferings of others is at the heart of ethics. It is this form of recognition of the other that makes the other feel human. When we empathize with the feelings of others, we treat humans humanely.

Yet, empathy tends to bind us to those closest to us and neglect others who are not as close. A principle of justice or universalization that demands that all people be treated as having equal worth overcomes the biases of empathy and is a necessary addition to the ethical perspective. The content of a principle of justice needs filling in by different cultures and peoples, but the abstract form remains the same: our actions need to be guided by principles that we would be willing to affirm in all their applications, even when we are the recipient rather than the perpetrator of their consequences.

The principle of justice can be justified, as Plato so wisely thought, as a necessary principle for the internal operation of the psyche. Unless the ego can treat all the needs and emotions with some degree of fairness, the psyche will become unbalanced and have to undergo either the underdevelopment or repression of some of its key functions. Justice is a character trait we need to develop in order to have a healthy functioning psyche, but once we have it, then we will also tend to treat not only ourselves but others justly.

The power of the ego to intellectually transcend the situatedness of the person has been so captivating to ethicists that they have forgotten that the ego is a product of development and that its critical powers are grounded in this development. This forgetfulness has led them to identify ethical values entirely with ego values, especially with reason, consciousness, universal principles, and objectivity. But as we have already seen, the ego cannot escape its developmental history and must recognize the importance and centrality of the nuclear and narrative selves. If these selves, especially the nuclear self, are injured, then the unifying powers of the ego are often used as a defensive exoderm to hold the fragmented nuclear self together.

In these instances the ego can, as Freud knew, repress emotions, conflicts, troublesome needs, and superego guilt to maintain the semblance of unity in consciousness. When the ego is not integrated with the nuclear and narrative selves, its values can appear as rationally justified, but they are not felt or embodied. One feels abstracted from the values of her narrative and nuclear self. Indeed, all of life seems distant when lived primarily from the viewpoint of the ego. Life is thought, but not experienced. Narratives, friends, values, families, homes, and so forth can all fall under the critical scrutiny of the ego and be given up, if the ego decides that there is a better job, better friends, or a better spouse. The ego exists in its cold, removed palace, surveying the world from on high. While such an ego fragmented off from the other workings of the psyche provides great powers of choice, freedom, and critical acumen, we know from Freud that its freedom and choices will be constantly undermined by the elements that it has repressed.

Hence, for the ego to be a healthy accretion to the self, it must both be integrated with and transcend the nuclear and narrative selves. When it does so, it can produce an "ego ideal" that embodies the most vital values of the individual nuclear self, the social embeddedness of these values in narrative, and the critical adjustment of these values in the recognition of the other and the constraints of reality. When our ego ideal is based on our identification with a nurturing calm selfobject rather than a controlling self-absorbed parent, expresses our individual talents and ambitions, locates a suitable place for the expression and realization of our individuality in the social order, and recognizes ethical constraints on the expressions of the self, then the self has the possibility of both lifelong fulfillment and moral agency. The two are not at odds, as in liberal theory, but grow out of one another when we take an ecological perspective on the self.

4. The Mature Self

The mature interweaving of the nuclear, narrative, and ego selves is what I term "the ecological self." The ecological

self is like a mandala whose inner patterns keep expand-
ing themselves endlessly outward into new variations of
color and shape. The core of the mandala is always the
nuclear self. When life goes well, the undaunted ambitions
of the grandiose pole are united by talent and character to
an archaic set of ideals that do not induce guilt. This coherent self then expands into a social context where it elabo-
rates itself in new shapes and expressions while retaining a
tie to its central structure. As this pattern expands outward
it encounters an inevitable border which limits it, forcing it
to reconceive its pattern so that it can function harmoniously within a bounded universe. In short, the ecological
self occurs when the joy of the grandiose pole unites with
stable, realizable values of the idealized pole in a narrative
that brings happiness to oneself and others in a life of increasing development and heightened complexity.

Here is a vision of the human person that acknowledges the biological core and community involvement of
Aristotle, the quest for ideals of Plato, the vivacity of individual existence in Nietzsche, the sentiments (empathy and
justice) of Hume, the use of universal principles as in Kant,
and the pragmatic bent of Dewey in understanding the
organism as engaged in a constant interchange with its
environment.

We are not simple nuclear selves, as Nietzsche sometimes has it, acting out of our sheer grandiose energies. Nor
are we just narrative constructions as MacIntyre and the
ethogenic sociologists think. Nor are we transcendent egos
critically adjudicating disputes and acting according to universal principles and scientific methodologies as Kant, the
utilitarians, and most contemporary ethicists hold. We are
all of these and cannot be neglectful of any of them. By
itself, narcissistic grandiosity is a disaster of non-concern for
others, but without it, life has little joy or individual assertion. Narratives bind our lives to the social order, but without them we have no continuity through time or a feeling of
social belonging. The ego distances us from the social order
and ourselves, but in so doing gives freedom and the possi-

bility of continued development to fuller and deeper forms of integration and expansion of the self. Full ethical life is, as Hegel said, a balancing of individuality, socialness, and universality. Such a balancing requires a constant interplay and ecological intertwining of these three factors of the mature self.

Most important, we have found a ground in the nuclear self for why normative ideals are necessary to life and a ground in the ego for why these ideals need to be ethical rather than merely narcissistic. Fully healthy selves are also ethical selves and a person cannot be a fully ethical self unless she has attained a large degree of health in her psyche.

CHAPTER 9

MATURE AGENCY
AND SOCIAL RESPONSIBILITY

We can complete our model of ecological maturity by inquiring into the question of what it means to be a responsible human agent. A review of the traditional notion of ethical agency, which has been more or less intact from the Greek philosophers to the present day, will reveal that we have been held responsible both for too much and too little. We are held responsible for who we become, as though we were fully free to choose our selves, and not held responsible for actions we do not consciously intend. This traditional model of agency has left us inured in guilt on the one hand and, on the other, let off the hook for actions we have not consciously intended.

1. The Traditional Concept of Agency

After surveying the most important recent Anglo-American literature on the concepts of agency, freedom, and autonomy, Richard Double concludes that five conditions must be met if a person's choice is to be considered free and the person an autonomous agent: (1) self-knowledge, (2) reasonability, (3) intelligence, (4) efficacy, and (5) unity.[1]

We need self-knowledge to be autonomous, for we would hardly be choosing freely if we were mistaken about what our desires, motivations, and beliefs really are. If I think I desire to be dean of the college because it pays more money and has more prestige than being a professor, but really desire it (unbeknownst to myself) in order to act out sadistic impulses on the one hand and escape intimacy at home on the other, then my choice is not free, for I do not know what I am doing nor why I am doing it.

The reasonability criterion requires that our choices be based on critically examined beliefs and values. If I decide to something on the basis of a certain belief about the world and that belief is false, then the choice is not free, since I would not have made the decision had I known what the world really was. According to this criterion, the psychotic who lives in a fantasy world cannot make free choices, nor can we to the extent that our beliefs about the world are clothed in fantasies. Charles Taylor would add that a crucial part of the critical examination process is judging the rightness and wrongness of our desires according to a set of values we hold.[2] For Taylor the essence of ethical agency is the ability to be self-monitoring, the ability to act according to a structure of critically determined values rather than being moved merely by immediate desire.

The intelligence requirement asks that our ethical deliberations be logical and coherent. "By intelligence I mean the ability to learn facts about the world, retain that information, and draw inferences from it. I also include the ability (rather than the desire) to reason well about ourselves and our mental states."[3]

The efficacy requirement means that we must have "the power to actually make self-knowledgeable, reasonable, and intelligent choices. . . . This entails the ability to resist non-rational factors in our choices, such as threats and bribes from the external world, as well as non-rational motivations from within the cranium."[4] In short, I am not free if I know what is driving me to drink, have logically determined that it has disastrous consequences for me and others, but, nonetheless, cannot control the desire to drink.

The unity requirement is necessary in order to assure that the person who has self-knowledge, critically examined beliefs and values, a rational deliberative process, and the power to act is the same person throughout the process. Plato saw unity as the crucial ground for ethical agency and asserted that the unity of the psyche was the highest value for agency, for only unity could prevent various aspects of the psyche from controlling choices rather than the person. When the psyche is not unified, then a fragmented sexual need can force it into erotic activity which we do not want or repressed anger can make us more aggressive and hurtful than our careful examinations tell us we ought to be.

These criteria state in the rigorous style of contemporary ethical theory the traditional concept of agency that was developed by the ancient Greek philosophers and has continued more or less intact until the present day. When humans are able to transcend the social and biological forces working on them, achieve knowledge of all the motivational factors affecting their actions, base their actions on values and beliefs that are rationally justified, and have power over all the motivational inputs, then they can be autonomous agents. The crucial factor in the achievement of this power over oneself is the attainment of unity in the psyche. In sum, Double finds that the old triumvirate of rationality, power, and unity are the keys to achieving ethical agency.

After stating these criteria for free choice, Double concludes that "freedom," "agency," and "responsibility" are incoherent terms because they require both that there be a break in the chain of causal efficacy (such that we are not mere pawns in the hands of social and biological forces), and that the causal chain be unbroken (the act must be caused by a person with a certain character and abilities and not be due to chance or spontaneous events). Double's problems with these concepts cannot be answered by any of the traditional theories of personal identity, for the same self cannot both be coherent with itself and break with itself.

The tripartite concept of the self developed here can partially answer Double's conceptual problems, for humans have both the powers of acting according to who they are (nuclear and narrative selves) and the power of critically distancing themselves from who they are (the ego). Hence, they are capable both of acting within a causal order and breaking that order. When the nuclear, narrative, and ego selves are conjoined we have the possibility of "delayed action" (John Dewey's term) or "right reason plus right desire" (Aristotle). It is the mature integrated self that is capable of both acting out of who it is and critically reviewing the act in question. Only the mature, developed, unified self can be free.[5]

Yet, we must qualify this conclusion, for the discovery of the unconscious makes it impossible to believe that all five of Double's criteria can be met in any act by any kind of self. The unconscious, even in healthy adults, can be manipulating choices without our knowledge. We never fully outgrow primary process thinking, emotional rootedness in the past, or certain fixations of belief and feeling. The unity of the psyche is never assured, self-knowledge is always partial, beliefs about reality are often touched by fantasy, and our power to control our actions is always in doubt. In short, all choices and actions are probably overdetermined to some degree. If Double's five variables are necessary for free and responsible agency, then we are not and cannot be free autonomous agents in the sense the tradition requires.

Such a conclusion appears regrettable, for it forces us to accept limitations on powers we heretofore thought were ours. However, it is in fact a boon. The traditional notion of ethical agency makes us both too responsible and not responsible enough. In identifying the psyche with consciousness, ethics holds us responsible not only for what we intentionally do but also for who we are. Since we supposedly have power over ourselves, we can in theory choose to be anything, including being full moral agents. Hence, if we are not moral agents, we have chosen to be such and are responsible for our immorality. While such an ideal of freedom is a lofty goal, it is a fiction. We do not and cannot choose fully who we are. What we are is largely determined in the first two years of life by biological, familial, and cultural forces outside of our control. What narratives are available to us is largely determined by the social order. The extent to which we are able to develop the critical capacities of the ego and have them be effective in directing life is partially determined by the educational systems of our social order.

In short, Western culture and its philosophers have been so dazzled by the powers of the conscious rational ego that they have not seen the extent to which the ego is a product of development and can be circumscribed by that development and other forces in the psyche. What the discovery of the unconscious has revealed is that cultures which worked according to the concept of fate understood more about human nature than we thought. Who we become is largely dependent upon the family we are born into, our gender (if the culture treats males and females differently, as every known culture does), ordinal position in the family, the family's socioeconomic status, and the structure of the culture. Traditional cultures imposed these fates by custom and law. One's birth determined one's social position and one's social position determined one's identity. With ethics and the rise of liberal democracy, external fatedness was greatly lessened, but in its place we have discovered how the society, especially as it is present in the family, is introjected into the unconscious. Although we may not be fated to a certain social position, we seem fated to hold the values and beliefs of our socioeconomic class. We may not be fated to marry a certain spouse, but seem fated to carry around how we resolved our erotic relations to our parents. We try desperately to escape the control of our parents only to discover that they have been introjected into the very heart of ourselves.

Of course, early ideals can be modified, injuries partially repaired, self-representations altered, and narratives changed. But one cannot put the entire nuclear self in question, for this would be equal to a psychosis. Like the nucleus of an atom, the nuclear self is the strongest, most vital part of a person. Electrons might come and go or change orbits, but the nucleus must remain more or less intact if the atom is not to explode into a fragmentation of particles or transmute into a different substance. The conscious ego might determine that the nuclear self has a negative self-representation and then follow various methods from self-help books to bolster its self-image, but they do not work, for conscious methodologies only operate at the level of electrons in the self—they can never penetrate the core of the unconscious nucleus. In general, an artificial repetition of the early childhood situation in which a practiced therapist or rare friend can become a genuine selfobject and enter into empathic selfobject transferences is needed for a person to receive some repair of the nuclear self. But the nuclear self can never be fully transformed. Innate talents and predispositions remain, early idealization colors all later ideals, fears of being crushed, neglected, or abused can abate but rarely disappear fully. William Ernest Henley's famous lines, "I am the master of my fate, I am the captain of my soul" express a Western fantasy. If there are captains of souls, there is also a crew capable of mutiny and a ship capable of being dashed to pieces on the rocks of a cruel fate.

In claiming that we have the freedom to become anything we wish, the traditional concept of autonomy placed us in an unfortunate dilemma: if we produce evil consequences then we either (a) consciously intended them, in which case we are guilty of evil motivations, or (b) did not consciously intend them, in which case we need assume no moral responsibility for the consequences. The first alternative leads to the negative psychic dynamics of guilt that Nietzsche and Freud so brilliantly elaborated, while the second leads to a complacency about a self that could be harboring powerfully destructive motivations in the unconscious.

Guilt is a natural emotion that has a crucial role to play in the psyche, for it tells us when the grandiose pole of the nuclear self has strayed from the idealized pole. That is, guilt gives us a warning that our actions have strayed from our ideals causing a rift between the two essential poles of the nuclear self that needs repair. However, when guilt is imposed because we fail to live up to a generalized social ideal rather than an individual ego ideal, then the self gets a double message: "you are bad" and "you must become other than you are." The first message promotes the identification with a negative self-image, while the second is highly frustrating, for if I could have done otherwise, then why didn't I? Together they give the message that I am the person who does evil and cannot be allowed to be who I am. If the ascription of guilt becomes commonplace in development, then the Freudian dynamics of a repressive, self-negating superego appear with the concomitant symptoms of depression, masochism, sadism, and a strong tendency to project one's guilt onto others and then find them wanting.

Supposedly, guilt is imposed in order to prevent further occurrences of antisocial behavior. Yet, insofar as guilt imposed by others creates negative identities and punishing superegos, it will tend to increase antisocial behavior. Probably the highest predictor of future crimes is a person's being found guilty of and punished for present crimes.

Along with making us too responsible for who we are and what we do and, thus, lessening of our abilities to be vital individuals acting with self-acceptance and without guilt, the traditional notion of agency has also made us less responsible than we could be, for it does not hold us responsible for that which we do not intend. Although we are expected to be in full control of our actions, we can be "let off the hook" if we can produce an "excuse" for objectionable actions. Excuses can be of varying kinds,[6] but essential to all of them is showing that we did not intend the undesirable consequences. "I didn't mean to hit you, I was just trying to scare you." "I did not intend to be late, the traffic was horrendous." If we can show that we did not consciously intend the negative effects of our acts, then we will, in most cases, be absolved of blame for them.

Such a paradigm of agency will have the obvious tendency to drive questionable motives into the unconscious where we need not be responsible for them. I upset you by being unintentionally late, by unintentionally forgetting our anniversary, by unintentionally spilling a drink on your new shirt. I am not to blame, but I get the satisfaction of aggressing against you.

Not only does the traditional model of responsibility tend to drive questionable intentions into the unconscious, it keeps us in a state of self-deception. If I knew that I was the kind of person who transferred my rage against my father onto authoritative men, then I couldn't do it so easily. If I knew that my seductive tendencies were actually an attempt to control and hurt women, then I would be under an obligation to stop this mode of behavior.

We have already seen how much human suffering and devastation is caused by unconscious intentions and compulsions working through overdetermined actions. The human tragedies wrought by projection, addictions, and the deadly acting out of unconscious rages, libidinal complexes, and early dependencies are so incalculably massive as to make consciously intended evils pale in comparison. Yet the traditional theory of responsibility allows us to claim innocence for these deeds, for they are not consciously intended.

Hence, the traditional notions of agency, responsibility, and freedom invented by the Greeks and continuing all the way to Sartre's radical existential freedom, infecting along the way institutions of law, social expectations, and theories of punishment, have given us both too much and too little responsibility. With the discovery of the unconscious we can now understand these difficulties and propose a theory of agency and responsibility that is based on who we really are as humans rather than a fantasy of the gods we hoped to be.

2. Fate

The discovery of the unconscious restores the ancient notion of fatedness: who we are is largely determined by a mixture of biological and social forces working in early childhood to produce a self. The self is not a primordial given, but the product of a developmental process that the child cannot direct or control. Since the ability to perform ethical actions depends on the coherence of the self, a large portion of the responsibility for the ability to be ethical must be attributed to environmental factors.

The understanding of this developmental process has led a number of recent thinkers to reassert Socrates' shocking claim that no one does evil voluntarily. If we act in ways that hurt others, it is because we have suffered early injuries that cause repressed rage, or have not been educated and/or trained to have moderate character traits by which we can delay our emotional responses. It is failures of the environment that cause failures in the development of the self, which then get rooted in the unconscious and infect our actions with antisocial motivations. We did not choose to be injured nor do we freely choose to hurt others; the unconscious merely conducts the injuries we have received onto others, for the fundamental law of the psyche says that one will do unto others as has been done unto one.

Ilham Dilman in *Freud and Human Nature* shows how arrogance, meanness, greed, vanity, envy, and avarice arise from failures in early childhood development and represent reactive, narcissistic, or impulsive defenses. "[E]vil always comes from a self that is immature in one respect or another."[7] Immaturity for Dilman results from developmental failures. While he goes on to say that a person could be both mature and morally mediocre, he holds to his uneasy conclusion that genuine evil is the result of failures in the developmental process.

In his *Love and its Place in Nature*, Jonathan Lear holds that people become cruel not out of free choice, but because they have been treated cruelly. "It is cruelty that breeds cruelty; and thus the possibility of a harmonious cruel soul, relatively free from inner conflict and sufficiently differentiated from the cruel environment, begins to look like science fiction."[8] Being "sufficiently differentiated" is the equivalent of what I (and Dilman) term maturity and the failure to achieve it results from the environment's not having been "good enough." Cruelty is possible only when the environment fails to offer a loving enough response to the developing child.

Although the psychoanalytic movement in general is not concerned with the problem of evil, its theory tends to support Dilman's and Lear's conclusion that we never do evil voluntarily, but only as the result of having innate aggressions and/or suffering deprivations and abuse during development. If we are evil, we are evil primarily by fate. Persons treated lovingly return the gift of love; those negated, neglected, and abused, turn to the world with rage and unsatisfiable dependency needs that must manipulate and control other people.

There is certainly a truth in this position. It is difficult to imagine why anyone who has received thoughtful empathic love and respect during development would turn to needless cruelty and aggression. This is not to say that psychologically healthy persons will not at times be insensitive and unjust in their dealings with others or that they will not overidentify with their social roles and commit evils out of its pressures, but they will not have as a primary unconscious project the destruction of other people.

While psychoanalytic theory provides a strong case for the claim that no one does evil voluntarily, there remains something offensive in this position. In denying that human beings are responsible for the evils they cause, we also deny the possibility of dignity and genuine agency. Agency becomes merely the ability to act out of the good human natures that have been produced by good enough environments. Such a position can lead to an overemphasis on fate and to a neverending stream of excuses pointing back to one's inadequate past. Excuses are demeaning, for they imply that we are the victims of forces outside of our control. They are the whimpers of a victim, not the statements of a dignified human agent who can say, "I did it and deserve what I get." Nietzsche says "pity offends the sense of shame."[9] Shame is what we feel when we do something wrong and know we had the power to act differently. Both pity and developmental theories of personality offend the archaic sense of freedom we feel as humans. As Sartre says, any being that is conscious is also free.

Yet, we have seen how disastrous it can be to assume that humans have the possibility of full control over their actions. Thus, we seem stuck in a dilemma. If we assume that humans are free, then we deny the reality of the unconscious. Individuality is lost in the face of having to meet an ideal of goodness and guilt ensues. But, if we assume that humans are fated to do what they do, then human dignity and freedom are lost as we become merely victims or beneficiaries of our developmental processes.

3. Mature Agency

In order to have a theory of agency that neither makes human beings too responsible for who they are nor too fated to take responsibility for their actions, we need to separate responsibility from the notions of free conscious intentionality, guilt, and the attainment of moral ideals. I think the only way to do this is to substitute, with modifications, the theory of responsibility from the world of fate: we are responsible for what we do and the consequences of our acts whether they were consciously intended or not. This is not an unheard of theory, for we use it every day in assessing accidental behavior. I hit a baseball farther than I have ever done before and break your window. I did not intend to do this and am not guilty of a crime, but I am responsible to pay the damages. This understanding of responsibility does not demand that we inflict the person doing the damage with a negative identity of guilt (since no intentions were involved), and yet reparation can be justly demanded.

Given that intentions are usually overdetermined, especially in antisocial acts, we can cut through the tangled Gordian knot of determining what is freely intended from what is unconsciously determined by separating the notion of responsibility from conscious intentionality altogether.

Are we to hold the boss responsible for harassment when he pats the employee's shoulder with a bit too much vigor and the tonalities in his voice indicate that he desires to communicate something other than professional approbation? He does not consciously intend to seduce the employee, so traditional ethics must find him innocent. Besides, finding the boss "guilty" of sexual harassment is a major indictment, and the evidence just isn't strong enough for this assessment. Hence, the employee's feelings of being harassed and degraded are unvalidated and the boss's unconscious fragmented sexual impulses and aggression remain unreformed. However, if we remove attempts to assess conscious intentionality and guilt and focus on what the employee felt, then we can ask the boss to accept responsibility for making the employee feel harassed. It does not matter that "he didn't mean to," for we now accept unconscious motivations as operative. The boss needs to assume responsibility for being the kind of person who makes his employee feel harassed and use this as an occasion for the exploration of his possible unconscious narratives. He is much more likely to do this if we do not also assess him with guilt for intending to seduce the employee.

If Peck and I are right in thinking that evil is caused primarily by persons suffering from narcissistic personality disorders, then we can more clearly see why guilt and blame are useless and harmful concepts. Should narcissists be found guilty for the misery they bring to the world and the countless lives they destroy? Are they to be blamed when their failures to be ethical stem from failures of their self-objects to give them enough love in the earliest stage of life? Are their parents to be blamed? The injuries to the nuclear self occur not so much through overt acts or occasional severe neglects, but through a chronically deformed relation of the parent to the child in which the parents use the child to satisfy their narcissistic needs rather than meeting the child's needs. The development of the nuclear self, according to Kohut, "will be less influenced by those responses of the selfobjects that are shaped by their philosophy of child rearing than by those that express the state of their own nuclear self. In other words, it is not so much what the parents *do* that will influence the character of the child's self, but what the parents *are*."[10] If parents are attempting to have their own narcissistic needs met by their children, it is because their needs were unmet by their parents. Here is a world in which blame, guilt, and intentionality do not make sense. It is a world of fate and fatedness, of good and ill luck. Not only are blame and guilt not called for, but they tend to make the narcissist even more self-negating and less able to see others as humans.

Rather than guilt, what is called for when we do wrong is remorse. Remorse is an emotion that acknowledges that a wrong has been done, we did it, and feel genuine grief for the suffering we have caused others and ourselves. Remorse is an uncomfortable feeling but not an identity-setting one. Thus, it can lead to change in a way that guilt cannot. If we renounce social guilt for ourselves, we must also give up the practice of blaming others. Rather than blame, a profound acceptance is called for—an acceptance that understands that persons doing wrong would be better if they could be. Such acceptance does not absolve us from determining the most appropriate response to wrongdoing, but leads us away from negative psychosocial dynamics of guilt that produce only harm and despair.

When responsibility is untethered from guilt, freedom, intentionality, and a general ideal for moral behavior, then we can accept responsibility for who we are and what we do without also having to feel guilty. This responsibility for self is, admittedly, paradoxical, for it asks that we accept responsibility for something we are not responsible for. We did not have the freedom to create ourselves. Who we are and what we do is largely determined by forces outside ourselves, and yet we must accept responsibility for ourselves and all we do, be it consciously or unconsciously intended.

This notion of accepting responsibility for who we are and what we do will be clearer if we can distinguish it from "taking responsibility," "being responsible," and "holding ourselves responsible."[11] When we take responsibility for an act or hold ourselves responsible for it, we imply that we are in control of ourselves and have freely chosen the act. If the act is negative, then we must admit that we have freely chosen to be evil and must punish that part of ourselves that bid us to do the evil.

In contrast, accepting responsibility means that one chooses to be responsible for who one is, knowing that in large part one has been fated to be this way. The nuclear self is primarily an internalized residue of the early social world of the child. Our narratives are given to us by the society. We can always legitimately excuse any act by saying "I could not have done otherwise, given my upbringing." Such approaches to personal responsibility rest on facts concerning development and are acceptable. They are also dead ends. If holding ourselves responsible for negative acts ends in guilt and self-punishment, excusing ourselves from responsibility fares no better, for it keeps the self that committed the acts fully intact. When we give excuses, we have no grounds for change. We retain a fantasized image of ourselves as good and deny the existence of that part of us which caused the evil. With excuses one remains a passivity willing to be manipulated by exterior forces. Jonathan Lear exemplifies this crucial distinction between taking responsibility for oneself and accepting it by referring to Oedipus. Why does Oedipus accept his fate when it was fated for him? In claiming responsibility, Oedipus declares himself to be an activity and not a passivity doomed by the forces of nature. "Holding oneself responsible is essentially a super-I [superego] activity; accepting responsibility is not. In accepting responsibility, Oedipus is making an all together more elemental claim: these acts are *my acts*. *Where it* [Id] *was, there I* [ego] *am*."[12] Only by accepting responsibility for who we are and all of what we do can we have the possibility for genuine ethical agency.

We are still, however, at a level of abstraction, for we do not yet know what it means to accept responsibility for who one is. Is it merely saying some words—"I accept responsibility for who I am"—or does it involve the undergoing of certain experiences? Words are often tendered by the conscious ego and have little relation to what is happening at the unconscious levels of the self. In order to fully accept responsibility for who we are, we must come to know, feel, and love who we have been fated to be. Nietzsche calls this process the "*amor fati*"—the love of one's fate.

> My formula for greatness in a human being is *amor fati*: that one wants nothing to be different, not forward, not backward, not in all eternity. Not merely bear what is necessary, still less conceal it—all idealism is mendaciousness in the face of what is necessary—but *love* it.[13]

Loving one's fate seems strange coming from the philosopher who preached ceaseless self-overcoming, but for Nietzsche, humans are primarily their bodies—their finite, particular, nonexchangeable bodies. We are not and never can be any set of values, for our bodies with their peculiar talents, predispositions, needs, emotions, and quirks are primary. To love one's singularness and stubborn unchangeableness is to love one's fate. Fate, in the deepest sense, is nothing other than particularity.

We cannot affirm our particular fates or accept responsibility for who we are unless we know who we are; otherwise, we are only affirming a fantasy. The core of our self-knowledge concerns the core of ourselves, namely, our nuclear selves. Yet, such selves lie below the level of consciousness and, even when healthy, contain the residues of abandoned love objects, the loss of the fantasized protectedness and immortality of childhood, and all the injuries that tell us we are not, in fact, the grandiose center of the universe. The journey into the dark areas of the self is not an intellectual fact-finding mission, but a suffering that is willing, once again, to experience the griefs, conflicts, injuries, and fatedness of growing up. These early sufferings, especially the ones that are still active and fermenting in the unconscious announce themselves in dreams, mistakes, failures, and unintended consequences to our actions. The only way we can really come to know and be our own particularities is to accept responsibility for our dreams, mistakes, failures, and unintended consequences—things we usually are excused for. Am I responsible for my dreams? How absurd. Yet, Freud once wrote that we must accept responsibility for the evil impulses in our dreams, for "what else is one to do with them?"[14] Obviously, this does not mean that I should turn myself into the police for committing a heinous murder in my dream, but it does mean that I need to ask "Why did I dream this murder?" "What does this murder mean about me and what I am unconsciously experiencing?" "Might these feelings affect my daily activities?" Without accepting such responsibility for our unconscious productions, we cannot know who we are or be fully ethical.

If the key to being ethical is accepting responsibility for one's particularity and this cannot be done without having an affective knowledge of one's unconscious, then the key ethical relation becomes a person's relation to his unconscious. The great moral principle that hung over the entrance to the Delphic oracle so long ago, "Gnothi Sauton"—know thyself—is still true today and always will be. As the oracle wisely understood, self-knowledge might appear to be the easiest kind of knowledge to achieve, but it is, in fact, the most difficult, for the sources of who we are lie deeply hidden in the unconscious and are covered over by such elaborate defenses and self-illusions that it takes all our sorcery, heroism, and skill to penetrate them.

All the discoverers of the unconscious held that humans can live fully within themselves and with others only when they are able to know, suffer, and accept their particular fates. Nietzsche's overmen must descend into the abyss of meaninglessness and despair in order to emerge as laughing children, capable of the sacred "Yes," and ready to play the game of life without resentment and the need to destroy others. For Freud we cannot mature into persons who can fully love and labor until we take a painful and anxiety-provoking journey into the libidinal traumas and fantasies of childhood and reexperience forces that almost doomed us to disintegration.

Freud said that neuroses were a fleeing from suffering. In neurosis we refuse to face conflict and anxiety, repress them, and defend against them. To become healthy and capable of ethical responsibility, we must undergo the suffering we once refused to experience, and integrate the conflicts, as best we can, into our personal fates. I cannot emphasize enough how terrifying the journey into the unconscious is, for we reexperience how difficult childhood really was, feeling the power of the needs and emotions of the id ever ready to overwhelm the nascent self.

Persons who know, suffer, and accept their fates—their injuries, failings, and blighted histories—are unlikely to needlessly aggress against others, seduce them, or addictively fill their emptinesses with things, alcohol, or excitement. With self-acceptance humans have no need to project their darknesses onto others. This does not mean that these people cannot get angry, aggressive, erotic, and sad, or be inconsiderate, thoughtless, and neglectful, for they are human. But they are not *driven* to be these ways and, hence, can see what they are doing without denial and meliorate it, if they so desire.

Perhaps we can best understand the kind of person who can accept his or her personal fate by looking at that character who struggled with his fate more profoundly than anyone else in Western literature, Oedipus. In *Oedipus the King*, Oedipus is determined to be master of his fate. Even after he learns that his prophesized fate has come true, he proclaims his ability to control his own destiny by controlling his punishment:

> Apollo, friends, Apollo—
> he ordained my agonies—these, my pains on pains!
> But the hand that struck my eyes was mine,
> mine alone—no one else—
> I did it all myself.[15]

However, Sophocles was not done with Oedipus. At the very end of his life, at approximately ninety-five years of age, Sophocles, who was born in Colonus, wrote *Oedipus at Colonus*. The play was produced posthumously in 401 B.C.E., after Athens had lost the Peloponessian Wars and two years before Socrates was to be put on trial by the restored democracy.

Although he has wandered as a blind man for years, Oedipus appears in many ways to be the same Oedipus: he is incestuously bonded with his daughters/sisters and violates the sacred thicket of the Furies—the mothers of the earth. He still rages at men—at the chorus of elders from Colonus, Creon, and his son Polyneices, all of whom he declares have not treated him fairly. He curses Creon to devastation and his sons to kill one another. Yet, where before Oedipus is a pollution, he is now a blessing who will give advantage to the land where his body will lie, for he has achieved a deep acceptance of his fate and nonacceptance of his guilt. At the beginning of the *Colonus* Oedipus says, "Acceptance—that is the great lesson suffering teaches,"[16] and also declares "you'll find no guilt to accuse me of—I am innocent."[17] He accepts responsibility for who he is and what he has done, but refuses to accept guilt. He could not have done other than he did. In giving up control, ceasing to fight his fate, accepting his destiny, and entering into the lonely inward emptiness of a blind exile, Oedipus has become himself, and, as such, is a blessing. He is still incestuous, but his merging with mother earth grants peace rather than pollution, for earth is our true mother and one with whom we can legitimately merge. He still attacks men, but his curses do not cause the downfall of his sons and Creon. They are merely statements that he knows the fates of all who play the games of control and power. When fellow sufferer Theseus empathizes with his pain, Oedipus' rage disappears and a bond is formed. Oedipus can now discriminate friends from foes and joyfully merge with the great mother that has birthed us all. Real freedom is gained only by submitting to our destinies, rejecting guilt, and being who we are.

Sophocles comprehended the enormous forces governing human beings and realized that the deepest joy and
most fundamental freedom is simply accepting who one
is. In accepting ourselves, we are free from the imposition of
general ideals, free from the guilt of not being someone
other than who we are, free to be ourselves.

Yet, this is only one side of the picture. Philosophy has
explored the other side: the immense power of the ego to
effect change. While the ego cannot totally transcend its situatedness, it has remarkable abilities to overcome forces of
desire and social pressure and act according to an ideal of
what is right, even when that principle contravenes both
desire and social demand. The power of the ego to achieve
such transcendence has never been adequately understood,
but its presence in human life is undeniable. We can and do
overcome ourselves and our cultures every day. Critical reason can wrench us out of social and economic fates. It allows
us to critique, in part, the cultures to which we belong
rather than merely being pawns acting out their values. It
can even, as Freud discovered, help overcome the enmeshed
fixations of the early childhood experience. There is no reason to live out an unfortunate "fate" if the ego can find other
possibilities for existence.

The freedom the ego creates is immense, but separated
from the nuclear and narrative selves and unresponsive to
the particular complex of basic needs and emotional webs of
the person, it is an empty freedom whose exercise gives little joy. It is also a false freedom, for even when we think
we have overcome the forces that molded us and controlled
our lives in childhood and youth, they are still at work in the
unconscious. The freedom of the ego is, in part, a self-deception.

We are fated and free. We cannot escape who we are or
our developmental histories, but we can choose how best to
express our particular natures. We cannot become anything
we wish, especially an abstract moral ideal, yet we do have
the freedom to choose how to live out the person we have
been fated to be. We can partially modify our characters,

smooth rough edges, balance unbalanced abilities, and so on. Mature agency is accepting that the freedom of the ego is limited by our fated natures and that our fated natures can be modified, redirected, and even partially transformed by the ego. We are responsible both for accepting who we are and for recognizing the freedom we have to express our fates in a number of different ways.

The son abused by his father might never be able to fully overcome the rage and aggression he feels toward men, but some ways of channeling this rage are far more productive, satisfying, and less self-defeating than others. Unresolved Oedipal desires need not always result in ambivalent, conflicted intimate relations; they can achieve some resolution and a stable intimacy can be enjoyed—not a perfect one, but one which is good enough, given that intimate partners are particular creatures with definite histories rather than idealized love objects.

If we hold ourselves responsible only for our intended conscious choices, then what is dark and unacceptable will act irresponsibly from the unconscious. If we accept responsibility for who we are, but fail to see that our fates may have alternative expressions and paths, then we fail to realize the freedom which is a genuine possibility in human life. We are both grounded in a particular nature but have the freedom to direct that nature.

4. Social Consequences

How should we deal with failures of responsibility, given that they are almost never willfully and freely chosen, but are driven, at least partially, by unconscious forces? For instance, how should we treat Bobby's parents, who drove Bobby's brother to suicide and were pushing Bobby to the same fate? Should we concentrate on their narcissistic personality disorders, say these failures are a disease, and attempt to treat them? Should we call them "evil"—"people of the lie"—and find them guilty of the heinous crime of destroying their own children? Are we to treat alcoholics as suffering from a disease or as evil people destroying themselves and others? If we say that these people are diseased, then we relieve them of guilt, but fail to locate any power of change in them. If we say they are evil, then we affirm their abilities to do otherwise, but imply that they are knowingly harming others and give them a negative identity through the production of guilt.

Neither approach seems adequate, especially if one of society's fundamental aims is to prevent further harm from occurring. Since our culture has only these two paradigms for dealing with failures of responsibility, it cannot adequately handle such failures. Given the incredible statistics of crime, recidivism, alcohol and drug abuse, and the millions of psychologically damaged persons, I think it is clear that our languages and ways of dealing with failures of agency and responsibility are themselves failures. The root cause for the failures of ethics and health to cope with social failures is primarily an ignorance concerning the complexities of psychological processes. The language of moral agency assigns human beings too much conscious control over their deeds; the language of disease sees humans as victims suffering from afflictions and has no theory of how agency can be achieved.

We have both less control over who we are and what we do than ethics ascribes to us and more control than medicine allows. We are both driven by our fates and can alter them. In our scheme of mature responsibility, we accept responsibility for who we are and what we do, but do not accept the verdict of guilt for misdeeds. This does not mean that punishment is never called for, for often this is part of what accepting responsibility means. I did not intend to commit adultery but was driven by erotic forces I did not understand. If it hurt you so much that you want a divorce, then I must suffer this consequence, just as I must pay for the window I did not intend to break. We do not create ourselves, yet must accept responsibility for who we are and suffer the consequences for being who we are.

What are we to do when we encounter people, like Bobby's parents or alcoholics in denial, who refuse to acknowledge their destructiveness or to accept responsibility for who they are? In cases where no law is broken and no moral code clearly violated, we can try to help these people see what they are doing through an empathic probing. Yet, such attempts often fail, for denial is a powerful, often impenetrable, defense. In such cases, I think Peck is right in advocating that we flee as fast as we can from the pollution before we, too, become infected. Sometimes victims like Bobby cannot flee or even understand what is being done to them. These are cases of personal tragedy. Sometimes the destructive person occupies an important role in our place of work and leaving is not desirable or economically feasible. The workplace suffers a pollution that lowers the vitality of everyone involved. If one knows how the unconscious works, one can try some mitigating techniques to lessen the stimuli that set off the pollution. Even if these don't work, knowledge of how the unconscious functions can at least make the situation intelligible and allow one to protect oneself as best one can against the destructiveness.

But shouldn't we punish people who harm others? What good will punishment do? More than likely it will simply intensify the negative psychic dynamics and produce further guilt, resentment, and aggression. This does not mean that the destructive person is to be indulged, for this, too, heightens chances for repeated behavior. Nonresponsiveness to what is evil or responsiveness to what is healthy in the person are the only helpful routes if what we desire is not simply an outlet for our own rage but a better person and community.

What are we to do with those who break the law? This is a complicated issue, for the law deals not only with the "just" punishment of those who break the law, but also with the protection of citizens and, as Nietzsche said, the collective need to vent rage on those who disrupt the social order. How psychology and law intersect is also complicated but extremely important, as much of criminal law revolves around the determination of a person's intentions. The psychology that seems to underlie criminal law, at least in the United States, is that if one is able to determine right from wrong, and one does wrong, then one intentionally does wrong. That is, law seems to accept the Socratic psychology that if one knows what is right, one is able to do what is right.

The discovery of the unconscious throws this psychology into grave doubt. Just because consciousness knows what is right does not mean that the ego can control its unconscious intentionalities. Especially in cases of criminal behavior, we must suspect some kind of failure in the developmental history of the person. Criminals have probably suffered social and psychological injuries that have caused unconscious rage, guilt, or emptiness that pushes them towards antisocial behavior. That is, it is hard to conceive of criminal acts as motivated only by conscious factors; they are always overdetermined.

Minimally, the psychology of the unconscious calls into question one of the primary tenets of the legal system—that we should not "punish" people unless they freely choose and intend to break the law. Given that most criminal actions involve unconscious motivating forces and are not freely chosen, it seems that we either should go back to a more Homeric legality and punish all who do illegal acts regardless of intentionality, and/or should be more humane in our understanding of criminal activity and help criminals with their psychological problems. Is intentionality really the crucial matter? The drunk driver does not intend to kill five persons, but he does. Is such a person less a criminal than someone who out of rage but quite intentionally kills the seducer of her husband? Who is more of a threat to society? Is it really evil intentionality that we want to eliminate or evil deeds?

The psychology of the unconscious also raises doubts concerning one of the primary aims of the legal system: to reduce criminality. The incredibly high rate of recidivism tells us that a system based upon ascription of guilt and harsh punishment leads to further criminal activity and the psychology of the unconscious shows us why. What should we do if we really want less crime?

Here there must be a crucial shift in questions. The major question for society at both moral and legal levels has been "What should we do with persons who do evil deeds?" Answers to this question are difficult; no solutions are obvious. Giving all criminals therapy seems to deny human freedom, dignity, and the role of ego choice in life. Treating criminals as though they were perfectly free denies the realities of human nature and leads to inhumane punishment that further promotes the rate of crime. Rather than focusing on the issue of what to do with people who commit criminal acts, we need rather to ask, "How can we best construct the social order so as to prevent significant failures of sociality?"

Here is a question that has some clear answers. We know that the formation of a robust nuclear self and the expression of this self in a recognized social narrative is crucial for human beings' achieving maturity. The most important years in development are the first few years of life in which children need care, psychological nourishment, and a firm sense of security. What is society doing to promote the kind of care and nourishment that children need? Instead of making it more possible for parents to be at home, the government currently rewards them for giving their children to others by allowing them a tax credit for childcare expenses. Where are the social policies that allow for paid leaves of absence during the child's crucial first months of life? Where is the social recognition for the parent who stays at home and nourishes the child? Where are the educational programs on the developmental needs of children? Unless we enhance and make central the values of early nurturance, then the society will continue having severe problems with antisocial activity.

The narrative structure of the culture also needs to change from one which gives great recognition and rewards to a few highly esteemed professions to one which is less hierarchical and provides more recognition and rewards for a greater variety of activities. People have genuinely different talents, complexes of needs and emotions, and directions they need to take to fulfill their nuclear selves. The more possibilities for esteemed and rewarded labor that the culture has, the more narrative satisfactions there can be and the less need to take from others.[18] The more narratives can be interpreted as part of an ecological network rather than in a hierarchical framework that overly values some professions and undervalues many others, the more happiness will be generally available for individuals.

The shift in questions away from what to do with anti-social offenders to how to construct a social order with lower amounts of unconscious aggression, neediness, arrogance, sexual impulse, and envy may seem simple and reasonable, but it involves an entire change of conceptual and value frameworks—a change of original projects in Sartre's terms—for it involves reconceiving our notions of agency, responsibility, human motivation, blame, guilt, intentionality, and freedom. The desires for revenge, for determination of who the guilty party is, and for punishing guilty offenders are profound and deep-seated. We have basic emotions of anger, contempt, and disgust that make us naturally want to aggress against those who injure us or those with whom we empathize. I suspect the virulence with which we want to locate guilt and punish offenders comes from the many injuries we have suffered and our having been blamed for misdeeds and punished severely when young. Incriminating others and punishing them is a way both of taking revenge on the world for sufferings inflicted on us and cleansing ourselves of our own evil intentionalities by projecting them onto others.

To ask as our primary question how to create a society that ameliorates unconscious propensities to evil means that we have to accept the unconscious—accept that we, too, are limited in our freedoms and have fates, dark intentions, injuries, and drives for revenge. Hence, although I think the shift in questions from how to best punish offenders to how to construct a society capable of living responsibly with unconscious motivations is necessary and vital, I have grave doubts that such a shift can be made. As a culture, we, too, have a fate.

Yet there are signs that such a shift of questions is occurring. I again point to one of the most successful organizations for helping with a form of severe and damaging antisocial behavior, Alcoholics Anonymous. The combination of not using guilt as a primary category, admitting that humans do not have complete control over their lives, accepting that human wills need to submit to a higher principle, giving community affirmation even in the face of backsliding and moral failure, and demanding that people accept moral responsibility for their lives regardless of what was done to them or what biological propensities were given to them within the context of a nonhierarchical community strikes me as a paradigm that might be used for helping many kinds of social and legal derelictions. AA sees humans as both fated and free, as both the victims of our upbringings and yet responsible for who we are and what we do. Is this a paradox? Yes, but it is a better way to live than saying either that we are entirely dependent on our developmental environments or that we are fully free and totally responsible for our actions.

CHAPTER 10

LIVING WITH THE UNCONSCIOUS

1. The Ecological Ideal of Maturity
and the Unconscious

We began with M. Scott Peck's insights into the psychological roots of evil and the philosophical invention of ethics in ancient Athens. Although vastly separated in time, both ancient philosophy and contemporary psychoanalytic theory hold in common that living well depends on the proper organization and development of the psyche. Where these two traditions disagree is on what constitutes the fundamental powers, dynamics, and structure of the psyche. The ideal of mature psychic functioning invented by the Greek philosophers denied the existence of the unconscious and thereby overemphasized the values of freedom, autonomy, and rational control. The discoverers of the unconscious, especially Nietzsche and Freud, uncovered the profound human costs of the Greek ideal of self-mastery in the repression of certain basic needs and emotions, the depressive effects of guilt, the replacement of a spontaneous human particularity with an abstract ideality, and the aggression that we inflict on both ourselves and others in being moral.

These great thinkers put ethics in question and turned to the values of psychological health as what might lead us

215

to a new world of freer, more spontaneous and joyful human living. Yet, such a move centered so much on the individual that it could not adequately confront "people of the lie" with failures of moral and community responsibility. The limitations of ethics and health have led us to attempt a dialectical interweaving of these two discourses in an ecological concept of maturity.

Like ancient ethics and contemporary psychoanalytic theory, the theory of ecological maturity holds that living well depends upon the optimal organization and functioning of the psyche, but conceives this optimal functioning in a more complex way than either of the two traditions on which it is based. It is an attempt to answer the question: "How can we accept the reality of unconscious motivation and still retain the possibilities for dignity, concern for others, and responsibility that ethics gives?"

In comparison to the hierarchical ideal of maturity which singled out reason and freedom as the highest values of human living and led to the repression of opposing elements, the ecological ideal of maturity is a complex, multifaceted affair involving the development of the basic needs, emotions, capacities, nuclear self, narrative self, and ego. Ecologically mature persons are those who have faced their own deaths and accepted the limitations of mortality, have a firm sexual identity and unambiguously inhabit their bodies, can sustain a requisite amount of order in their lives while infusing them with lively adventure, can act autonomously while being connected to a role structure in the social order and deeply committed to intimate friendships, have a keen knowledge of their particular environments and a wider interest in the world, are responsive to beauty, and acknowledge the sacred as an essential part of life. Their emotional lives are keenly responsive to both interior and exterior environments, for they have character traits that neither repress nor indulge the emotions. The needs, emotions, and character traits function well because they are grounded in a self that has retained the vital self-assertiveness and ideals of childhood, found a suitable narrative which connects the self's unique talents and values with the social order, and developed the capacities of the ego in a such a way that the self can be self-monitoring, live in reality, and empathically recognize the equal rights and needs of others. Ecologically mature people accept responsibility for their fates—their particular gifts, talents, lacks, weaknesses, strengths, and the biological, personal and cultural histories that form their unconscious—while at the same time realizing that they have the freedom to make profound adjustments to these fates.

The ecological self represents an ideal of excellence for both health and ethics. In terms of health, the ecological self defines the optimal functioning of all the psychic systems of an individual. In terms of ethics, ecologically mature people respect the rights of others, empathically respond to their needs, and accept responsibility for all the consequences of their actions. Justice is a crucial principle and virtue for these people, for they understand that one cannot achieve an intrapsychic balance nor satisfy the needs without being just to themselves and others. However, unlike the traditional moral person, they do not accept ascriptions of guilt for evil consequences of their actions, although they can be remorseful and be willing to make amends and reparations when such are called for.

What the ecological self gives us is a fullness of human experience that makes life genuinely meaningful. Experience is both emotionally felt and rationally thought. We are not present merely as abstract minds organizing variables in decision-making processes, but as mortal, sexual, adventurous beings woven into the dense fabrics of our social and natural environments. The distancing forces of the ego are balanced by the binding ties of the nuclear and narrative selves. The great critical forces of reason are balanced by the vitality of the emotions rooted in a particular life history.

The riches of the ecological self require a price. Something must be sacrificed in order for this self to come into being, and that something is a lessening of the highest values of our culture: freedom, self-mastery, and rational control. The ego that has no binding emotional ties to others or place, no deep commitment to a certain narrative, and no strong attachment to any ideals or particular needs simply has more options, rational control, and mastery than the ecological self which must respond to the plethora of voices in the psyche. However, the price we have paid for our freedom is too high, for it has involved the negation of the emotions, certain needs, the èlan of the nuclear self, and the social groundedness of the narrative self. The ego is free, but empty. The ecological self is full, but lacks the ability to easily transcend its situatedness. The hierarchical ego loved mastery above all else; the ecological self balances freedom with fate.

In many ways, the ecological self is akin to the decentered self championed by postmodern theorists. Both call for the overthrow of an overauthoritative ego and the discovery of the multiple sources of desire, motivation, and response that human organisms have. Both see the acceptance of the variety of psychic motivations within us as linked to the recognition of and respect for cultures that are different from those which we ordinarily inhabit.

How is the mature ecological self to come into being? While the answer to such a question involves many complex variables, I feel that the key for unlocking the possibilities for mature ecological living is the discovery of one's unconscious. It is injuries in the personal unconscious that typically block expression of certain needs and emotions, make our narrative and ego functioning defensively rigid, and lead to enervating constrictions of the nuclear self. It is the social unconscious that can fill us with resentment and guilt, decrease our personal spontaneity, blind us to the limitations that our societies impress upon us, and turn us into mere variables within a social web. The discovery of the unconscious both frees us from these constrictions and reveals our fates. To become ecologically mature, then, is to learn how to discover and live with the unconscious.

2. Living with the Unconscious

It is a terrible blow to realize that we are not masters of our fates nor rulers of our own psychic households. I will never forget the day when my own unconscious was revealed to me and it became clear how my life had been haunted and demeaned by severe unconscious narratives and intentionalities. The insight was both completely deflating and exhilarating, for it held the promise that with a substantial exploration of my unconscious, I could overcome the devastations that brought me to that therapist's office. I could now really become a master of my fate and captain of my soul. Where there was now a fixated id and a domineering superego, there would soon be a masterful ego.

With these traditional ethical ideals in mind, I set out to live with the unconscious—to journey into its darkest nooks and most severe repressions. I lived with the unconscious by remembering dreams, writing them down, and dwelling on their symbolic meanings. I caught my daydreams and penetrated their narcissistic fantasies. I became acutely aware of what experiences aroused anxiety, and probed mistakes, failures, and overdetermined actions. I took responsibility for my dreams and the negative consequences of my acts, past and present, as difficult as this was given all that I had excused myself for. I then took all of these thoughts and feelings to a sensitive and insightful psychotherapist, who, like Vergil leading Dante, guided me through the layers of my Inferno.

I was shocked in two ways by this process. The first shock was the amount of suffering that I had to undergo. My preconception of psychotherapy was to see it, as many do, as a wonderfully narcissistic indulgence in which one gets full attention focused on oneself. In reality, psychotherapy involves the reliving of early horrors with all the fear, anxiety, rage, and incestuous longings that were experienced by a very fragile self that felt constantly on the edge of disintegration. Favored defenses were destroyed, and I found myself with questions and doubts about all my previous life choices, unsure of myself in almost all social settings, and lonely for the previous friends who did not want to be around someone struggling with his unconscious. If the pain of real life that brought me into psychotherapy had not been as monumental as it had been, I do not think I would have endured the unanesthetized psychological surgery.

The second shock occurred when I came to more fully appreciate what primary process thinking was. I had anticipated that my ego with its logical, reality-based thinking would take increased control of my psyche the more I learned and reexperienced my unconscious past. While this happened to a degree, I also found that the unconscious was far more profound, complex, sensitive, emotionally involved, creative, and thoughtful (in its own way) than was the ego. It constantly revealed depths of understanding and richnesses of feeling which I had no idea I was experiencing—feelings and thoughts that the ego could neither produce nor reproduce.

In short, I found that the ego could not replace the unconscious or control it, nor was this desirable, for the unconscious had added an immense wealth, vitality, and depth to my life that I did not want to lose. The journey into the unconscious was like going through the looking-glass into a myth in which great dangers threatened my very existence and the discovery of secret treasures made life rich and full. I have met the Cyclops and eaten the witch's poisoned apple. I have been awakened by the kiss of love and survived overwhelming tidal waves. I have flown to the stars and wrestled with giants. I was once eaten by a huge snake—the great dragon—but have returned to tell the tale.

Are these just fantasies and dreams? Not to my unconscious. They are as important as any event in the conscious world, for they affect the self at a primal level of development. While it is of utmost importance to distinguish reality from illusion, it is equally important to give the world of fantasy the respect and interest we usually reserve for reality, for it is only in fantasy that our deepest realities are revealed.

Here is a world that constantly surprised me, that constantly made me wonder about who I was—both as a unique person and in my humanity. Rich, profound symbols poured into my life, threatening, nourishing, and complexifying it far beyond anything I had previously imagined life could be in my earlier ego-dominated existence.

The interpretations of my dreams, fantasies, and overdetermined responses led me not to self-mastery or a realm of freedom in which I could autonomously choose to become an ideal moral agent, but to my fate. The rage arising from a father's sexual abuse and fear of being seduced into a mother's endless depression will probably never leave, nor will my identifications with a father's liveliness and a mother's gentle love of nature. I will probably always tend to intellectualize life rather than experience it in the richness of its chaos, for I have a low tolerance for chaos. Such is my fate. The discovery of the unconscious has not made me captain of my soul, but a traveler into the vast psychic world that surrounds the little island of ego consciousness.

Yet, with the increasing interplay of the conscious ego with the unconscious, I found my life slowly but profoundly transforming. Levels of intimacy were now available that I had previously feared and avoided. Needs I had previously never recognized began announcing themselves. No longer could I avoid death or sexuality, live in hidden morbid dependencies, deny the sacred, or go without love. Dormant emotions rose to life and caused myriads of problems, but also made me feel alive and connected to the world and to myself. Perhaps most importantly, while unconscious narratives and motivations did not disappear altogether with increased understanding and integration, I found their power had lessened enough to be redirected into suitable outlets or simply be suffered and accepted without having to be acted out.

I further discovered that the quality of my ethical life was significantly affected by my living with the unconscious. Unwarranted aggressions and debilitating fears abated and I was better able to see others as humans and deal with them without distorting overdeterminations. My abilities to give and receive love slowly, but perceptibly, deepened. In short, I came to realize that my relation to the unconscious was the central factor determining the extent to which I could become an ethical person capable of treating others as ends and bringing happiness rather than misery into the world.

In his remarkable autobiographical statement, *Memories, Dreams, Reflections,* Carl Jung captures the profound interconnections between ethics and an exploration of the unconscious:

> I took great care to try to understand every single image, every item of my psychic inventory, and to classify them scientifically—so far as this was possible—and, above all, to realize them in actual life. That is what we usually neglect to do. We allow the images to rise up, and maybe we wonder about them, but that is all. We do not take the trouble to understand them, let alone draw ethical conclusions from them. This stopping-short conjures up the negative effects of the unconscious.
>
> It is equally a grave mistake to think that it is enough to gain some understanding of the images and that knowledge can here make a halt. Insight into them must be converted into an ethical obligation. Not to do so is to fall prey to the power principle, and this produces dangerous effects which are destructive not only to others but even to the knower. The images of the unconscious place a great responsibility upon a man. Failure to understand them, or a shirking of ethical responsibility, deprives him of his wholeness and imposes a painful fragmentariness on his life.[1]

Above all, the ecological ideal of maturity stresses that it is people who have attained wholeness—who are fully in communication with all aspects of themselves and willing to interweave unconscious products and conscious intentions—that have the capability of being ethical agents. Unless both the social and personal unconscious are explored and taken up into thought and deed, ethical agents will, as Nietzsche and Freud so poignantly demonstrated, perpetrate ills on the world and themselves in the very acts by which they are attempting to overcome these ills.

If one really wishes to be a moral agent, then the first and most fundamental act is the commitment to live with and explore one's unconscious.

3. The Paradoxes of Ecological Maturity

The concept of ecological maturity may appear to be a new ethical ideal that all human beings should attempt to achieve, for it seems that moral goodness is now equated with being an ecologically mature person. This is both true and not true, for the ecological ideal of maturity is a paradox. It is both a way of being ethical and, at the same time, placing ethics in question. It is both a variation of Nietzsche's enterprise to live "beyond good and evil" and a development of the Western ethical tradition.

Ecological maturity is an ethical ideal in the sense that it is able to pass the two key tests of ethics: it fits with our prephilosophical moral intuitions and is capable of being universalized. Ecological maturity incorporates not only the intuitions of value that have been regnant in the Western tradition—autonomy, reason, knowledge, and ego development, but balances these with values that have been central in women's experience and the experience of more traditional cultures. These values include the centrality of social life, intimate friendships, empathy, connectedness with others and with nature, the primacy of emotional response, and a recognition of the sacred. The ideal combines Nietzsche's intuition that the spontaneity of an original self (the nuclear self) must be the foundation for all personal value with Plato's insight that order and universal ideals are crucial for maturity. It weaves the insights of the discoverers of the unconscious together with what is of genuine worth within the ethical tradition. It couples the profound human insights of the world of fate with the extraordinary enpowerment of the ego's possibilities that philosophy and science have revealed and developed.

Can I will to live in a world populated by ecologically mature beings? I could not will to live in Kant's kingdom of mature rational beings, for it might not involve intimacy, sexuality, beauty, emotions, and a myriad of other crucial aspects of human nature. I could not will to live with mature utilitarians, for the weighing of pleasures and pains has little relation to genuine happiness and the fulfillment of the self and its basic needs. I could not will to live in Aristotle's or Plato's community of mature citizens, for there is no recognition of the unconscious or of Nietzsche's zestful irrational individuality, and no way to include genuine diversity.

However, when I ask "Can I will to live with women and men who accept their mortality, have healthy sexual lives, relate well to the social order, autonomously direct their lives, are capable of genuine friendship, inquire into their worlds, respond to and create beauty, and recognize that the personal will is not the most sacred thing in the world," I reply, "Yes, for these are the kind of full rich people that make life so wonderful." When I ask, "Can I will to live with persons who do not have significant repression of the needs and emotions and who, therefore, do not engage in compulsive projections and aggressions?" I again say, "Yes, for these people are not likely to be evil." When I ask whether I would like to live with people who strongly assert their unique daimonic selves but do so within recognized social narratives and with respect and care for how their actions affect others, I again say, "Yes, for I admire self-assertive people but need my own self respected and cared for." When I ask, "Do I want to live with people who have entered their own darknesses and suffered the knowledge of their limitations, injuries, and fates," I say, "Yes, for these are the kind of people who do not need to make others suffer."

It is important to see that what I am trying to universalize is not a principle, as Kant did, but a form of life—a way of being human. No principle has been found that one could universalize without exceptions, nor, in general, do people usually act from abstract principles. Rather, they act from who they are as concretely formed, situated human beings. Perhaps this exercise in universalization is most like Rawls "original position" in which people choose the structure of their society without knowing what positions they will occupy in it. While Rawls has them ignorant of their situations, he cannot have them ignorant of what it means to be human, or there would be no grounds for choices at all. Rawls assumes a typical liberal understanding that the maximal satisfaction of desire is what it means to be human. If instead of this meager understanding of the human being, people in the original position knew the basic needs, the emotional system, psychological dynamics, and so forth of what it means to be human, then I think they would want themselves and others to be ecological persons rather than any other kind of human being, for this kind of person can both optimally develop a human fullness and be treated well by other humans.

Since the concept of ecological maturity represents the embodiment of widespread moral intuitions and can be universalized, it is an ethical ideal. It represents the highest form of human life, the zenith that humans are capable of attaining. Yet, the ideal of ecological maturity cannot be an ethical ideal, for as such it would deny the very particularity of fate that it recognizes. It would fall victim to the criticism of assuming that it is equally available to all humans and that all humans are equally free to achieve the ideal.

Ethical ideals usually assume that particular human beings are not as yet ideal or moral but can become so if they undergo certain transforming experiences and/or follow a certain way of life. The optimal human life pattern is seen as moving from particularity to universality, from a brute existence to ethical worth, from unformed potentiality to fully realized actuality. In the typical ethical scheme the particular person must be molded to fit the universal ideal. All value is in the universal; the particular will only be good insofar as it embodies the universal. According to Plato, the ordinary person is ruled by irrational passions, but with the aid of philosophy he can attain a life of moral wisdom. For Augustine, we are born into a state of original sin but can be led through a process of Christian confession to holiness.

In contrast, the ecological conception of maturity understands the relation between the particular and universal as a dialectical interplay. The particular person is not fully free to become a universal ideal, for she has a definite fate rooted in a particular nuclear self and a particular social order which in turn is located within a wider cultural tradition. Yet, a general ideal can stand in opposition to this particularity and lure it into development. The particular self can be partially changed to meet an ideal of maturity, but the ideal of maturity must also be adjusted to meet the concrete particularity of the person. The ecological ideal differs from an ethical ideal in that it gives value to both the particular and the universal, hence admitting that as a universal ideal it is an abstraction and an imposition that must be adjusted to the concrete values of the personal ego ideal and fatedness of the actual self. In short, the ecological ideal of maturity is a mere abstraction that has concrete and pragmatic worth only in relation to a particular person with a certain fate.

For example, to be ecologically mature one should have an unambivalent relation to one's sexuality. However, if I have been sexually abused as a child, then I might never be fully at ease or resolved about my sexuality, may never fully overcome the damage this abuse has done to the nuclear self. This is my fate. Do these facts mean that I cannot be ideal, that I must fail to be fully mature? The ecological ideal calls on me both to recognize my injured sexuality and its distance from the ideal and also to accept my fate as someone who has been abused and may never have a fully resolved sexuality. The ideal of sexual maturity for me is not an abstract universal of full unambivalent sexuality, but the particular goal that I can achieve, given who I am. I see that I cannot be the mature ideal but also see that in accepting my fate, I am the ideal. This is the paradox of the ecological ideal.

Thus, we cannot speak about "realizing" the ecological ideal of maturity, but only realizing the ideal as it applies to individuals in their concrete situatedness and fatedness. What needs to be realized are our concrete personal ideals that are informed both by the universal ideal of ecological maturity and by an understanding our own particularities.

The second way the ecological ideal of maturity is not an ethical ideal is that achieving it does not make us good and failure to achieve it does not make us evil. Being ecologically mature allows one to be good, but does not make one good. What makes one good is acting with respect and empathy for others. Likewise, failure to achieve the ideal might not be a failure if one has realized the ideal as best one can, given one's fate. One need not feel guilty for not being ideal. We can not be ideals for we are particularities. Guilt is a healthy emotion when it indicates a bridgeable gap between a person's concrete ego ideal and the actuality of who she is; it is a diseased emotion when it negates the self for failure to reach a general moral ideal that cannot be realized, given the self's fate.

The ecological ideal of maturity, therefore, must be seen both as a legitimate ethical ideal and as an unjustified abstraction. We need it as a genuine and commanding ethical ideal in order to inspire human beings to fuller realizations of their potentialities and achieve the abilities to treat others morally. We need to see the ecological ideal as an abstraction so as not to deny the concrete realities of our particular fates.

Similarly, the ecological ideal of maturity is and is not an ideal of health. It satisfies health's primary test of being based on the best empirical evidence we have to date concerning the functional dynamics of the psyche and represents what it means to be an optimally functioning human being. Ecological maturity is a full vision of what constitutes personal self-actualization and its realization issues into the profoundest personal happiness. Yet, it can not be an ideal of health, for it demands that we recognize and respond to the needs and rights of others. Ecologically mature people often sacrifice what might be optimal for their health in order to help others. It is not optimal for my health to give one of my kidneys to my child who has a severe kidney disease, but as an ecologically mature person grounded in the situatedness of my life, I do.

In being both ideal and not ideal, the ecological ideal of maturity is a paradox. How are we to deal with this paradox? First, we can treat the ideal as a reminder of the fullness that we can be as human beings. Philosophers, psychologists, and ordinary people can get captured by particular aspects of human nature and come to believe that life must be focused on freedom, love, social narrative, feeling good about oneself, moral uprighteousness, or any of the needs and capacities. What the ecological ideal does is to remind us of all the needs, structures of the self, emotions, character traits, conscious capacities, and unconscious dynamics that must be taken into account in a fully mature life. As such, the ecological ideal is meant as a gift to memory, an aide to help us recall the fullness that we are. Wittgenstein wrote that philosophy was at best "a set of reminders." This is an essay in that vision of philosophy.

Second, the ecological ideal of maturity is meant as a stimulus for becoming aware of and enhancing one's particular ego ideal. Despite what a number of philosophers and psychologists say, not all ego ideals are good ideals, even when they are grounded in healthy early experience. Insofar as one's ego ideal does not recognize an essential part of who one is as a human being, it can be repressive or simply less powerful a tool in helping us develop our human potentialities. That is, ego ideals can be more or less conventional repetitions of the ordinary styles of adulthood in a culture, blind to a number of facets of human nature, mediocre in the vision they have of what the self might become, and so on. The ecological ideal of maturity is not meant as a replacement for a particular ego ideal (for then it would be a full ethical ideal), but as a challenge for people to deepen, broaden, and enliven their ego ideals.

Finally, the ecological ideal of maturity is a plea for us to take human development seriously and to see how vulnerable and delicate the process of creating human beings is. Fostering the growth of a human self is a difficult task involving tremendous amounts of energy, time, care, and thoughtfulness. It is a process that will not go well unless we give it utmost priority and devote more of our personal and social resources toward it than is common today. Our primary values must revolve around the production of healthy, self-affirming human beings capable of profound human happiness and full ethical existences.

Our journey now comes to an end. We began in the age of the gods and heroes in a land of fate where self-determination was but a mere glimmer on the horizon. We saw that glimmer grow to a radiant ideal that helped give birth to Western culture. But the radiance also blinded us to the limitations and darknesses of the ideal. As the ideal became increasingly dominant, the gods died, the emotions atrophied, symbolic language gave way to science, life became pragmatic activity governed by rational decision-making procedures, and idiosyncratic particularities were eliminated. The discoverers of the unconscious recovered our lost worlds, restored possibilities for heroism and forays with the gods, and pointed toward a kind of human existence that was fuller and more complex than any hitherto imagined. Our journey ends sometime in the future, for we are not yet able to live with the unconscious or transform our patterns of hierarchical structurings into ecological webs of mature functioning. For now, we must be content with being on the way. Such is our fate.

NOTES

Chapter 1: Introduction: Ethics and Psychotherapy

1. Alasdaire MacIntyre, *After Virtue* (South Bend, IN: Notre Dame University Press, 1981), chapter 3. The other two defining types of lives are those of the rich aesthete and the middle manager.

2. Erwin Singer, *Key Concepts in Psychotherapy* (New York: Basic Books, 1970), 18.

3. Rem B. Edwards, "Mental Health as Rational Autonomy," in Rem B. Edwards, *Psychiatry and Ethics* (Buffalo, NY: Prometheus Books, 1982), 68–78.

4. M. Scott Peck, *People of the Lie* (New York: Simon and Schuster, 1983), 53.

5. ——— , *People of the Lie*, 55.

6. ——— , *People of the Lie*, 56–57.

7. ——— , *People of the Lie*, 57.

8. ——— , *People of the Lie*, 43.

9. ——— , *People of the Lie*, 43.

10. ——— , *People of the Lie*, 75.

11. Peck does not explain how such injured people can make "choices" concerning how to live. This reminds one of Freud's talk

about a psyche choosing its neurosis as though it could weigh options and decide which neurosis was best. If these are choices, they seem to be quite different from what we ordinarily call choices, which are not compelled by unconscious forces and are made with full consciousness of the essential factors of the options.

12. M. Scott Peck, *People of the Lie*, 38.

13. Peck's attempt to handle these problems centers on trying to show that narcissists are themselves victims and hence suffering from a disease, even though they do not consciously recognize that they are suffering. But even if we grant that narcissistic personality disorders are diseases, this does nothing to overcome the conceptual problems involved in equating a moral state with a medical one.

14. Alasdaire MacIntyre, *The Unconscious* (London: Routledge and Kegan Paul, 1958) found the concept of the unconscious so vague and illusory as to not warrant serious attention by philosophers. Stuart Hampshire, *Thought and Action* (London: Chatto and Windus, 1959) argued that all intentional acts must be conscious. See ch. 9 for further discussion.

15. The charges of overabstractness, unworkable generality, and inability to justify itself as the way humans should live are brought against ethics by Bernard Williams in *Ethics and the Limits of Philosophy* (Cambridge, MA: Harvard University Press, 1985). This is one of those difficult books that is so thorough in its critique of traditional ethics that it must be responded to by all those who now hope to do ethics.

16. See Ross Poole, *Morality and Modernity* (London: Routledge, 1991), ch. 4.

Chapter 2: The Birth of Ethics

1. Richard Shweder, *Thinking Through Culture* (Cambridge, MA: Harvard University Press, 1991), 113.

2. See Marcia Dobson, "Herodotus 1.47.1 and the Hymn to Hermes," *American Journal of Philology*; Winter, 1980, for a full account of how the Delphic oracle could have known that Croesus was boiling a turtle and lamb on a particular day.

3. Herodotus, *The Histories*, tr. Aubrey de Selincourt (New York: Penguin, 1972), Book VII, 16.

4. Herodotus, *The Histories*, Book VII, 17.

5. One might ask what kind of wisdom might be available to Agamemnon, given his place as king in the world of fate. There is a sense in the *Iliad* that such a wisdom is possible, for Achilles achieves it when he is "king" at the games in book XXIII. Later, Aeschylus in the *Agamemnon* and Euripides in *Iphigenia at Aulis* portray Agamemnon as struggling with the issue of what he must do as king versus what it is right for a human being to do. Such a wisdom seems necessary in order for the world of fate to function and yet is destructive of it, since wisdom can see through the artificiality of fated categories.

6. "Overdetermination" is also a technical term in psychoanalytic theory. An action or belief is overdetermined if it has both conscious and unconscious determinations. That is, we can give accounts of overdetermined actions from the viewpoints of both conscious intentions and unconscious determinations, each of which is complete and makes sense. I deliberately use "overdetermination" as a primary category of the world of fate in order to show how the worlds of fate and the unconscious have close connections.

7. Plato, *Gorgias* in *Collected Dialogues of Plato*, Edith Hamilton and Hunnington Cairns, eds. (New York: Pantheon Books, 1961), 491–93. All references to Platonic dialogues will be from the translations in the Hunnington and Cairns collection with page references according to standard pagination.

8. Plato, *Republic*, 343–44.

9. Plutarch, *The Lives of the Noble Grecians and Romans* (Chicago: Great Books of Encyclopedia Britannica, 1952), vol. 14, 161.

10. Plato, *Symposium*, 212e.

11. The *Symposium* is a notoriously difficult, complex, ambiguous work, and no episode in it is more difficult to interpret than the Alcibiades one. The interpretation I offer is by no means the only possible one, but it fits well with how I understand the central structure of Plato's moral thought.

12. Plutrarch, *Lives*, 161.

13. See Plato, *Republic*, Book VIII.

14. Plato, *Meno*, 72a.

15. ———, *Meno*, 77b.

16. Perhaps the clearest statement of this psychology occurs in Book VI of the *Republic* (500c): "For surely, Adimantus, the man whose mind is truly fixed on eternal realities has no leisure to turn his eyes downward upon the petty affairs of men, and so engaging in strife with them to be filled with envy and hate, but he fixes his gaze upon the things of the eternal and unchanging order, and seeing that they neither wrong nor are wronged by one another, but all abide in harmony as reason bids, he will endeavor to imitate them and, as far as may be, to fashion himself in their likeness and assimilate himself to them. Or do you think it possible not to imitate the things to which anyone attaches himself with admiration?"

Augustine also holds this psychology that one becomes what one intends (loves) when he says, "Everyone becomes like what he loves. Dost thou love the earth? Thou shalt be earth. Dost thou love God? then I say, thou shalt be God". Quoted by Charles Taylor, *Sources of the Self* (Cambridge, MA: Harvard University Press, 1989), 128.

17. Plato, *Phaedrus*, 245d.

18. Plato, *Symposium*, 212a.

19. Plato, *Apology*, 30b.

20. ———, *Apology*, 41d.

21. Aristotle, *Nicomachean Ethics*, tr. Martin Ostwald (Indianapolis, IN: Bobbs–Merrill, 1962), 1105a.

Chapter 3: The Discovery of the Social Unconscious

1. Alfred Mele, *Irrationality: An Essay on Akrasia, Self-Deception, and Self-Control* (Oxford: Oxford University Press, 1987) defines akratic action as "free, intentional action contrary to the agent's (decisive) better judgment" (7). Mele, along with a

number of important thinkers such as Donald Davidson, Amelie Rorty, and David Pears understand *akrasia* as failings in the structure of consciousness. That is, *akrasia* is a failure to structure consciousness in such a way as to act on one's best judgment. Consciousness becomes akratic when it gives too much attention to the immediate situation, allows one subsystem of reasons to become dominant in forgetfulness of a more important set, and so on. The solution Mele gives to the problem of *akrasia* is to develop better methods of self-control such that consciousness does not get too focused on the immediate or lose track of its primary values. Insofar as *akrasia* is understood primarily in terms of problems with the structure of consciousness, these thinkers follow the Enlightenment tradition established by Descartes which sees *akrasia* as due to a nonalignment of the faculties of reason and will.

While there is truth in what these thinkers say, I think that the most serious examples of *akrasia* point to unconscious forces that limit and abrogate the freedom and power of conscious willing. That is, powerlessness to do the good when we know it and are seemingly able to do it are best explained in terms of unconscious forces working on consciousness rather than failures in the structure of consciousness. It should be noted that Mele would not call such events cases of *akrasia*, for they do not satisfy the condition that we really are free to direct our activities.

2. Aristotle, *Nicomachean Ethics*, Book II, chapters 1–4.

3. Aristotle, *Nicomachean Ethics*, 1114b26–1115a4.

4. Aristotle, *Ethica Eudemia*, tr. W. D. Ross (Oxford: Oxford University Press, 1925), 1249b22–4.

5. The one major exception to the Enlightenment glorification of reason is, of course, David Hume. For Hume, reason not only could not direct the passions, it was their slave. However, Hume has a very different concept of the passions from that which comes from the ancient world, for there is a certain orderliness and self-regulation to them. Indeed, they have so much self-regulation that they can do a better job directing human life than reason could, if it could.

6. Spinoza, *Ethics*, Book V, Prop. II.

7. ——— , *Ethics*, Book IV, prop. 38.

8. Karl Marx, Thesis # 1, *Theses on Feuerbach* in *Karl Marx, The Essential Writings*, ed. Frederic Bender (Boulder, CO: Westview Press, 1972), 152.

9. Nietzsche, *The Genealogy of Morals*, in *The Birth of Tragedy and the Genealogy of Morals*, tr. Francis Golffing (Garden City, NY: Doubleday and Co., 1956), 172.

10. Nietzsche, *The Genealogy of Morals*, 173. Here Nietzsche is uncannily close to Freud's explanation of neurotic symptom-formation. When emotions and desires cannot be spontaneously expressed, they become repressed and then become symptoms.

11. Nietzsche, *The Genealogy of Morals*, 189.

12. ――――, *The Genealogy of Morals*, 189.

13. ――――, *The Genealogy of Morals*, 190–91.

14. ――――, *The Genealogy of Morals*, 192–93.

15. ――――, *The Genealogy of Morals*, 217.

16. ――――, *The Genealogy of Morals*, 217–18.

17. ――――, *The Genealogy of Morals*, 194.

18. ――――, *The Genealogy of Morals*, 231.

19. ――――, *The Genealogy of Morals*, 256.

20. ――――, *The Genealogy of Morals*, 247.

21. I draw heavily from Charles Scott, *The Question of Ethics* (Bloomington, IN: Indiana University Press, 1990) in this discussion of whether Nietzsche is asserting a new ethic. Scott's book is a profound and careful exegesis on the relation of Nietzsche, Heidegger, and Foucault to ethics.

Chapter 4: Freud and the Discovery of the Personal Unconscious

1. Sigmund Freud, *Introductory Lectures on Psychoanalysis* (1917) in *The Standard Edition of the Complete Psychological Works of Sigmund Freud*, trans. and ed. James Strachey et al., 24 volumes (London: Hogarth, 1953–74), vol. 16, 284–85. Hereafter the *Standard Edition* will be abbreviated SE, followed by the volume number.

2. For a detailed history of these predecessors of Freud, see Henri Ellenberger, *The Discovery of the Unconscious* (New York: Basic Books, 1970).

3. Spoken by Freud on his seventieth birthday. Quoted by Ilham Dilman, *Freud and the Mind* (Oxford: Basil Blackwell, 1984), 16.

4. Freud, "An Autobiographical Study" (1925), SE 20, 47.

5. ———, "Instincts and their Vicissitudes" (1915), SE 14, 120.

6. ———, "The Unconscious" (1915), SE 14, 187.

7. ———, "On Narcissism: An Introduction" (1914), SE 14, 85.

8. ———, *Introductory Lectures on Psychoanalysis* (1917), SE 16, 382.

9. ———, *Introductory Lectures on Psychoanalysis* (1917), SE 16, 356.

10. ———, "Mourning and Melancholia" (1917), SE 14, 244.

11. ———, "Formulations on the Two Principles of Mental Functioning" (1911), SE 12, 222.

12. ———, *Introductory Lectures on Psychoanalysis* (1917), SE 16, 383–84.

13. ———, *The Future of an Illusion* (1927), SE 21, 15.

14. The quotation reveals Freud's sexism and his constant tendency to interpret the world from the viewpoint of male experience. This sexism will reappear in our examination of the Oedipus complex in section 4.

15. Freud, *Civilization and its Discontents* (1930), SE 21, 139.

16. Freud, *Civilization and it Discontents* (1930), SE 21, 112.

17. Sigmund Freud, "Two Encyclopedia Articles, vol. 28, Coll. Works, p. 258. Also quoted in Jonathan Lear, *Love and its Place in Nature* (New York: Farrar, Strauss, and Giroux, 1990), 148.

18. Freud, *The Ego and the Id* (1923), SE 19, 40.

19. ——, *The Ego and the Id* (1923), SE 19, 40.

20. ——, *Three Essays on the Theory of Sexuality* (1905), SE 7, 163.

21. ——, "Fragment of an Analysis of a Case of Hysteria" (1905), SE 7, 83–84.

22. ——, *The Ego and the Id* (1923), SE 19, 17.

23. ——, *Introductory Lectures on Psychoanalysis* (1917), SE 16, 453–54.

24. ——, *Totem and Taboo* (1913), SE 13, 141–46.

25. ——, *Totem and Taboo* (1913), SE 13, 146.

26. ——, *The Future of an Illusion* (1927), SE 21, 15.

27. ——, *The Future of an Illusion* (1927), SE 21, 15.

28. ——, *Civilization and its Discontents* (1930), SE 21, 115.

29. ——, *The Ego and the Id* (1923), SE 23, 30.

30. ——, *The Ego and the Id* (1923), SE 19, 29.

31. ——, *The Ego and the Id* (1923), SE 19, 35.

32. ——, *The Ego and the Id* (1923), SE 19, 34.

33. I find Freud's theory of penis envy, the Oedipus complex for girls, and his relating their lack of participation in the creation of culture and morality to biological tendencies rather than unjust social and cultural restrictions to be one of the least successful parts of his theory. For a fine corrective to Freudian theory that is more understanding of the social and value aspects in the differential development of boys and girls in Western society, see Nancy Chodorow, *The Reproduction of Mothering* (Berkeley: University of California Press, 1978).

34. The one exception to the non-teleological functioning of ideals occurs when humans identify strongly with a group ideal. However, the cost of such an identification is the loss of individuality. One identifies with the group ideal only as a mem-

ber of a group, and, hence, it still holds that individuals are not moved by ideals. It is in *Group Psychology and the Analysis of the Ego* (1921) that Freud makes his most positive statement about the relation of the ego to the ego ideal: "There is always something of triumph when something in the ego coincides with the ego ideal." (SE 18, 131) I will develop the teleological functioning of the ego ideal in chapter 8.

35. Freud, *Group Psychology and the Analysis of the Ego* (1921), SE 18, 131.

36. ———, *The Ego and the Id* (1923), SE 23, 53. Also quoted in R. D. Chessick, "The Death Instinct Revisited," in *The Journal of the American Academy of Psychoanalysis*, vol. 20, #1, Spring 1992.

37. ———, *The Future of an Illusion* (1927), SE 21, 11.

38. ———, *Civilization and its Discontents* (1930), SE 21, 128.

39. ———, *The Ego and the Id* (1923), SE 19, 34–35.

40. ———, *Civilization and its Discontents* (1930), SE 21, 134.

41. ———, "'Civilized' Sexual Morality and Modern Nervousness" (1908), SE 9.

42. Nietzsche, *Genealogy of Morals*, 218.

43. Freud, *The Ego and the Id* (1923), SE 19, 56.

44. Ilham Dilman, *Freud and Human Nature* (Oxford: Basil Blackwell, 1983), 101. He is quoting Helen Puner, *Freud: His Life and Mind* (New York: Dell, 1959), 199.

45. Freud, *New Introductory Lectures in Psychoanalysis* (1933), SE 22, 171.

46. ———, *Introductory Lectures on Psychoanalysis* (1917), SE 16, 281.

47. ———, *The Future of an Illusion* (1927), SE 21, 8.

48. ———, *The Ego and the Id* (1923), SE 19, 48.

49. ———, *Introductory Lectures on Psychoanalysis* (1917), SE 16, 285.

50. ———, "Moral Responsibility for the Content of Dreams" (1925), SE 19, 131–34.

51. ———, "The Question of Lay Analysis" (1926), SE 20, 221–22.

52. ———, "An Autobiographical Study" (1925), SE 20, 47.

53. Ilham Dilman, *Freud and the Mind* and *Freud and Human Nature*, Jonathan Lear, *Love and its Place in Nature*, and Ernest Wallwork, *Psychoanalysis and Ethics*.

54. Freud, *New Introductory Lectures on Psychoanalysis* (1933), SE 22, 167.

Chapter 5: The Case Against Ethics

1. Ernest Wallwork has an excellent defense for seeing Freud as believing in the possibility of freedom in *Psychoanalysis and Ethics* (New Haven: Yale University Press, 1991), chs. 3 and 4. See also Ilham Dilman, *Freud and the Mind* (Oxford: Basil Blackwell, 1984), ch. 10.

2. This is one of the central themes of Freud's *Civilization and its Discontents*.

3. Sandra Bartky, *Femininity and Domination* (New York: Routledge, 1990), ch. 5.

4. Stuart Hampshire, *Thought and Action* (London: Chattus and Windus, 1959), 94. Quoted in Ilham Dilman, *Freud and the Mind* (Oxford: Basil Blackwell, 1984), 63. See also Alasdaire MacIntyre, *The Unconscious* (London: Routledge and Kegan Paul, 1958).

5. Freud, "The Unconscious" (1915) SE 14, 167–68.

6. See Alasdaire MacIntyre, *After Virtue* (South Bend, IN: Notre Dame, 1981), ch 15.

7. Ilham Dilman, *Freud and the Mind*, 79.

8. Nietzsche, *The Genealogy of Morals*, 280.

Chapter 6: Psychological Health

1. See Allan Bloom, *The Closing of the American Mind* (New York: Simon & Schuster, 1987), Robert Bellah, et. al., *Habits of the Heart* (New York: Harper and Row, 1985), and Christopher Lasch, *The Culture of Narcissism* (New York: Norton, 1978).

2. Over the past decade or so I have consumed numerous books in the personal health field, especially in psychological health and addiction theory. None of these books strikes me as canonical, but together they seem to contain a number of similar elements that add up to a canonical set of values. I do not support my claims as to what the theorists of personal health say by reference to any texts since they are so numerous and none of them has struck me as so wonderful that I want readers to make sure they read it. Yet, the field itself is worth exploring and an afternoon's browse at the local bookstore should turn up any number of texts that substantiate what I call the values of personal health.

3. Erik Erikson, *Identity and the Life Cycle* (New York: Norton, 1980), 53.

4. See David Norton, *Personal Destinies* (Princeton, NJ: Princeton University Press, 1977) for an excellent differentiation of developmental values from standard ethical or moral values.

5. The strongest attempt to show how values of individual self-realization do imply obligations to others is David Norton's *Personal Destinies*, chs. 9 and 10.

6. See Bernard Williams, *Ethics and the Limits of Philosophy*.

7. Defining maturity in terms of treating others as equals works best for liberal democracies. In cultures with strong systems of fate, it may not be possible to act in this way, for people in different castes or positions have different rights and responsibilities. Treating everyone as "equals" in such a society is highly problematical and might involve willing the destruction of the whole social order.

8. See Daniel Stern, *The Interpersonal World of the Infant* (New York: Basic Books, 1985).

9. Ilham Dilman, *Freud and Human Nature* (Oxford: Basil Blackwell, 1983), 187.

10. Lawrence Kohlberg, "Moral Stages and Moralization: The Cognitive-Developmental Approach," in *Moral Development and Behavior*, ed. Thomas Lickona (New York: Holt, Rinehart, and Winston, 1976), 35.

11. Kohlberg's theory can be found in numerous places, including Lawrence Kohlberg, "Moral Stages and Moralization: The Cognitive-Developmental Approach," in Thomas Lickona, ed., *Moral Development and Behavior*. Kolhberg's theory draws heavily from Kant's understanding of ethics and has both influenced and been influenced by two of the most important contemporary social/political theorists: John Rawls and Jürgen Habermas.

12. In her account of early childhood development, Gilligan draws heavily on Nancy Chodorow, *The Reproduction of Mothering* (Berkeley: University of California Press, 1978). Chodorow's reconstruction of Freud's account of early psychosexual development is far more sensitive to social issues than Freud. Indeed, she sees that the differential development of males and females is not biologically engendered, but the result of one salient social fact: that our society has "mothering" done solely by women.

13. Anthony Cortese, *Ethnic Ethics* (Albany, NY: State University of New York Press, 1990), 96.

14. Anthony Cortese, *Ethnic Ethics* , 97.

15. Ilham Dilman, *Freud and Human Nature*, 196–97.

16. Jonathan Lear, *Love and its Place in Nature*, 189.

17. Kathleen Whalen FitzGerald, *Alcoholism: The Genetic Inheritance* (New York: Doubleday, 1988), xii.

18. Donald Gallant, *Alcoholism*, (Cambridge, MA: Harvard University Press, 1988), xi.

19. C. D. Chaudron and D. A. Wilkinson, *Theories of Alcoholism* (Toronto: Addiction Research Foundation, 1988), xxxi.

20. See Fitzgerald, *Alcoholism: The Genetic Inheritance*, 13–15. For a critique of the genetic theory, see David Lester, "Genetic Theory—An Assessment of the Heritability of Alcoholism," in C. D. Chaudron, *Theories of Alcoholism*.

21. Fitzgerald, *Alcoholism: The Genetic Inheritance*, 7–11.

22. Gary Forrest, *Alcoholism, Narcissism, and Psychopathology* (Springfield, IL: Charles C Thomas, 1983).

23. See chapter 1 for a further description of narcissistic personality disorders.

24. Arthur Knauert, "Basic Evaluation of Alcoholism and Substance Abuse," audiocassette copyright 1985, Art Knauert, M.D.

25. Roy Hoskins, *Rational Madness* (Blue Ridge Summit, PA: Tab Books, 1989).

26. Herbert Fingarette in his *Heavy Drinking* (Berkeley: University of California Press, 1988) is one of the few philosophers who has looked carefully at alcoholism. He argues that most heavy drinkers do not fit the disease model of alcoholism and do not need to stop drinking in order to be cured. They have simply chosen an unsuccessful life-style (here he is close to Hoskins) and need to learn how to change it—not how to stop drinking altogether. He feels that heavy drinkers have been "forgotten" with the vast attention going to the few heavy drinkers who do fit the disease model. I hope to show in this section that there is a strong case for the disease concept of alcohol dependency and why such a model can be effective in treating addictions. Some of the early studies that Fingarette refers to to support the theory of controlled drinking as a viable option for problem drinkers have been strongly challenged in recent literature. Yet, research is fairly new in this field; we are only beginning to understand the process of addiction.

27. See Herbert Fingarette, *Heavy Drinking*, 87–91.

28. See my *Human Excellence and an Ecological Conception of the Psyche* (Albany, NY: State University of New York Press, 1991) for a full development of this notion.

Chapter 7: Mature Needs and Emotions:
A Reconstruction of the Id

1. It should be emphasized that genital heterosexuality in Freud's *Three Essays on the Theory of Sexuality* is not seen as normative, but as a description of sexual development.

2. Freud, *Beyond the Pleasure Principle* (1920), SE 18, 42.

3. What follows in this chapter and the next concerning the organization of the psyche receives a fuller elaboration and justification in part 2 of my *Human Excellence and an Ecological Conception of the Psyche.*

4. This critique of Freud is also raised by Theodore Roszak, *The Voice of the Earth* (New York: Simon and Schuster, 1992), 289–91.

5. For an important study in how the psyche demands cognitive order, see Leon Festinger, *Conflict, Decision, and Dissonance* (Palo Alto, CA: Stanford University Press, 1964).

6. Aristotle, *Nicomachean Ethics*, 1155a5.

7. Nietzsche, *Thus Spoke Zarathustra*, tr. W. Kaufmann (New York: Penguin Books, 1978). The first few words of *Zarathustra*, "When he was thirty he left his home" makes a parallel to the life of Christ. Other parallels include his wandering from town to town to find "disciples," the use of parables to give meaning, and a kind of death and rebirth in part 4. Of course, the news Christ brings is that of God and the Kingdom of Heaven, while Zarathustra is the anti-Christ bringing us the good news that God is dead and that we are to live on the earth.

8. Contemporary emotion theory is divided among those who think that the emotions are socially constructed and those who follow Darwin in finding the emotions to be genetic and explained in terms of adaptation. I think the biologists clearly have the best of this argument as physiological expressions of the emotions seem to be ubiquitous and infants have definite emotional responses to situations of nurturance, neglect, danger, and injury without having learned such responses. For excellent accounts of a theory of basic emotions, I suggest Carroll Izard, *Human Emotions* (New York: Plenum Books, 1977), Kellerman

and Plutchik, *Emotion: Theory, Research, and Experience* (New York: Academic Press, 1980), and Magda Arnold, *Feelings and Emotions* (New York: Academic Press, 1980).

9. For a recent set of beautiful vignettes from an existential psychotherapeutic perspective dealing with how the repression of mortality can lead to neurosis, see Irvin Yalom, *Love's Executioner* (New York: Basic Books, 1989).

10. See *Human Excellence and an Ecological Conception of the Psyche*, ch. 11, for a fuller account of the meaning of *sophrosyne*.

Chapter 8: The Mature Self: A Reconstruction of the Ego and Superego

1. Others find that Kohut's work has important philosophical implications. See in particular C. Fred Alford, *The Self in Social Theory* (New Haven: Yale University Press, 1991).

2. I take this terminology from Samuel Scheffler's *Human Morality* (New York: Oxford University Press, 1992). Scheffler uses Freud's analysis of the superego to show that sophisticated theories of naturalism can have moral motivation as part of the natural psychological structures of human beings.

3. Freud, *Group Psychology and an Analysis of the Ego*, SE 18, 131.

4. See Janine Chasseguet-Smirgel, *The Ego Ideal: A Psychoanalytic Essay on the Malady of the Ideal* (New York: W. W. Norton, 1985) for a continuation and deepening of Freud's thoughts on the ego ideal in comparison to the superego.

5. See Karen Horney, *The Neurotic Personality of our Times* (New York: W. W. Norton, 1937).

6. See Kohut, *The Restoration of the Self* (New York: International University Press, 1977), 63.

7. Kohut, *The Restoration of the Self*, 45.

8. ———— , *The Restoration of the Self*, p. 128. Here Kohut also differs from the object relations theorists who see aggression as a primary drive.

9. Otto Kernberg, "Factors in the Treatment of Narcissistic Personalities," in *Essential Papers on Narcissism*, ed. A. P. Morrison (New York: New York University Press, 1986), p. 213–14.

10. See David Carr, *Time, Narrative, and History* (Bloomington, IN: Indiana University Press, 1986) for a thorough phenomenological exploration of the role of narrative in human experience.

11. See in particular Alasdaire MacIntyre, *After Virtue* (South Bend, IN: University of Notre Dame Press, 1981), Irving Goffman, *The Presentation of Self in Everyday Life* (New York: Doubleday, 1959), and Rom Harré, *Social Being* (Totowa, NJ: Littlefield, Adams, 1980).

12. Plato, *Republic*, Book IV.

13. M. Scott Peck, *People of the Lie*, 78.

14. Bernard Williams, *Ethics and the Limits of Philosophy*.

15. Samuel Scheffler in *Human Morality* gives a strong argument for why morality should not be considered either as always overriding or as stringent (unable to accommodate individual interests). I believe the view of morality put forth here fits into his "moderate" category of moral theories in that it both accommodates individual aims and demands that all people receive equal consideration.

16. See my *Human Excellence and an Ecological Conception of the Psyche*, ch. 10, for a fuller account of how I conceive of the ethical perspective.

17. See Heinz Kohut, *How Does Analysis Cure?* (Chicago: University of Chicago Press, 1984).

Chapter 9: Mature Agency and Social Responsibility

1. Richard Double, *The Non-Reality of Free Will* (New York: Oxford University Press, 1991), 48.

2. Charles Taylor, "What is Human Agency?" in T. Mischel, ed., *The Self* (Totowa, NJ: Rowman and Littlefield, 1977), 103–35.

3. Richard Double, *The Non-Reality of Free Will*, 43.

4. ———, *The Non-Reality of Free Will*, 44–45.

5. I realize that we have not yet understood how the ego can achieve transcendence from other factors in the person to gain a critical perspective. Freud found this so improbable that he disallowed it as a possibility for human nature. Yet, phenomenologically, it seems to be a genuine facet of developed human beings that they can question themselves and oppose certain desires and needs on the basis of principles or critical knowledge. I tend to agree with Dewey that the social conditions that are capable of producing such an ego are ones that are diverse enough to free us from a rigorous conformity but not so diverse as to cause massive confusion and indirection. Metaphysically, I am a Whiteheadean and believe that certain events can be the focus of such a massive amount of energy that they can freely rearrange what the past has pushed into the present.

6. The master for understanding how excuses work in moral discourse is, of course, J. L. Austin. See his "A Plea for Excuses" and "Three Ways of Spilling Ink" in *Philosophical Papers*, second edition (Oxford: Oxford University Press, 1970).

7. Ilham Dilman, *Freud and Human Nature*, 196–97.

8. Jonathan Lear, *Love and its Place in Nature*, 189.

9. Nietzsche, *Thus Spoke Zarathustra*, 265.

10. "The Disorders of the Self and Their Treatment: An Outline," Heinz Kohut and Ernest Wolf, *Essential Papers on Narcissism*, ed. A. P. Morrison (New York: New York University Press, 1986), p. 182.

11. I was helped with these distinctions by Jonathan Lear, *Love and its Place in Nature*, 170–77.

12. Jonathan Lear, *Love and its Place in Nature*, 171.

13. Friedrich Nietzsche, *Ecce Homo*, in *On the Genealogy of Morals and Ecce Homo*, ed. and trans. Walter Kaufmann (New York: Vintage, 1989), 258.

14. Freud, "Some Additional Notes on Dream Interpretation as a Whole," SE 19, 133.

15. Sophocles, *Oedipus the King*, in *The Three Theban Plays*, trans. Robert Fagles (New York: Penguin, 1982), 1467–71.

16. ———, *Oedipus at Colonus*, in *The Three Theban Plays*, trans. Robert Fagles (New York: Penguin, 1982), 6–8.

17. ———, *Oedipus at Colonus*, 1105.

18. The most important recent work written on the relation between unique individuals, work, and justice is David Norton, *Democracy and Moral Development* (Berkeley, CA: University of California Press, 1991).

Chapter 10: Living with the Unconscious

1. Carl Jung, *Memories, Dreams, Reflections* (New York: Vintage Books, 1965), 192–93.

INDEX

249